The Elements of Academic Style

The Elements
of Academic Style

WRITING FOR THE HUMANITIES

Eric Hayot

Columbia University Press
New York

Columbia University Press
Publishers Since 1893
New York   Chichester, West Sussex
cup.columbia.edu

Library of Congress Cataloging-in-Publication Data
Hayot, Eric, 1972–
The elements of academic style : writing for the humanities / Eric Hayot.
pages cm
Includes bibliographical references.
ISBN 978-0-231-16800-7 (cloth : alk. paper) — ISBN 978-0-231-16801-4 (pbk. : alk. paper) —
ISBN 978-0-231-53741-4 (e-book)
1. English language—Rhetoric—Study and teaching (Higher) 2. Academic writing—
Study and teaching (Higher) 3. Humanities—Study and teaching (Higher)
4. Critical thinking—Study and teaching (Higher) I. Title.

PE1404.H3943 2014
808.06'6378—dc23
2013048155

Columbia University Press books are printed on permanent and durable acid-free paper.
This book is printed on paper with recycled content.
Printed in the United States of America
c 10 9 8 7 6 5 4 3
p 10 9 8 7 6 5 4

COVER DESIGN: Julia Kushnirsky
COVER IMAGE: © Corbis

Contents

CONTENTS

CONTENTS

The Elements of Academic Style

One

Why Read This Book?

Writing is not the memorialization of ideas. Writing distills, crafts, and pressure-tests ideas—it *creates* ideas. Active, engaged writing makes works from words. And these works belong, in turn, to the means that made them. They emerge from a process; they represent their becoming, and that emergence, in their final form.

Writing is, therefore, a kind of learning. I say so to oppose writing to dictation, to a conception of writing as a necessary but tedious step in the distribution and fixation of ideas. Conceiving of writing as the process whereby you put down thoughts you already have will give you a bad theory of what writing does and can do. As an idea of writing's purpose, it tends to make for mediocre writers and mediocre prose. Writing as though you already know what you have to say hinders it as a medium for research and discovery; it blocks the possibilities—the openings—that appear at the intersection of an intention and an audience, and constitute themselves, there, as a larger, complete performance. Active writing should not involve saying things you already understand and know, but instead let you think new things. And that is why, this book will argue, you cannot know what your ideas are, mean, or do until you set them down in sentences, whether on paper or on screen. It is also why the essay or the book you write will not be, if you are open and generous and unafraid, the essay or book you started with. To understand that process as a good thing and to develop a writing practice that helps you inhabit it: those are the two projects of this book.

Why read this book instead of any other book about academic writing? To answer that question, let's look at the three major types of books of this type that scholars in literary studies might be tempted to read:

1. *Books addressing nonfiction style, especially at the level of the paragraph and the sentence, though often including a general ethos of writing as well.* This category, the largest of the three, includes Strunk and White's famous *Elements of Style*, Jacques Barzun's *Simple and Direct*, Arthur Plotnik's *Spunk & Bite*, Roy Peter Clark's *Writing Tools*, William Zinsser's *On Writing Well*, and Joseph Williams's *Style*. Most of these books assume a college-educated audience; almost all focus heavily on semi-journalistic forms like the magazine essay. None of them address scholarly writing at all. The exceptions are Helen Sword's recently published *Stylish Academic Writing*, whose focus on major features of nonfictional style (storytelling, sentencing, jargon, etc.) draws from examples from across the academic disciplines, from the humanities to the hard sciences, and Michael Billig's *Learn to Write Badly*, which deals almost exclusively with academic writing in the social sciences.

2. *Books focused on the psychological and working structures that help people write.* Some of these are for lay audiences and undergraduate students, including Peter Elbow's *Writing Without Teachers* and Natalie Goldberg's *Writing Down the Bones*. Others focus specifically on the kinds of problems the academic professoriate faces, such as Robert Boice's *Professors as Writers*, Paul Silvia's *How to Write a Lot*, and Joan Bolker's *Writing Your Dissertation in Fifteen Minutes a Day* (a sentence from the introduction of that book: "I don't actually know anyone who's [written a dissertation] in only fifteen minutes a day.").

3. *Books that cover the formal patterns and structure necessary to produce specific academic genres.* Books like William Germano's *From Dissertation to Book* or *The Thesis and the Book*, edited by Eleanor Harman and her colleagues, follow this format. In this category you will also find something like Wendy Belcher's excellent *Writing Your Journal Article in Twelve Weeks*, which includes advice about work patterns alongside its highly detailed analysis about the journal article as a genre.

The Elements of Academic Style covers ground from all three of these areas. The first part of the book, "Writing as Practice," frames the discussion of academic style by talking about how writing is currently taught (implicitly and explicitly) in graduate school. It goes on to offer advice about psychological and social structures designed to promote writing and looks at the institutional contexts that govern the major genres in humanistic style (mainly the kind of thing that appears in books of the second and third type). I also present an ethos of writing—a way of thinking about what writing does, and how it should work—that aims to help you understand *why* you might write a certain way, or why I recommend certain structural strategies or sentence-level choices. Together, these pieces of advice guide you toward an understanding of writing as an extensively lived practice governed by (and governing in turn) a wide variety of behaviors, attitudes, institutional patterns, and personal and social regimes.

The book's second part, "Strategy," examines large-scale structures that govern the production of scholarship in literary and cultural studies, including introductions, conclusions, structural rhythm, transitions, and so on. The third part, "Tactics," covers lower-level aspects of writing practice: footnotes, figurative language, diction, ventilation, and a variety of other concepts that usually operate below the level of a writer's conscious activity. I know of no other book that gives this kind of detailed guidance for scholarly writers in the humanities (Helen Sword's book comes closest, but flies at a higher altitude). It's in the detailed, writing instruction about scholarship—breaking down the "Uneven U" paragraph, demonstrating how to "show your iceberg," laying out a continuum of metadiscursive practice, or working through three major types of transitions, all of these specifically focused on scholarship in literary and cultural studies—that this book offers things you can't find anywhere else.

The Elements of Academic Style is mostly written for scholars in literary and cultural studies, whether graduate students or members of the faculty. At its most particular, it is a book about how to write "theory," or rather, how to write literary scholarship in the mode that was born out of the influence of philosophy and cultural studies on literary criticism over the last three decades. I make no guarantees as to its general applicability! Might these lessons only work for someone with my idiosyncratic educational trajectory; my Continental, soupless childhood; or my suspiciously comedic history of psychological disasters? Perhaps. But perhaps again you and I share, happily, a history of psychological disasters. In which case what works for me may well work, *mutatis mutandis*, for you as well.

I do think that, regardless of who you are, many of the lessons here are abstractable for general use. Readers outside the literature Ph.D. sweet spot—interested undergraduates and amateurs, or professional historians and philosophers of all stripes—will undoubtedly find lessons to take home, if they are willing to account on their own dime for field-specific differences in style. Because in the long run I don't care whether you write just like me. I care whether you write just like you—that you come to scholarly prose with both purpose and intention, that you take it seriously as a craft, that you understand how and why you do what you do, that you strive to do more than reproduce the stylistic average of your age and experience. And that you follow, in the long run, the path that you make.

This is a book for finding your way.

Part I

Writing as Practice

Two

Unlearning What You (Probably) Know

Why write a book on scholarly writing for graduate students and faculty in the humanities? Partly because no such book exists.

Other volumes, most famously Strunk and White's *Elements of Style*, cover aspects of writing essayistic nonfiction style at the sentence level. Even fewer cover structure; Joseph M. Williams's *Style* stands out in that arena. Fewer still focus specifically on academic style, and those that do tend to cover broad swaths of the social sciences and humanities, and even, like Helen Sword's *Stylish Academic Writing*, the sciences as well. A number of books help with psychology and time management; still others are geared toward making dissertations into books. All are useful, yet all aim broader, narrower, or to the side of what this book wants to do. What's more, some of these books are written by people who seem to be jerks, or at least are perfectly happy to take on that role in prose. Being the ideal reader of Jacques Barzun's *Simple & Direct*, for instance, entails reading a sentence like "we are forced to notice our contemporaries' fumbling purpose in the choice and manufacture of words" and feeling like you want to belong to that "we." I don't. Writing is hard, and it gives me little pleasure to feel contempt for those who don't do it well. I'm among them often enough.

But the main reason to write for faculty and students in literature is to counteract the current state of writing instruction in graduate programs. Mostly such instruction doesn't happen at all. This is startling when you consider that writing well in two or three major professional forms—the conference paper, the twenty-five- to thirty-five-page journal article or longer book chapter, and the complete book—is one of the most important things you should know how to do, and how to do well, as an academic. It is more startling to realize that even when writing is taught—and it is, though usually unconsciously and implicitly—what little instruction that does happen doesn't actually teach students how to write in those important professional formats, instead often inculcating habits that make it more difficult to write well in them. All in all, much of what graduate school teaches about writing and writing practice makes things harder and worse.

Let me explain. Many writing assignments given in graduate courses in literary and cultural studies (and in their upper-level undergraduate cousins) involve asking students to write an end-of-term essay, usually twenty to thirty pages in length, that connects thematically to the course material. Students usually conceive of and write these essays in the final three to four weeks of the semester. All of these essays receive grades, but only a small subset of them ever gets marked up and commented on. (Many are simply never seen again.) If you are a student like I was, you will, after reading the professor's comments, put the essay away and never think about it again. The new semester follows; you have new reading and work to do; summer teaching begins; or you have to study for your comprehensive exams.

Yet everything we know about writing tells us that lessons about style, structure, and argument don't take without commentary or revision. In fact, if you've been a graduate student in English, you've spent quite a bit of time trying to convince recalcitrant undergraduates to believe and practice that very thing. So why does the vast majority of graduate education in U.S. programs in literature happen without extensive discussion of writing, or any active, institutionally structured revision?

Let us recognize the exceptions. Many professors do bring writing instruction into the classroom, and a number of graduate programs have a course dedicated specifically to writing practice. A friend of mine speaks of a wonderful intro-to-grad-school class (his was taught by taught by Sam Otter, at UC Berkeley, in English), where students wrote a critical review of scholarship, an argumentative essay, and a final ten- to fifteen-page work of literary criticism. Another colleague at the University of Arizona some years ago had students produce an abstract, a conference paper, and a final essay, with one assignment leading into the other as a way of showing students how to carve a developmental path through professional forms. (He then set up a mini-conference for his students, so that they could practice giving conference papers—extra work for him, but how generous and serious!) And so on. There are good people, trying hard, almost everywhere, in the cause of good writing.

My argument here is, accordingly, with the *institutional* patterns, not the individual faculty. That's because, though I hope that every student gets to study with a faculty member who teaches writing well, I know that the sheer luck of the draw (or the necessity of choosing an advisor in your field) will in many cases mean that students get almost no writing instruction at all. (Even if, as a faculty member, you are one of the "good guys," ask yourself: to what degree has your graduate faculty ever had serious discussions about the institutional patterns of teaching writing, or asked how your program could better integrate the teaching of writing in professionally normative forms into the intellectual and professional development of your students? To what degree have you been willing to subordinate the pedagogical choices of any single faculty member to some institutional or developmental logic that you have discussed together and allowed to become part of the nature of your graduate program?) The problem is structural rather than personal. It has to do with the relationship between the entire pattern of graduate-level pedagogy on one hand, and professional life after graduate school on the other.

To understand this more clearly let's look at one specific instance of that overall pattern: the seminar paper. What, we might ask, does the seminar paper teach?

Let's start answering this question by concentrating on what the seminar paper teaches as a matter of writing *practice*, asking what kinds of behavior it trains graduate students to do. It's perhaps easiest to begin by noticing that the patterns and practices of the seminar paper bear no resemblance to the ways professors write. No one I know writes publishable essays in three weeks, much less when simultaneously working on one or two other essays over the same time period. Most of us write a single essay over the course of a steady, longer period of work—a summer, a semester, or a year—while engaging in extensive periods of research and rewriting. During this time we will often present pieces of this larger work at conferences, share portions with friends and colleagues, or pass some of our ideas through our teaching, using the feedback from those arenas to refine and focus concepts and intuitions or to find new directions and patterns of thought. Once complete, essays submitted to journals always go through periods of more or less serious revision in response to anonymous or editorial review or to suggestions made by copyeditors. The process of publishing an essay in a journal or book rarely takes less than a year from start to finish and usually involves a complex and iterative series of thinking, writing, and revision.

Note the differences between this drawn-out practice and that of the seminar paper. The way things work now, a visitor from Mars might reasonably guess that the purpose of the first two or three years of graduate coursework is to train students in a writing practice designed to generate seventy-five pages or so over three to four weeks. Which would be great if that were what the profession actually asked for. Since it's not, you would minimally want some assurance from someone that the frequent training in this particular skill—writing seventy-five pages over three weeks— actually helps prepare graduate students for the kinds of work they will be asked to do when they begin writing their dissertations.

The most obvious assurance I can think of would claim that the value of the seminar paper is that it acts as a "junior," or "practice," article— it's about the same length as an article, is written in sentences and paragraphs, makes an argument, uses evidence, and so on. Such a response usefully allows us to see some of the specific virtues of the seminar paper, namely that it can teach students to organize and manage an argument of an appropriate length; that it helps give students a intuitive sense of the shape of a twenty-five-page idea; and that it requires them (usually) to manage both primary and secondary sources. Fair enough.

But seminar papers differ from articles or book chapters in some important ways. Because they are written in three or so weeks, seminar papers tend to have far less research in them than in publishable articles. This means that they're not very densely citational, rarely use narrative footnotes, and cannot address existing professional debates in a significant way. Also, since they're written in a hurry, they are likely to have horizontal (paratactic) rather than subordinating (hypotactic) structures, in which one simply says the next big thing one can think of while trying desperately to get to the minimum page length requirement. For similar reasons, seminar papers usually involve close readings of two to three texts in the course, and their intellectual center often lies somewhere in the set of questions and texts organized by the course's professor. Reviewers who encounter such essays as journal submissions recognize them immediately because the basic question they address has an unspoken justification in the logic of the course for which the paper was originally written, about which the essays themselves cannot, of course, speak. The result is that even very good seminar papers need a summer or semester of work to approach the form and structure necessary to get published.

There may be, then, some good reasons to occasionally assign seminar papers, but they do not justify assigning them in every class. There's actually quite a bit to learn about academic writing that the seminar paper cannot really teach. Consider a list of the things you will need to learn to write publishable (and interesting) articles and books:

Psychology and Ethos

1. To adapt to the rhythms and psychological pressures of how professors work.
2. To develop a repertoire of habits that make writing possible.
3. To construct an ethos of writing as a form of social practice (to know *why* you write).

Format and Structure

4. To clearly understand the standard formats of academic style (the conference paper, the article, and the book) and the differences among them.
5. To know, for each format, the various stylistic and structural options governing argumentative and scholarly logic (introductions, conclusions, etc.).
6. To have a sense of the different ways of using evidence, and to know how those ways create a comprehensive citational practice.

Discourse and Metadiscourse

7. To deploy paratextual and metadiscursive language to frame and organize an argument or arguments.
8. To have a basic sense of the sentence- and paragraph-level effects of grammar, diction, figural language, and other aspects of style.
9. To understand how all these aspects of writing come together to create an intellectual or writerly style; to make one's own style.

The seminar paper teaches some aspects (such as skills 4 and 5), and may involve practice in skills 6, 7, and 8. These successes are mitigated, however, by the fact that it *un*-teaches the first skill and can do a good deal of damage when it comes to skills 2, 4, 5, 6, 7, and 8.

How so? Well, the speed at which the seminar paper is written means that you get some practice in putting together sentences and paragraphs (skill 5) and will have to use quotations and other forms of evidence (skill 6). But because the paper is long, both you and your professor will understand its major value as stemming from the validity and clarity of its argument as a whole, so the sentences and paragraphs will matter less, relatively speaking, than they would in a one-page assignment. As a result seminar papers do not draw your attention to the basic formal patterns that compose academic style; instead, they suggest that the writing is the thing you pass through on your way to the real ideas. (But the professor can't focus on students' sentences because the seminar papers are written so quickly that allowances must be made for awkwardness of style! Exactly.) Similarly, comparing any seminar paper to any published article will show you that the latter cites far more densely and has more footnotes than the former. What you learn while writing seminar papers, though correct for any single citation, is wrong for citational practice as a whole. At the macro, structural level, the seminar paper has you repeatedly practice a style of citation and notation that is professionally *wrong*.

A problem like this is solvable, even within the semester constraint. You can start by asking yourself, what do I need to learn how to do to write successful articles and books? Among other things you will need to learn to cite and footnote appropriately. I have recently begun asking my students to practice this task by having them write final papers with citational densities approaching those of published articles. Since they don't have time to do the concrete research it would take to fill their work with real notes, I simply have them make the quotations and citations up. (Seriously. I just have them invent the quotations, allowing them to practice using them at the right moment; to learn how to transition in and out of block or full-sentence quotes, or in-line citations; to manage agreement and disagreement with sources; and to handle different theoretical, historical, or critical supports.) Simultaneously, I ask students to identify three or four kinds of notes that academics commonly use, and require them to use at least one of each type in their papers. Voila! They're practicing appropriate citational structure. Not exactly how the pros do it, but close enough for *practice*. Just as professional basketball players don't train by exclusively playing five-on-five games, or concert violinists by only playing full scores, academics don't have to improve at writing articles only by writing articles. Writing a good article requires a number of different skills, only one of which is learning to manage a twenty-five-page idea. Graduate school should give you the opportunity to learn them all.

The point here is not that all seminar papers should require their writers to practice citational density. Sometimes you want a paper to focus on close reading a single text; at others you might want to practice integrating historical research with literary material. Different kinds of writing assignments teach different kinds of things. A good, coherent education ought to train graduate students in the wide spectrum of skills necessary to produce scholarly articles and books, which means that it should include a variety of writing assignments, that it should involve metadiscourse about the forms and practices of writing that allow students to put those assignments together in some larger picture of professional and writerly development, and that it should be understood as an overarching process whose responsibility is the faculty's and the department's as a whole.

Such a process begins with two simple questions: What do faculty need to teach Ph.D. students in literature to *do?* What, that is, are the specific forms of professional practice that will allow students to succeed as writers and scholars?

These are mainly the dissertation, the journal article, and the book.

And how much time do students spend practicing or leaning how to write journal articles or dissertations in graduate school? Not very much— especially during the first two to three "coursework" years. What would it take to prepare students to work in those genres, not simply as a matter of format, but as a matter of writing practice? How do you teach people accustomed to short-term writing assignments to develop the psychological and behavioral patterns needed to produce an article or a dissertation?

Let's remember some basic things about the dissertation. It has no deadlines. It will not be written in three weeks. Dissertation chapters stem from weeks to months of intense research, followed by months (or years) of writing. Instead of being judged relative to other seminar papers ("This is good, for something written in three weeks!"), dissertations are judged relative to published scholarship, altering expected standards for citation, structure, and novelty ("This is good, relative to important published work on the subject."). And instead of being done when the deadline comes, dissertations are finished when they're deemed good enough. Writing a dissertation thus presents a set of very particular psychological and professional challenges. Much of the struggle my students have when dissertating, especially with their first chapters, does not come from having to master unfamiliar subject material but from having to learn to write, and to think about writing, in a completely new way.

How could you modify the first years of graduate school to prepare students for that challenge? Here we run into some practical obstacles. We can't start first-year students out writing journal articles because they don't know enough yet, and because such articles themselves take too long to write and hence don't fit in a single semester. Fair enough. But what if students in their second or third year were required to do a year-long independent study whose outcome was a publishable essay? (That standard is a requirement of the comprehensive exam in the political science Ph.D. program at Duke University and of the M.A. program in English at Penn State University.) Or what if we delayed the start of the spring semester courses by two weeks, thereby creating a "revision" period in which students rework one of their seminar papers from the previous fall, or put together a précis describing how they would turn that paper into a publishable article?

Some places are already thinking about this as they attempt to cope with the problems caused by the dominance of seminar paper requirements. Recently the Department of Literatures, Cultures, and Languages at Stanford University decided that too many of its students were struggling with three end-of-quarter seminar papers, which resulted in too many incompletes and too many summers spent making them up. As a result, for 2012–2013 year the department offered students and faculty a chance to experiment with a new format. Students, in consultation with their advisors, chose one of their three classes for which to write a longer assignment and did shorter writing assignments in the other two.

We can push this idea farther. Imagine that the faculty in a Ph.D. program would identify three pedagogically useful formats for producing writing in a semester-length course: the seminar paper (designed to maximize the student's opportunity to think of a twenty-five-page idea); a series of short papers (designed to maximize critical reading practices, paragraphing, or style at the sentence level); and the "excerpt," a ten-page piece of writing that would imagine itself as a piece of a fully publishable article (designed to maximize citational learning, dealing with scholarship, and structure). Then imagine that, in each semester, students (in consultation with their advisors and with the thematic opportunities of their courses in mind) would assign each format to one of their courses. Outside the regular classroom, the department would then offer special sessions over the course of the year that would describe and teach the three genres, with discussions of how they correspond to pedagogical goals and how they prepare students for professional-level writing. These sessions might involve handing out successful examples in the various genres, workshopping student work, or analyzing the patterns and structures of the major professional types of writing that the formats teach. Now think about the difference between the average level of thought and institutional awareness surrounding professional writing in such a department, and the one that obtains in most departments now.

No one knows whether such an experiment, or the new process at Stanford, will produce better writing in the long run; in fact the Stanford experiment seems to be less about writing than about avoiding incompletes. I describe them here because they show how the institutional structure of graduate education communicates a theory of writing and teaches a set of habits involving writing practice, and because they open the door to thinking in a more holistic way about what writing is and how it is taught.

More practically, I am trying to help you understand—if you have not yet started your dissertation—how you might even now begin thinking about preparing yourself for that challenge. You do not need to wait for your graduate program to change. You can always take on an independent study with a professor in your field, or get together with a group of friends to create a writing group. Minimally you need to be thinking of yourself as someone who is moving beyond a highly familiar genre and mode of practice—the end-of-term paper that you have been writing since high school—into a new and unfamiliar one, and asking what it will take to prepare yourself for a career as a writer in your chosen professional modes.

As for those of you in or beyond the dissertation, I will say simply that I hope some of this explains why scholarly writing is so damn hard. You are the product of a system that, though it thinks incredibly well about other people's writing (literature, for example), does not think well—or act or institutionalize thoughtfully—about its own. The reality is, the difference between those who "succeed" and "fail" in the profession has as much to do with luck and mentoring as it has to do with ability or hard work. Better writing instruction cannot create more jobs for literature Ph.Ds but it can change *who* makes it to the tenure track and who publishes good work. When you treat writing as something that needs no instruction—or when your institutional patterns around writing actually make it harder to students to succeed—you reinforce the advantages of those students who come to graduate school already prepared to write. You double down on luck and class privilege; you make the system more arbitrary and unfair. Reading this book is designed to put you in a position to resist that unfortunate accomplishment.

I make no promises about outcomes in individual cases. But I am sure that I can help you understand what and how publishing scholars write, give you the tools you need to think about what scholarly writing is and what it does, and offer some helpful practical advice for putting together dissertations, articles, and books. I don't think you should waste time feeling angry or depressed about the way the system currently works. But I do think you can alter your relation to it by taking control of your own writing practice. I also hope that you will, if you ever get the chance, help change things for the next generation of students.

Three

Eight Strategies for Getting Writing Done

Different people have different ways of getting writing done. A colleague of mine swears that he spends months planning out an essay, laying out its evidence, structuring its arguments, and mortaring its outline. Then he sits down and writes the thing, all in order, in the course of a few days. Another friend doesn't write for months, then goes on two- or three-day sleepless writing binges; she emerges from her cave bearing the living body of an annunciated Jesus.

Neither of these strategies works for me. In fact I think they're a little bit crazy, and wouldn't recommend them to an enemy. But both these friends have published as much work as I have, so . . . your mileage may vary. The advice that follows borrows extensively from the history of my own writing practice, and has been good, so far as I know, for that of a number of friends and former students. If you can get things done by binge-writing or planning meticulously ahead, go for it; we're all just skinning cats in whatever way possible. If not, however, the following might help.

Let's start with fear. I am terrified—seriously terrified—of academic writing. Nothing that I do confronts me as strongly with a fear of total, consuming incompetence and inadequacy. The problem is that I am trying to be great, and I am (quite reasonably, unfortunately) afraid that I am not great. As a result I am occasionally tempted to take the advice the doctor gives the man who says, "It hurts when I do this": "Stop doing that." And it is probably true that giving up on being great would make writing easier for me. When I write for *Printculture,* or when I worked as a journalist at the Associated Press, I never felt the anxiety I associate with scholarly writing. I also don't feel it when writing e-mails, annual reports, grant applications, or grocery lists. Those kinds of writing can be boring or institutionally complicated, but they don't involve a confrontation with the fear that I am not as good as I would like to be.

Unfortunately, at some level the ambition to do great work—to write something that matters not just to me but also to the community of peers I care most about, the people whose work I respect and admire most—is central to the ethos of why I write scholarship at all. I cannot imagine giving up on it, since to do so would be to settle for producing mediocre essays. As a matter of career survival, it *is* possible to get by on work one knows is mediocre, but, for me at least, such a thing would make it impossible to go on. I don't have to be great, but I have to be *trying* for greatness.

What this means is that everything that is weak in me—everything that would have me sleep another hour, avoid working out, put off cleaning the house, or delay a necessary apology to a friend—struggles to keep me from writing, fights to have me give up and be satisfied with the sentences I already have or the essays I've already published.

Your own psychological structure may differ—you may be afraid of something entirely different—but in general all academic writers suffer from some kind of writing fear. Students often hear that half of the people who start graduate school don't finish. One of the main stumbling blocks is the dissertation, which is the first encounter students have to the kinds of professional writing demands and practices that will govern the rest of their academic careers. Those demands and practices produce a specific form of anxiety. The ultimate truth about graduate school is that successful academics are not always the smartest ones in their cohorts. They're the ones who manage that anxiety well, who learn to live with their fears and continue, despite everything, to write.

Here follow eight rules that have helped me realize that continuance.

1. *Write daily*. This is the oldest trick in the book: accomplish psychologically difficult tasks by making them habitual. Habits mitigate much of the difficulty in the psychological *choice* to do something unpleasant, instead turning it into the kind of automatic behavior that allows us all to

continue brushing our teeth on a daily basis (and flossing on the morning before a visit to the dentist). Building habits, however, can be difficult: a 2009 study by Phillippa Lally and her collaborators at University College, London, found that habitual automaticity takes on average sixty-six days to build—meaning that it takes about two months until something is as habitual as it's going to get. Automaticity, the research suggested, takes longer for tasks requiring more self-discipline; making a habit of daily sit-ups will be harder than eating a daily piece of fruit. (Overall, participants in Lally's study took between 18 and 254 days to form a habit, but some did not form a habit at all, suggesting that individual differences will matter a great deal when developing habit automaticity.) What all this suggests is that you should plan on at least two months of steady, solid self-discipline to create a new habit. But the good news for most people is that, at some point, automaticity will kick in and make things much, much easier.

Writing every day is difficult because everyone has any number of other things to do, most of which frighten them much less than writing. The key is to carve out a very small period of time for writing each day, putting it in both your physical and mental calendars, and convincing yourself that having that time is a way of *taking care of yourself*. Once that is done, you need to protect your writing time vigorously, both from others and from yourself. This means definitively scheduling this time and not moving it around or interrupting it, even when it seems perfectly reasonable to do so. Doctors, plumbers, teachers, friends, students, and even your family and children will all live, and live happily, if you consistently refuse to be available from, say, 9 to 10 every morning. Or even 9 to 9:30.

I recommend the morning for two reasons: first, research by Stanford University's Kelly McGonigal has shown that willpower is a finite psychological resource that gets used up over the course of a day and replenished in sleep. This means that you have more willpower in the morning than you do in the afternoon. As a result it's far easier to build and keep difficult habits in the morning. You can save your willpower-depleted evenings for other, easier habits, like having a drink after dinner. Second, practicing virtuous behavior in the morning lets you feel good about yourself for the rest of the day. I've found that it's impossible to really enjoy your afternoon if you have an unpleasant task waiting for you at 5:00 P.M. Whereas having coffee with friends or watching a show on TV at the end of a day in which you've faced and bested your demons feels like an appropriate reward for your matinal virtue.

How long should you write? During the school year, when you're teaching, thirty minutes a day is fantastic. If you manage to average slightly more than that—by writing for an hour or two, perhaps, on days when you don't teach—you're doing incredibly well. During the summer or on school breaks I tend to write for three to four-and-a-half hours a day, always in a sequence of three sessions: 9:30–11:00 A.M, a break for lunch, 11:45 A.M to 1:00 P.M., another break for a snack and internet, and then 1:30–3:00 P.M. I've found that I can't really concentrate for much longer than ninety minutes, and sometimes I actually can't make it through the third session. When that happens I switch over to reading, or sometimes I just take a break. But that's just me. Other friends have been using and praising Francesco Cirillo's "Pomodoro Technique," which involves breaking work up into 25-minute chunks followed by short breaks. You might try, during the school year, writing for one or two Pomodoros a day, and expanding those periods during breaks. What both patterns have in common is that they are patterns. I suspect that the fact of having a pattern matters more than which pattern it really is.

Part of building this habit involves speaking about it others. Narrating your process (I do X for Y minutes a day; I do X for Z minutes during breaks; then I start again) by sharing it with friends helps externalize it, and makes it something that exists outside your own drive and desire. A pattern's external existence makes it easier for you to feel responsible to it, rather than treating it as an easily modifiable expression of your current mood or state of affairs. In other words, it makes it a habit.

For about eight years I gave myself word-count goals, but I've since stopped focusing so much on counts because it was making me nervous. In summer I still aim for around two pages a day, and on days I reach that aim early I sometimes call it quits to celebrate. I essentially have two goals: two pages or three sessions of writing, whichever comes first. That way I can be assured of accomplishing something, without putting pressure on myself to write 600 words of new material. Some days what you already have written needs to be worked on before you can move forward; concentrating on that labor, and allowing it to count as

Fortifying Your Habit

A writing habit will benefit from being located inside a series of actions and spaces, both physical and temporal, that function as its enabling context. Together these can create a pattern of physical and mental activity that enables you to get work done. For instance, I only write in my office. I begin serious writing days by establishing a sensory space governed by white "noise": I put on headphones (always listening to something I know well, usually Radiohead, seven or eight albums in a row on repeat) and I begin chewing gum (this helps me concentrate; it's like white noise for your mouth). I then start playing Freecell (a solitaire card game); the focus it requires helps me begin to shut out other noises and concerns. After about fifteen minutes, I open the relevant document files and begin to work. For lunch I eat the same thing every day (a bagel with cream cheese); likewise for the snack that comes after the second writing session. I only leave my office to go to the bathroom, but I keep my headphones on and avoid talking to people. I have the phone, internet browser, and e-mail shut down (though I do browse, and sometimes check e-mail, during breaks). Together these practices aim to put me into what Mihaly Csikszentmihalyi has called a "flow" state, in which I become fully immersed in the writing task, essentially unaware of the passage of time or of the world outside my work. The micro-habits associated with the larger habit of writing help protect and insulate my writing practice; they create a pathway into, and out of, the mental discipline I need to get over my anxieties and begin to write.

meeting a goal, helps prevent tying yourself to unrealistic and unproductive goal-making.

Nonetheless I want to point out that if you can average two pages a day when you are not teaching—which shouldn't sound like much to someone who can write three seminar papers in three weeks—you can finish a full draft of a dissertation in one hundred days of writing, or roughly five months of work; or you can get a hundred pages of writing done in a summer. (This is assuming you don't write on the weekends; I generally don't). You'll have to rewrite and revise that dissertation, which will take at least another five or six months. Throw in another six to eight months of reading and you're at about a year and a half. Give yourself another half year for things to go wrong and get fixed, and your total time invested reaches roughly two years.

Though that may sound reasonable, almost no one I know has written a dissertation in less time than that. Why not? Mostly, I think, because they came into the dissertation having to learn how to really write one—not only how to write the actual chapters as chapters (and not as seminar papers), but how to develop a practice of writing that would support the sustained, longer process of production and revision that dissertations needed. As a result much of their time was spent learning both a new writing practice and a new written genre. Their first chapters became the laboratories of that practice, and thus often took a full year to write. If graduate programs taught writing more comprehensively and responsibly, we could avoid some of that wasted time and especially avoid the cruelty of its psychological effects on students, who spend that first chapter wondering whether they're going to make it, whether they're good enough, whether they'll run out of funding, and so on, when they should be working on their research, their sentences, and their arguments. If your dissertation is still ahead of you, the best thing you can do for yourself is to develop a set of writing habits now that will allow you to come into that challenge as a successful writer.

Another advantage of writing to a rule each day is that it frees you, psychologically, from one of the more difficult forms of anxiety in our profession: not knowing when it's ok to not be writing. I struggled a great deal in graduate school with guilt and unease over how much I wrote because, of course, I could *always* have been writing. I could have slept less; I could have played fewer computer games; I could have gone out less often with friends. At its worst that guilt made it hard for me to enjoy the fun things I was doing. By doing my writing first and establishing a set of habits that validated my own work process, I not only knew when I should be working, I also knew when I didn't have to be working. That I was good company at all during those years owes itself largely to the fact that, having written my two pages a day, usually by sometime around 3:00 P.M., I knew I was allowed to enjoy myself. This is also, by the way, why I prefer to write in the office: it helps build habit automaticity by giving me a standard place to write, but it also helps me know that when I am not in the office, I don't have to be working, leaving me free to enjoy home life.

2. *Make small goals and meet them.* Whether you choose to write for a time or to a word count, you will sometimes not reach your goal for the day. One of the most important things my advisor Jane Gallop taught me was that unmet goals don't create habits. For this reason you absolutely need to focus on giving yourself *small, easily achievable* goals. Don't plan to write four pages a day; don't try to write eight hours a day (or two hours a day when you're teaching). Focus on the slow and steady. Your job is to making meeting goals a regular part of your life, to become a *goal-meeting person.*

Among other things this principle determines how you behave when you miss a goal. Lally's research shows that people who miss occasional goals do not suffer much when it came to automating habits. It's only when you make a huge deal of the missed goal that it can become one. So you should try to forgive yourself immediately if you fail to meet a daily goal. For the same reason that you don't desert a diet because you had three hamburgers at the barbeque, or give up on mastering a step-over move because you missed a day of soccer practice, you cannot allow small lapses in habit-creating behavior to alter the general structure governing your work process. Look forward: if you can't eliminate your guilt by forgiving yourself, concentrate on meeting today's goal, and feeling good about doing so.

Above all, don't add today's "gap" to tomorrow's task. If you only wrote one page today, that does not mean you have to write three pages tomorrow. Sitting down to write three pages is harder than sitting down to write two, which makes your habit-creating pattern that much harder to begin. Those extra pages have a way of spiraling out of control, leading to a day when, faced with the idea that you have to "catch up" by ten pages or so, you simply give up and eat a bag of Doritos instead. (I have done this, by the way. The chips were delicious.)

Making and meeting small goals also determines the kind of relationship you have with yourself. I don't want to live in a world in which some part of me regularly punishes another part of me for not behaving well, in which I simultaneously occupy the roles of Marine drill sergeant and recruit ("Get up maggot!! If you're not puking, you're not working!!"). I find it more helpful (and this really is true) to imagine that the part of me

that knuckles down is working on behalf of the part of me that would prefer to avoid the writing scene entirely, and I do my best to be grateful for
all the things that first part of me has helped the complete entity known as
"Eric Hayot" accomplish. (I realize this is a little weird, but honestly, it's
how it works for me. When I write I occasionally leave notes to myself in
my file at the end of the day offering encouragement to the me of tomorrow. The most embarrassing of these, written sometime in 2006, read:
"Good job, Eric. You are a very good boy.") Knowing what I am and am
not capable of helps me set goals that I can reach, and creates a pattern of
self-motivation and self-reward that keeps me happy.

For that same reason you should also reward yourself for meeting goals.
If you have ten pages by Thursday, take a Friday off to celebrate. Or spend
the day writing, but without any pressure to reach a limit or to continue
when you're tired. Such "windfall" writing (the term is Paul Silva's) often
turns out to be the best of your week. Go easy. Focus on building the habits, not on defeating or overmastering them. Treat yourself as though you
care about yourself (even if, as is so often true, you sometimes can't, or
don't). Developing a two-page-a-day habit during breaks from school will
be enough to finish a dissertation, get tenure, and have a significant and
serious career as a publishing writer.

3. *When you're stuck, keep writing.* Of course, you will get stuck. You
will get stuck on a macro level, when after three or four months of work
you lose faith in your article or chapter and fear that you may need to
start over. And you will get stuck on a micro level, having days where it
feels like you're going backwards, or ones when you simply can't write
anything at all.

The solution to both problems is the same: keep writing. Many micro-
level problems can be solved by opening up a new file and freewriting for
five to ten minutes. Freewriting is typing or handwriting, nonstop, whatever comes into your head. I usually start with, "Eric, you are now beginning to freewrite. You are stuck in the article because you cannot . . . "
Don't stop typing or moving your pen; don't censor yourself; don't correct
spelling errors. Just commit to writing nonstop for a set period of time.
Often over the course of ten minutes you will write your way into a solution, or find that at some point your prose switches over from "free" to
focused and engaged, adopting midstream the vocabulary and sentence

structures of your project. For less serious problems, you may simply want to force yourself to sit at your desk for just a bit longer. (One of my automatic responses to feeling stuck is to want to walk away from the computer. Whenever I feel my leg muscles beginning to lift me off the chair, I force myself to sit and stare at the screen for five more minutes. Sometimes I freewrite a few sentences. Nine out of ten times this gets me through the problem.)

For larger problems, I recommend two approaches: first, go back and reread everything you have. Initially you may simply want to do this as a way of revising and rethinking, so that you spend your time reworking sentences and paragraphs, adding or removing metalanguage, and seeing more clearly the structure that you have so far. At some point you may want to create an outline of the work you have, describing as clearly as you can to yourself the logic of your argument and the organization of its evidence (read more on structure in part 2). Then spend some time writing a description (in sentences) of the outline of your piece, discussing the ways in which what you have sets up later parts of the structure, or creates promises and obligations to fulfill. Sometimes the answer to being stuck lies not in the sentences but in the structure. Seeing how the structure may be causing your problem will be enough to allow you to alter it and make the problem disappear.

If you are still stuck, a good second approach is to have a friend, colleague, or advisor read your work and talk the problem through. We all have a tendency to only show our writing to people when we're happy with it. I can always tell when my graduate students are struggling because they start avoiding me in the hallways or on e-mail. Their writing is not going well; they miss a few days of work in despair; they begin to feel guilty; they want to solve the problem before they see me again. But this is crazy behavior, like only going to see the doctor when you're well. Part of my *job*, I tell students, is to help them write their dissertations. If they avoid me when things are going badly, I cannot help. And I want to help!

If you don't have a helpful advisor, try very hard to build up a network of peers with whom to share work. I believe in and have enjoyed writing groups, including an excellent one in Los Angeles, though often I get more out of group discussions from commenting on the work of others than I do from hearing about my own. (Part of the problem is that more than two

The Writing Camp

One of the things I've done over the years is to organize a writing weekend with a good friend. We do the reading ahead of time, then get together and devote one day to one person's work, the next to the other's. (Two chapters are usually about enough for a weekend.) With more time, I've done something weeklong, in which a friend and I wrote in the mornings, read each other's material in the early afternoons, and talked about the work over drinks in the evening. These camps have been great both for improving my work and for strengthening friendships; they're as much about the pleasure of being engaged with one another as about the writing that they help make possible.

or three people talking about writing makes everyone too nice, and usually not specific enough.) I prefer to share writing one-on-one with close friends, people whose opinions I trust and, most importantly, who give me the kind of writing advice I know will be useful to me. Lucky people will make such friends in graduate school, though I did it mostly afterwards— and in fact still continue to collect new friends with whom I share work.

Above all, do not give up. Two especially pernicious fantasies lie at the root of many forms of blockage: the idea that you are supposed to get everything right the first time around (because everyone else does, allegedly), and the fear that you have somehow reached a limit (of ability) beyond which you cannot pass. Try not to make up crazy rules about how long it should take you to finish or what your process should look like. Don't hold yourself to imaginary standards: I once told my teacher Kristie Kaufman that I was hoping the third chapter of my dissertation would only take me four drafts, since the previous two had taken five each and I thought four would be an improvement. "Why do you care?" she asked. "Maybe it just takes you five drafts to make things good." "Good" is the standard. No one ever got any bonus points for finishing in three drafts instead of five, or three weeks instead of two months; no one has ever praised or published a bad book on the grounds that it only took a year to write. And try not to despair unreasonably. My friend Greg Jackson once told me that he wouldn't allow himself to get depressed until he had spent as long on a new project as he had on the previous successful one.

If your last thing took you a year to get right (and it probably did) then it's actually *not rational* to worry too much before that much time has passed. Maybe it just takes you a year to make things good.

4. *Avoid virtuous procrastination.* Academics who procrastinate have a hard time noticing that they're doing so, mainly because they have moved beyond the more obvious forms of undergraduate procrastination (going out with friends, playing video games, frequent tanning, etc.) to its advanced and subtler virtuous modes. The classic structure of virtuous procrastination involves cleaning the house or doing the dishes instead of writing. Unpleasantness is relative: if the chapter terrifies you, cleaning your house feels like a walk in the park. Whatever *looks* like an obstacle to your writing—a filthy house, for example—is most likely a problem you yourself have imagined into being to keep from having to write.

The most common form of virtuous procrastination for well-meaning academics is teaching: I can't write, because I have to prep for class; I didn't work today, because I had so many papers to grade. And so on. The special appeal of teaching as a form of procrastination stems from three things: its capacity to make us feel knowledgeable and powerful; its virtuous service to others; and the institutional inexorability of its weekly rhythms. Writing by contrast makes us feel weak and afraid; serves only ourselves; and is not, on a weekly basis, the subject of any institutional demand. That teaching and writing are both parts of the general academic "job" makes it easy to shift effort and justification from one to the other; most people wouldn't bat an eye at the idea that you had to do one part of your job instead of a different part of your job. Unlike taking care of the kids or waiting at home for the plumber, teaching and writing belong (or seem to belong) to the same field of activity. But this apparent fungibility conceals the deep emotional differences between them. It is because teaching is so much *easier* than writing that we choose to do it instead.

When I talk to students about this, I repeat advice given to me in graduate school by Gregory Jay: your job in graduate school is not to become the best graduate teacher ever. No one ever got a Ph.D. for teaching well. Your job is to write a good dissertation and to develop the skills that will allow you to have a successful career. You will be tempted to deeply immerse yourself in your teaching; having spent some eighteen years as students, you identify heavily with the classroom, and you dream of one day being a professor. For that reason the lure of teaching will be especially strong. Resist! Though accounting may make it look like the university is paying you to teach (you're called a "teaching assistant," after all), these jobs were only given to people the faculty thought could become great scholars. Do a good, decent job in the classroom, but do not forget what got you admitted into graduate school and what will get you out: your ability to do scholarly research in your field.

The same advice holds for faculty on the tenure track. Their job responsibilities are clearer, but the temptation to use power and strength in the classroom as compensation for feelings of weakness or inadequacy on the page is no less strong. If you want to have a successful publishing career, you absolutely must resist this tendency and especially resist the impingements on your writing time created by department meetings, student advising, or informal chats with colleagues. These things do matter, but they will cease to matter if you lose your job for not publishing enough. Good colleagues will give you similar advice, and good department heads will protect you from the most egregious demands upon your time. In the absence of a good head or decent colleagues, take care of yourself, and chat with friends when you're dead. (Kidding. But seriously, chat *after* writing.)

None of this is intended to be dismissive or contemptuous of teaching. I love teaching, and have benefited tremendously from a series of generous and devoted teachers. Teaching well has positive pragmatic consequences, both for your ability to get tenure and for your own sense of power and pride in your professional life. I have never found it helpful to think of teaching as a drag on writing, as a useless task to be shed as quickly as possible so that I can get back to my real (research) work. The idea that writing is real work and teaching is not makes me totally crazy. The students are our work too.

So please understand: I am warning you against making teaching a *substitute* for writing, against using teaching as an excuse not to write, and against letting teaching fill all your available free time so that it feels like you literally cannot write. If you can manage not to do that, and if you can build some good habits around your writing practice, you will enjoy your teaching more because you will know that it is not keeping you from meeting your other professional goals.

Most forms of procrastination come from not forcing yourself to start writing. But another kind, quite common among academics, has to do with people who cannot stop working on their projects. People who get stuck this way often fear the criticism that comes with evaluation; sometimes they believe (consciously or unconsciously) that their work must be perfect before it can be finished. As long as they have not quite finished, as long more research can be done and more revising and polishing can take place, the work is not "complete." Since it is incomplete, its flaws do not yet count—they are, in fact, not flaws but successes-in-waiting. By avoiding placing their work before its final juries (like editors of journals or dissertation committees), such procrastinators postpone the moment of judgment for as long as they can. One person I know postponed it all the way through the tenure decision—and was denied tenure, having written hundreds of pages without ever having submitted an article to a journal or a book manuscript to a press.

Unwillingness to finish is especially dangerous in graduate school, where students who conceive of their dissertations as magnum opuses will spend endless years polishing and extending 300-, 400-, or 500-page manuscripts. (Such students should be stopped by caring faculty, but are often not.) Your dissertation is not, you should hope, your only book and certainly not your best book; it's not even, or not exactly, your first book. Letting it go and having it be evaluated—as painful as that moment can be—will push you closer to writing something that will meet the standards of the profession, which will allow you to graduate, and (*inshallah*) to begin a career.

As with most psychological structures, patterns of procrastination or impatience can be quite difficult to catch in process. But your goal need not be never to procrastinate. Instead, it should be to get slowly better at recognizing the patterns of your own virtuous deferrals and to catch them within days or a week instead of letting them stop you up for months. Today, a decade and more since my graduation, I still procrastinate, usually by reading too much or by letting administrative work use up my writing days. The difference between now and then is that I catch myself sooner and faster, and have developed habits that allow me to quickly return to positive, productive writing practices. Among the most important of these is regular conversation with friends about how my writing is going. Lies you use to protect yourself from fear ring falser, and louder, when you tell them to someone else.

Beyond teaching and housework, the other major form of virtuous procrastination involves caring for children and other family members. Here the warning is, again, not to neglect doing these things, but to avoid doing them as substitutes for writing. But you will also recognize in the coming together of these three forms of affective labor the bleak shadow of the gender system. Given that these forms of work and care fall most often and hardest on women, people who care about ending sexism ought to work to build departments and universities that mitigate the conflicts between personal and professional life. Along the way you will understand that no psychological analysis like the one attempted here happens free of the institutional patterns that govern it, whether from above or below. Since this book is focused mainly on what you can do to get yourself to write, I will allow this brief mention of that fact to stand in for a general reading of the institutions, and, therefore, as a nod towards a certain incompleteness.

5. *Make fear an ally.* Most people imagine that their goal is to stop being afraid of writing. I am saying something quite different: any writing that aims to be great or even good will be by nature frightening, because it challenges you to do your very best work and forces you to acknowledge that your very best work may not live up to your most ambitious vision of yourself. Fear of writing is therefore inevitable. Your job is to manage that fear, not destroy it.

(It is possible, I suppose, that someone out there writes without fear. For no one is it all fear, all the time. My fear, for example, is mixed at times with a great deal of self-belief or even arrogance, both of which help me break through the impulse to give up. But I imagine wholly fearless writing as complacent writing—writing that is too self-assured, too confident about what it is doing to be ready for intellectual or stylistic surprise. Such fearless writing would be writing that wasn't learning anything. This is why no one fears writing e-mail.)

One way to manage fear is to use it to recognize opportunities within the framework of your argument or your prose. Another is to let it protect you from complacency.

On the first count, you must move from a general fear of writing to a specific fear located in the piece you're currently working on. If you are stuck, ask: What am I most afraid of here? What scares me the most about this paragraph, this transition, this paragraph, or this essay? Freewrite on the question for a few minutes. Then, instead of thinking of the fear as an obstacle to be overcome, begin imagining it as the solution to an intellectual problem. Open by addressing the fear, not as fear but as a knot or interpretive conundrum that has laid itself out before the reader. You can do this with metalanguage, writing something like, "The thing I was most afraid of when I wrote this chapter was that the analysis would be unable to bring together in a coherent whole the various pieces of evidence collected here." This is a high-risk strategy requiring delicate handling and best used rarely. But you can change that metadiscursive statement into the beginning of a problem and an argument, like so: "How can we connect Smith's writings on metallurgy with his literary works? What kind of historical or contextual responsibility emerges when we recognize that as a writer, Smith spent far more time detailing his experiments with alum and lead than he ever did with the poems in *Constellations of Miranda*?" Something like this allows your fear to point you toward an intellectual problem; it recognizes fear as a kind of scholarly labor. Treat fear as a productive instinct, a preconscious awareness that something interesting lies before you. Spending your time overmastering fear, or ignoring it, and you will lose out on the insights it grants.

Another way to use your fear is to keep it just enough alive to make your writing life interesting. If you set out to write an article or a chapter without knowing exactly what you will conclude, leaving yourself open to learning through the writing process—as I have said, I think this is the better way to write—then you will naturally worry that by essay's end you will in fact have nothing to say. When I am writing I occasionally encounter this as I come up with, somewhere around the tenth or eleventh page, a really good idea, one with the right size and shape to close out the entire piece. My initial impulse is at that point to keep the idea in reserve, to organize the rest of the essay around it, and to write in full confidence that I will, some ten or fifteen pages later, finish with something to say. But when that happens I make myself write the idea down immediately—right there or page 10 or 11 or wherever I am. If it closes a paragraph or a section, so be it. Doing so forces me to push past this first idea to something better; since the best idea of the essay cannot (for structural reasons) be on the tenth page, I must somehow over the next fifteen pages or so get to an even better or more interesting idea, or manage to put that idea in a frame that will surround, elevate, or contextualize it in ways that justify asking the reader to read the second half of the piece. If the reader must keep learning, so must I. In this way I am always holding open the ground before me, using the fear of falling to motivate new thought. (I imagine myself driving a train over a cliff, leaning out ahead of the locomotive like a cartoon rabbit, building a bridge just ahead of the wheels' encounter with the open air.)

6. *Start poor, finish rich.* Many books on style will tell you to be concise and avoid jargon. Don't use two words where one will do; replace long words with short ones; trim the fat; make your writing simple and direct. Such books are fond of quoting Blaise Pascal's classic humble-brag, "The present letter is a very long one, simply because I had no leisure to make it shorter" (417). All this counts as decent advice (I'll have more to say about it in chapter 24), but it's wrong about one thing: you should not, and cannot afford to, worry about concision when you are just starting to write.

Think of it like this: it's hard to buy a friend a sandwich when you're feeling poor because you barely have anything yourself. When you're rich on the other hand, it's sandwiches all around. Similarly for writing: the time to worry about concision comes when you can *afford* it. Cutting ten pages from a twenty-page manuscript is a disaster; cutting fifty pages from a 210-page manuscript no big deal. If you cut and prune too early, you'll slow yourself down (and run the risk of not meeting goals), and you'll lose out on the chance that one of your loose or wordy paragraphs will turn out, in hindsight, to contain a crucial new idea.

Psychologically, a dangerous pattern can emerge around cutting, in which it becomes a form of abnegation or self-denial: I'm being really tough on myself by being ruthlessly dismissive of my own work. Like anorexics who know that they hold themselves to standards others don't dare achieve, such writers victimize themselves in the name of values no one else believes in. This is self-punishment in the name being "realistic" (as opposed to all those soft, unrealistic idiots who think their writing is any good, or those fat people who dare to call themselves "thin"), an assault on one's own happiness or sense of self-worth that is compensated for by the feeling of virtuous denial that accompanies it. In the long run, people caught up in this pattern can end up seeing their entire career as a series of failures to live up to their best dreams. Of course this might be true! Maybe some of your writing is no good; maybe you won't be read in a hundred years. But you are almost certainly *not* the best judge of either your writing or the emotions that come with it. Part of building a good writing practice is recognizing that fact, being suspicious of your emotional states (especially when they hurt you), and recognizing how much of the lying you tell yourself relies on the false production of virtue. The lie that you tell yourself as a form of self-denial will be the hardest to see as a lie. But in reality, the truth—the truth that you can do good work, that you have done it in the past and that you will do so again—is, counterintuitively, on the side of your *happiness*, not your despair. (Occasionally, when I am caught up in this form of sadness, I will simply list out loud, as a mantra, all of the things I've accomplished that I'm proud of. Those accomplishments are far realer, more actual and in the world, than how I am feeling today, or this week, about my latest piece of writing.)

More pragmatically, when you write without knowing exactly how things will turn out, you will be learning as you write. This kind of writing process turns back on itself, recursively; as you write new pages you will also return to what you have already written, discovering the path it makes and following it forward. It's therefore important not to censor lines of thought in the initial stages, especially when you have so little writing done. Follow your ideas where they take you, then return to what you have written and think about how it hangs together, how it might be structured and organized so as to function as a single, coherent whole. When that happens you will realize that some of your pages no longer fit—that the best path through what you have written does not include every sentence or every section. And that's ok—because at this point you will have lots of pages, you can be generous, even profligate, in your cutting and revision.

7. *Treat revision (and even research) as writing.* Though the advice to finish rich is partly about self-preservation, about freeing you up to write at the beginning of your process, it also highlights the fundamentally recursive nature of learning as you write. As I work, I will pause every once in a while—usually after each subsection, then each section, then each chapter—and work back through what I have written so far. This allows me to conceive of and evaluate what I have done, and to begin to trace a structural outline of the work as a whole. It also helps me identify my

best thoughts. Because I don't censor much in the first draft, my writing will tend to have a number of different ideas, some of which are properly subordinated or connected to one other and others that are outliers. As I reread and revise, locating my best ideas, I start building the structure of the revised section around those concepts—even as I cut, or save for later, some of their subordinated or outlying instances. That structure, which grows throughout the revision, then lays down a potential line of advance for new sentences and new sections.

Revising and rewriting this way allows me to make sure that I am properly managing the relation of various subsections, sections, and chapters of a work—that their order makes sense, that the transitions among them work, and that the reader's experience of reading has good rhythm, pace, and energy. It also means that the closer I get to the close of an article, a chapter, or a book, the more constrained I will be by what has come before, and the more I will know about what my already existing material *needs* to be complete.

I will have more to say about structure, rhythm, pace, and other practical aspects of academic prose later on, but for now I want you to notice that if you write this way, it does not make sense to think of writing and revision as separate processes. Most people educated in the United States will have a sense of revision that covers amending sentence-level errors and occasionally adding or removing material; this is because most of the revision they practice in high school and in college amounts to little more than correcting what the teacher has asked them to fix. When you begin to write like a professor—to write, that is, within the constraints of scholarly ethos and scholarly time—such thinking does you no good and no favors. It inculcates a model of writing in which "revision" happens to a static, preexisting text, rather than one in which the act of revising, like the act of writing, creates the text that the writing becomes. Revision is not something that happens *after* writing. It constitutes the core of the dynamic writing process I am trying to teach.

Some of you may find it helpful to think of research in the same way. I have tended to separate research and writing days, but that does imply, a bit weirdly, that the main work of discovering and learning happens only on the writing days. Everyone who's spent time paging through documents knows that some of your best ideas can come from browsing, reading, or taking notes. So you may want to develop a habit pattern that includes research as part of the general act of "writing," in which you have days or goals that recognize the work you're doing in the archives, or simply reading and taking notes. Giving yourself credit for that labor, integrating it into your goal-making and goal-meeting process, may be a useful way to conceive of yourself as a writer and a scholar. (But be careful: doing research is one of the classic forms of virtuous procrastination.)

8. *Take this advice!* I assume that most readers of this book will not take most of this advice, mainly because I do not take most of the advice I get from books. Nonetheless I wish to assert against the tsunami of indifference and resistance that *you really should try some of this stuff.* I have had students over the years listen carefully and excitedly to a number of these suggestions, and even agree that, for instance, writing for an hour a day would be a good idea. But do they actually go and do it? Usually not. I imagine this happens for two reasons: first, because they don't quite believe that I myself do these things—they think, perhaps, that these suggestions are for beginners, or for people who somehow don't have it together; that because their goal is eventually to not need any of this advice, they should start practicing living without it right now. Honestly, this is crazy. When I am writing scholarship, I do everything I describe here, exactly as I describe it. This really is my grown-up, professional writing practice. I'm not just making things up for kids.

The second reason is that following this advice regularly is hard. If it takes two or more months to automate a habit, which means two months of the serious exercise of willpower and discipline, with frequent opportunities to backslide, to get caught in emotional traps, or to have life get in the way. I know that when I have taken a break from writing—in a semester, for instance, where I am teaching new courses—returning to the habits I describe here can be really difficult. On my most recent first day back (after a three-month break), I started with the gum, played Freecell for an hour, wrote for forty-five minutes, and collapsed in exhaustion. It took me a full week to get back to normal. And that's after fifteen years of relatively continuous practice. So I know how difficult all this can be. The only advice I can give you is to trust yourself enough to try it, and to never let small lapses stop you. Be good to yourself; befriend your anxiety and fear. It does, in the long run, get easier.

Four

Institutional Contexts

Writing well begins with knowing who, and what, you are writing for. Anything you do as a writer will only be unusual or ordinary, exciting or dismal, novel or tired, in relation to the expectations of an intended audience. There is no universally good writing, just good writing in a specific context.

For academic writers this means understanding two things: the intellectual habits and patterns of thought of the journal or press with which you hope to publish, and the general scholarly norms, usually national or linguistic, that surround it. Writing an essay for a general-audience academic journal like *PMLA* is quite different from writing for the field-specific *Modern Chinese Literature and Culture* (*MCLC*), most obviously because *PMLA*'s readers will know much less about modern Chinese literature than *MCLC*'s do. If you want to publish on Chinese literature in *PMLA*, you not only will have to provide more background information than you would for *MCLC*; you will also need to connect whatever argument you make to some larger theoretical, historical, or institutional context that will engage readers from outside your field.

I know that this is annoying advice. Writing is already hard enough, and we are all constrained enough for time, that hearing that we should go out and study the journals we want to publish in feels like a weird kind of hazing. Can't you just write what you want? Shouldn't good work just get published? Well, unfortunately, no. All published work is published *somewhere*. That "somewhere" will have a set of intellectual and stylistic norms that determine how your work is received.

So let's discuss those norms. First, journals. Let's say you have an essay on the intersection between biography and fiction in the work of the modern Chinese writer Ding Ling. You could frame the essay as an intervention into twentieth-century debates about the problem of authorship, putting Ding Ling into the conversation with Barthes and Foucault, but adding material on, say, the ways in which the history of literary translation in modern China has altered the position and social role of the author, and the ways in which that history affected, in turn, Ding Ling's fiction. You could then use this new evidence to make a more general (= European, most of the time unfortunately) theoretical argument that might interest French medievalists or contemporary Americanists. Alternatively, for *MCLC*, you could frame the essay as a discussion of the authority of women in modern Chinese feminism, contrasting the semi-autobiographical material in *Miss Sophia's Diary* with other diary-like or notebook-like texts from China's May Fourth period. Between these two versions maybe 60 percent of the essay's content could remain. You would mainly keep the close readings and their setups; you could also keep most of your background material (though you would have to add more for the readers of *PMLA*). But you would need to replace almost the entire meta-discourse—all the sentences in which you talked about what your article was about, how it intervened in its field, or explained what it had done. This would mean writing completely new introductions and conclusions, and producing new section openings and closings. Even a close reading of a very small passage in Ding Ling's work would have to be reframed at its close if it were setting you up for a shift to Foucault instead of a shift to some other Chinese diarist. That's a serious amount of work, and you can save yourself time by knowing in advance who you are writing for. (You will find a wonderful and detailed guide designed to help you figure out which journals to send your work to in Wendy Belcher's *Writing Your Journal Article in Twelve Weeks*. I highly recommend it.)

What's true for the differences among journals with various types of specialization (genre, theory, literary history, generalist, narrow, and so on) also holds for journals of the same type in the same field. A quick look through recent issues of *American Literature* and *American Literary History*, or *Modern Language Notes* and *Modern Language Quarterly*, will immediately show a pattern of differences in tone, style, and theoretical approach. So before you submit something to a journal, go back and page through a few recent issues. Sending your essay to a journal that seems to match its already existing structure and approach is easier than having to go back and modify what you have to match your sense of what a certain journal wants: fit the shoe to the foot, not the foot to the shoe.

The same is true, though less so, for university presses. A general sense of what the press has been publishing, especially as it relates to specific fields (Penn State in art history, North Carolina in American literature, Duke in cultural studies, etc.) and especially book series, can be helpful. It's rarely the case that you can modify a book for a press (writing a "Duke" book); more likely you will want to consider these issues as you think about which presses to contact regarding your manuscript, or as you consider adapting your book proposal, however slightly, to one press or another. On these matters of professional conduct—meeting editors, sending in book proposals, receiving contracts, responding to readers' reports, and more, all of which exceed the scope of a book on writing proper—I send you off to William Germano's *Getting It Published,* an excellent resource.

Beyond the demands of specific journals and presses are larger forces that govern expectations for scholarly proses. All publishing outlets operate within larger normative frameworks, linguistic or national, that govern expectations about writing. For most readers, this will be obvious; having grown up in the American academic system, they will feel confident that they understand the ways that academic work published in U.S. journals should look and feel. (This is probably less true than you think, I suggest later.) But for one group of writers in the U.S., those norms will feel radically unfamiliar. Anyone trained outside the United States will have gone to school in a system whose basic presumptions about the goals and patterns of academic writing may differ substantially from American ones. In France, for instance, academic writing is far less hypotactic—less vertically organized, less structural—than in the United States. Heavy subordination, especially when it comes to obvious introductions and conclusions, exacerbated by explicit "signposting" in the metadiscourse (first I will do this, then this, then that), can strike French readers as either juvenile or arrogant. French style in literary criticism places a stronger emphasis than U.S. criticism does on the visible originality of a "line" of thought—a more horizontal, paratactic pattern of development that reveals the author's unique process and mental patterns as much as it exposes some original piece of research. Literary critical work in French also tends to be more "casually" footnoted than American work; a French essay is more about the act of its writing, the activity that happens in the writing and reading of it, than about reporting on research done or ideas the essay knows in advance. (The Anglophone emphasis on concision and the vigorous marshaling of evidence—on saying things plainly and supporting them well—thus stages from a certain French perspective a sad, parsimonious moralism, a typically amaroidal form of English self-praise.)

Because most Anglophone literary critics have spent a lot of time reading French theory in translation, they will be accustomed to some of the habits of the paratactic style. But, as always, if you're going to use such a style, you should know why you're doing so, and be aware of the ways in which your practice plays with or violates the norms of the readerly community you wish to address. (True story: a person who reviewed the manuscript for my first book told the editor that though the book was good, it would have to be edited to remove Gallicisms, since English was obviously not my first language. [It is.] I had written parts of the book in a deliberate stylistic homage to the [translated] voices of Roland Barthes, though I hadn't said so anywhere. So I didn't remove the Gallicisms.)

If you grew up in China, on the other hand, you will have learned that one of the most epistemologically powerful things an essay can do—especially if written by a junior scholar—is to show that its arguments resemble those of an existing authority figure. This is usually proved by parallel citation. Unfortunately, that structure has little truth-value in the U.S. context, where a strong emphasis on originality (and on telling the reader how exactly you are original) means that you produce epistemological strength by *distancing* yourself from at least some of the experts in your field. In general American essays find rhetorical power in articulating their novelty, which can often appear in an explicitly antagonistic form (other people have talked about this, and they're all wrong), or in a gentler, discovery-oriented variety (people have talked about A, and they have talked about B, but they have never discussed A *and* B).

No one's right or wrong about any of this, or at least not in any way that matters. But if you want to publish in the United States, you would do well to understand the underlying assumptions that govern what editors and reviewers think academic writing should do ("prove something new by extending or even exploding an existing tradition" vs. "demonstrate the value of the new by showing how it recapitulates the tradition"), and how they feel academic writing should be structured and written. Though I have directed this advice specifically to writers trained in another system, anyone who writes could stand to be more thoughtful and more conscious about the overarching norms that help decide how we decide what's interesting or what's true. Much of the rest of this book describes how to write for a U.S.-based academic audience. But this narrow ambition leads to a final recommendation: if you want to be serious about writing, read academic work from other languages. Like traveling abroad, the dislocation provided by unfamiliar sights and rhythms will make you more conscious of how you think and work where you are most at "home."

Five

Dissertations and Books

One of the major types of books on academic writing focuses on the transition from dissertation to book. The transition matters because for most research-oriented academics, whether your dissertation becomes your first book will determine whether you get tenure at the first place that hires you. (If, I should add, the first place that hires you requires a book for tenure.) People who substantially revise their dissertations (or mine them for articles and write whole new projects) tend, in my experience, to need to change jobs at least once before going up for tenure, simply because they need the extra time to work. Their books also tend to be better, more polished and more vigorously located in contemporary debates, than those written by people, like me, whose first books were revised dissertations.

That said, if you can, write a dissertation that can become a book. The easy way to do this is to try to write a book for your dissertation.

Let me explain. If the dissertation-to-book books are to be believed—and here I am referring mainly to William Germano's *From Dissertation to Book* and Beth Luey's collection of essays, *Revising Your Dissertation*—there is a genre of writing called the "Dissertation." Many dissertations are Dissertations, in the sense that they obey the rules of this genre, which differ in important ways from those that govern the genre known as the book. Your job in moving from dissertation to book is to take a piece of writing that is a Dissertation and turn it into a piece of writing that is a book.

How does a Dissertation differ from a book? Jennifer Crewe (of Columbia University Press) tells us that "the audience for a dissertation usually consists of four or five people, the student's doctoral committee," while audiences for books are larger and more diverse. As a result "revising your dissertation is not just a matter of removing the literature review, trimming the notes, and toning down the jargon. A dissertation must in many cases be reconceptualized and expanded in scope before it can become a successful—or even a publishable—book" (Luey 133). Germano for his part makes the difference between Dissertation and book a function of professional standing: the primary function of the Dissertation "is to demonstrate that you are able to undertake professional-level work. . . . A dissertation demonstrates technical competence more often than an original theory or a genuine argument" (19).

All this makes Dissertations sound terrible! They're narrow, boring, self-indulgent, and overwritten; they're competent rather than scintillating. If we told students up front that this was what they were setting out to do for the next couple years, who in their right mind would ever want to write one?

No one. For this reason I recommend writing your dissertation as a *book* and leaving the genre of the Dissertation behind entirely. Don't write your dissertation for an audience of five; don't do a literature review (a special genre of chapter that only exists in the humanities dissertation, though it is a common format for parts of articles in the sciences and social sciences); don't produce merely technical competence. *Do* create an original theory and/or a genuine argument. Writing this way will save you an immense amount of time, and spare you years mastering an intellectual form (the Dissertation) that is unpublishable and naïve (and which, to boot, you will only ever write one of in your entire academic career). This doesn't mean, of course, that your dissertation-written-as-a-book will be a good book. But it seems much better to me to write a mediocre book than a great Dissertation since your goal in the long run is to write a good book, and it's easier to get there from something that resembles it than something that doesn't.

The really good news is that in many respects writing a book is easier than writing a Dissertation, since you already know what books look like, whereas you have probably never read a Dissertation. With that in mind it behooves you to think, as you approach your dissertation, about what a good book does—what it is, if it is not simply a collection of articles linked by an introduction. Looking at books you admire *as books*, ask yourself what they do that seems admirably book-like. This is not just a question about the content, style, or argument of the work, but also of its structure, the connections it establishes among chapters, the long arc of its development, and the relation of the parts to the whole. You will want to be able to distinguish a good argument from a good book, while recognizing that part of what makes a strong book has to do with the arrangement of argument, structure, and time, or with the forcefulness or stylistic originality of its prose. As you poke around for good books, pay special attention to first books, since those will likely have originally been written to fulfill dissertation requirements, and will therefore tend to have some structural similarities that stem from the writing situation that produced them (especially true when it comes to the number and type of chapters; the quality and length of the conclusion; and metadiscursive management of originality and authority). The other thing you should absolutely do is look at the previously mentioned books by Beth Luey (an edited collection) and William Germano: because both tell you so much about how to make a Dissertation into a book, they end up giving lots of great advice about what good books should and should not be. Between the examples of actually existing books you admire and specific advice designed to help you learn how to write and recognize good book-ness, you should be able to develop a solid feel for what a book ought to be, both ethically and structurally. Do this *before* you start writing your dissertation.

My own take: a book must be more than the sum of its parts. A book should gather meaning over time, and should accumulate that meaning into a whole that necessarily includes all its pages. Books that give away all their answers in the introduction, leaving the pages to just lay out a continuum of evidence and examples; books whose chapters relate to one another only thematically or topically ("immigrant literature in Albania"; "immigrant literature in Belgium"; "immigrant literature in Ireland"); books whose chapters can be reordered without affecting the argument; books that don't think they need a conclusion; books whose only logic is a kind of endless piling on: all these run the risk of producing a whole that is less than what it contains. Such books are books-as-containers, books

Dissertations Becoming Books

Shouldn't my book have more chapters than my dissertation? Yes, it probably should. Most books do. And of course that makes life difficult, since graduate funding is limited and your program probably wants you to graduate and get out of there to make room for new people. You don't want to set yourself up to write a six-chapter dissertation (with your eye on the six-chapter book that it will become) if doing so will take an extra year or two (and make you scramble for funding). You're better off finishing a reasonable, three- or four-chapter dissertation, while publishing a couple articles, getting a job, and graduating. (I say this like it's uncomplicated; I know it's not.)

With my students these days I have been working on conceiving the book project (as something that will probably have four to six chapters; see more on average chapters per book in part 2) and then working backwards from there to a reasonably sized dissertation. That means my students are writing dissertations that are essentially *parts* of books, and thus that they have a plan that will allow them to answer the inevitable job-market questions about what they will do to turn their dissertations into books. Now, I make no guarantee that what the student (and his or her committee and I) thinks will be the book will turn out, after two or three years of writing, to actually be the book. We all have to be willing to be surprised by the directions a project takes. But working within this framework has two major advantages: (1) it gives students a dissertation project that can be done in a normal amount of time, and (2) it gives them, and me, lots of opportunities to be thinking and talking about what books look like, what this book might look like, and so on, all of which helps them learn more about how to accomplish the fundamental task of their pre-tenure years.

whose ethical justification ("How, or why, is this a book?") stems from the material fact of their bound pages rather than from the concept that grows from having *these* pages bound together in *this* order. To finish writing a book is to see and communicate the book-concept. Much of the labor of the last months of writing/revision involves grasping the concept from the pages you have, figuring out how to get the reader excited about that concept, and then keeping the promise of that excitement as the reader moves through each page of the work. (I say more about the structure of books in chapter 10.)

As you think about a dissertation or a book, you need to consider how the chapters fit together to make a whole that establishes meaning over and above the sum of the contents. Some of this is simply practical: when I was working on my dissertation, I knew I was going to write a chapter on Ezra Pound whose chronological high point would be 1915, and I knew I had another chapter on a 1974 visit to China by several prominent French theorists associated with the journal *Tel quel*. I also knew I could not write a two-chapter dissertation. So I had two choices: the first would be to split the Pound and *Tel quel* sections into two, giving me four chapters and a balanced project. This would have forced to me to articulate a strong principle of connection between Pound and the *Tel quel* group, lest the project appear to be internally unjustified—lest, that is, the combination of Pound and *Tel quel* look purely arbitrary. (This is a frequent problem with seminar papers turned articles, where the justification stems from the academic course the two or three particular authors were taught in, but you also get this problem sometimes with comparative literature dissertations that bring together two writers who don't seem to have much in common—Jorge Luis Borges and Sarah Orne Jewett, or something—thus obligating the writer to begin the whole thing by saying something like, "Everyone thinks that Borges and Jewett have nothing in common, and of course there's no evidence that the former ever knew of the latter. But they are surprisingly connected because both traveled widely, and both had mothers that died young," etc., etc. This is almost always terribly unconvincing.)

The alternative was to come up with a third (or fourth) chapter. Tricky, because given the material I had, I could not reasonably come up with a second French or second Anglo-American chapter; the resulting project would have been oddly weighted. It could possibly have been justified, but I would have had to work hard to manage the relationships so that the selection of the chapters did not seem arbitrary, and so that the general claims the dissertation made could be appropriately defended. (If you are going to talk about "Chinese dreams" in general, then having two examples from one part of the world and only one from another is a weird thing to do.) For similar reasons I couldn't really have a third chapter from anywhere too close to 1915 or 1974; I needed something either about halfway between them, earlier in the 1860s/1870s, or later in the 1990s. So I went to the library and spent several weeks digging around for material before coming across Bertolt Brecht, who fit the bill perfectly (German, with evidentiary high points in 1935 and 1953). Brecht also had the advantage of being roughly as famous and important as Pound and the *Tel quel* theorists.

I've used a fairly pragmatic example to illustrate an ethical argument—that books should create wholes. The contrast is typical: high-blown talk about the meaning of writing comes down to, when the rubber meets the road, highly practical decisions about what to do and how to write, and how to balance a project historically, geographically, and otherwise. Feelings and practice intersect. The finished work is their adjudication.

Six

A Materialist Theory of Writing

Ideas don't exist except when they're communicable. The best idea in the world will do almost no one any good if it can't be spoken or written down or drawn or sung or danced or carved or otherwise passed on.

This is especially true for the professional scholar, since in that realm the ideas *are*, effectively, the sentences they're in. From this perspective people don't have ideas; they have sentences that communicate ideas. Thinking of the ideas as somehow separate from the sentences—either "before" or "after" them, as most writers tend to do for academic prose—means having a fairly dismal theory of language, believing that the actual stuff of language makes no significant difference to the meaning it communicates. No serious person has that theory of language for literature—otherwise we'd read "thou still unravished bride of quietness" as the emotional and intellectual equivalent of "Hey there, tongue-tied virgin." If you believe that the poetic, grammatical, and rhetorical impact of language accounts for at least some of the force of literary work, then you should believe it for scholarly writing too, especially because, among other reasons, what we call "literature" contains a good deal of writing (Ben Jonson, Michel de Montaigne, Confucius, for example) that thought of itself as scholarly at the time. QED.

How do ideas materialize? Or rather, how do sentences materialize ideas? Only in relation to a receiver, who is, barring genuine debility (and even so!), the final arbiter of what was *actually* communicated by any given utterance. Whether this is true in a final ontological sense matters less than that it's true in a professional one: if everyone but you thinks your sentences express uninteresting or incomprehensible ideas, that's your problem, not theirs. (At least in this lifetime. Being recognized as a genius after you're dead is surely worth something, but it's hard to tell what, exactly, from this side of the morbid border.) This means that when you are writing, you are writing for one or more specific readers, about whom you must be at least reasonably well informed. This is trivially the case when one considers that all academic essays are primarily monolingual, that all writers expect their readers to be conversant with some basic professional vocabulary, and so on. It's more interestingly the case when you begin to account, as a writer, for the emotional and mental structures that govern the way your expected readers read, and begin to use prose to manage and manipulate those structures as you make meaning. The reader is the *home* of your ideas. Writing is a performance that happens in the intersection between your work and the reader's experience of it. The ethos of good writing begins with that recognition.

Though this does mean that all writers are to some extent trapped by the audience they want to reach, the good news is that you can also use your writing to shape your audience, to nudge your readers one way or another, thus creating a new audience that belongs specifically to your work. Easy enough for most of us who have loved novels, plays, or poems to imagine how a work of art trains the eyes, ears, and minds of its audience to new tastes, or creates new modes of aesthetic perception and social awareness. And there's no good reason to exclude nonfiction in general or literary criticism in particular from such a possibility. Indeed, if you are in this profession it is, I hope, because at some point you loved some piece of scholarly work you read: something moved you, exploded you with joy and possibility and apish, desperate desire. I get those feelings when I read work by Susan Stewart, Fredric Jameson, or Mark McGurl (among others)—happiness at the sheer wonderfulness and brilliance of it, overlain by the fear that I'll never write anything as good. That's what being someone's audience feels like: a transformation that leaves neither the reader nor the work unchanged.

(The strength of that mutual becoming is why I have no time for the folks who complain about how terrible or boring or stupid or self-absorbed academic writing is. Sure, some of it is terrible. Some of everything is terrible. But some of it is wonderful, and much of it is trying very hard to be wonderful. If we recognize how hard good writing is, how fraught with professional and personal anxieties it can be, we might be a bit more generous to ourselves and to one another about it. Yes, our failures are collective, but so are our triumphs: great writing is only great for an occasion and an audience that exists to be changed by it. We readers are the audience that makes that joyous changing possible.)

As the poet said: no ideas but in things. And "things," sentences and paragraphs, only in relation to readers, who establish the structures of change, comprehensibility, and import that frame any act of communication. This is what I meant when, in chapter 1, I described writing as a process that transformed your "best ideas" into something better than your best ideas: good writing makes ideas better not only by improving their best qualities (their fineness, their structural integrity, their evidentiary support) but by making them available to a community of readers, whose response determines, in the long run, whether your sentences (or the ideas they encode and express) matter at all.

I am not suggesting here that you must always bow to some concept of the reader, that there can be nothing in your work that indulges your own aesthetic or intellectual faith, your beliefs about what makes good scholarship or prose, or your commitment to making the work your own. What you publish will have your name on it; it ought to make you happy and proud. The sentences are *yours* too, and so you must, readers be damned, also write for yourself, in concordance with your goals as a maker of things. Don't write to the lowest common denominator; don't consistently embrace the audience's deepest habits or shallowest expectations; don't treat scholarship as little more than marketing or advertising (though some aspects of its rhetorical and performative work overlap with those fields). Scholarly work that gets made for the audience's easiest pleasures doesn't change minds, or lives. Many audiences *want* to be startled, engaged, disturbed, and otherwise shocked out of their familiar habits. (This is why the clarity fetishists, chanting over the preserved bodies of Strunk and White, are wrong to make concision or plainness the panacea for all communication's ills.) Sometimes the difficulty of a piece of writing comes from how much in its audience it seeks to remake or undo. Such work—like the best paintings, poems, sculpture, or music—rewards the thicket-clearing struggle with visions of improbable, darkling horizons. Those horizons, when they come, come at least sometimes *from* the struggle. This means that your writing can *use* difficulty, that managing clarity and difficulty can become an aspect of a given style. What matters is to know what you're doing and why, which will allow you to be bold in your ambition and clear-eyed in your pursuit of its effect on your readers, to prepare your audience for an experience that will belong to the performance of its reading. All of this amounts to your signature on the work.

Seven

How Do Readers Work?

Your experience of the text differs in one deeply significant and structural way from that of your readers: while the reader reads the article or book in order, from start to finish, over time, you know the finished project as an unfolding whole. You see on a single plane, as though from a great height, what the reader will experience as a passage and a journey. As you write and revise, this synchronic, overarching perspective will appear to you gradually, unfolding slowly its transitions, its emotional low and high points, its structure, and its argument in the lines as you work them. By the project's end you have no excuse not to know your project backwards and forwards.

But you are not writing for someone who will know your project in those ways. You are writing for those who will in most cases read your work only once and who, if you are lucky, will only occasionally skip or skim paragraphs or sections, only sometimes read while distracted by the radio, a demanding student (or colleague), their own desperate unhappiness, or an alarming rash. You can hope for an attentive reader who will be game and willing to hear those things in your book that you have addressed to such a rigorous attention. (You should in fact be this reader for others, if you can.) You cannot, however, expect it.

The challenge of a reader who reads only once also faces many novelists, who organize the fiction from beginning to end with an eye on the first-time reader's experience, adjusting for its sake the patterns of silence and unveiling that make for irony, suspense, comedy, or drama. It would be odd if all novels began with a few paragraphs announcing in meta-discourse the point they were trying to make or the rough conclusion to their plots. (Some do, but they gain energy precisely from their violation of a generic norm; in general, anticipation, not surprise, makes the magic of much great literature.) While you may not need to organize your article or book as though it were a murder mystery, the sheer pleasure one-time readers take in fiction's revelations suggests a parallel for authors of academic work: you need to write for, and think continually of, a reader whose basic temporal experience of the work will be radically different from your own, and for whose pleasure you are essentially responsible. This is why the work should not be a simple expression of "your" "ideas." The relation you have to that expression in prose is unique: no one else wrote your work, and no one else will ever read it the way you do. Any piece of scholarly writing is, therefore, an expression of thought designed to communicate to readers who have not yet thought it.

This simple truth lies behind the standard advice to go back and revise your introduction when you're finished with something. You thought you were writing about René Descartes; turns out you wrote a book about Renée, the Duchess of Chartres. You don't hold yourself to the introduction you wrote weeks or months ago; you go back, you change what you said, and you set up readers' expectations so that they match what the work actually does. In so doing you see the work from that synchronic height, managing and adjusting it so that it creates single meaningful experience for the reader who comes at the pages one by one.

The insights that lead you to alter the introduction apply to the work as a whole. Your job is to create an encounter for a reader who will experience your work from start to finish, diachronically. The synchronic writer manages the ordering of the text with that reader in mind. So if, for instance, you know that on page 45 you will be introducing an important concept, "diegetic rectitude," you can go back to the earlier sections of the work and sprinkle in various cognates or synonyms of those terms (using "right" or "rectify" for "rectitude," for example) so as to prepare your readers' ears (semi-consciously) for the eventual arrival of your master term. If they encounter "diegetic rectitude" for the first time after having read sentences like, "Thompson's actions set right the pattern of the diegesis," or "Malory thus rectifies what we might think of as James's diegetic 'mistake,' adjusting narrative space to the purposes of plot," they will find the new term a comfortable resolution of a concept that, in hindsight, they will recognize had been developing for ten pages or so. Whereas if "diegetic rectitude" shows up more or less out of nowhere, the reader will have a harder time grasping it, and you may have to do more work on the back end laying it out than you would have otherwise. Neither of these choices is necessarily the better one, but we often write as though the second were the only option because we tend to write as though earlier pages were unalterable rock. They are, for the reader. But for the writer, the first page is just as malleable as the last; the writing process makes no formal difference between them. Put plainly: every sentence in your work should *know* about every other sentence in it. No sentence stands alone. Each sentence plays its role within a system and pattern of development that leads inexorably from the first page to the last one.

Once you get that writing creates diachronic experiences for a reader, understanding your audience's psychological needs and practical habits becomes a central part of writing practice. You may consider, for instance, what I call the psychological arc of your article, chapter, or book. What are the points of highest energy? Lowest energy? Where do you expect the reader to be surprised? Where do you *want* the reader to be surprised? Are there moments in which you need to lighten the tone, to give your reader a break? Can you change the spacing of your quotations to affect the reader's experience of argumentative pace? Are there places where you'd like the reader to speed up? To slow down? What should the graph of the ideal reader's emotions look like, start to finish?

Some of these questions are diagnostic—such as, what is my essay doing?—and help you understand the pattern of writing you have. They also let you analyze and describe the academic prose of others, which helps you help friends and colleagues with their writing and makes you a finer critic and reader in your field. Understanding how, for instance, the pattern of energetic development in Derrida's *Limited Inc* differs from the one in *Of Grammatology* can help you understand the larger structures of both works, which have to do partly with the ways they think about evidence, and their rhetorical uses of provocation and humor. More pragmatically, diagnostic questions will point you to your own patterns of development, allowing you to begin thinking of those features as extensions of the work you are doing, opportunities to manage or manipulate the reader's experience in useful ways.

Diagnostic questions thus lead to prognostic ones. What do I want my essay to be doing? Where does the emotional pattern I have developed go from here? This type of question considers the psychological structure as a feature of your prose partially independent from its argument, allowing you to decide something like, *I need a surprise here,* or *This section needs to be slower,* not because the content requires it (you have an especially new or complex idea, for example) but because the psychological or rhetorical pattern you are building does.

Let me give you an example from my own writing. In the conclusion of *Chinese Dreams* I introduce the term "sinography" to describe the kind of intellectual approach to the study of China justified by the book's examples and analyses. (I didn't invent the term; it came out of discussions between me and a few other people, but I knew the reader would not have seen it before.) Let me give you a sense of the prose: "I take sinography, literally the 'writing' of 'China,' to be the study not simply of how China is written *about,* but the ways in which that writing constitutes itself simultaneously as a *form* of writing and as a *form* of Chineseness, in a gesture whose style and content are always already turned back of themselves in an (un)concealment of their own origin." Heavy stuff. I go on like that for the rest of a long paragraph. By paragraph's end, I thought, the reader would be on the verge of understanding the argument, but would still need a few more sentences of explanation. The obvious move at that point was to begin the next paragraph, "That is, . . . " and then explain the whole thing again in different language, counting on the time the reader would spend on both paragraphs to allow the argument to sink in and become comfortable.

What I did instead was to switch over to a new paragraph, with no obvious transition: "In the Freudian model of the dream as a wish fulfillment, the dream is divided into its manifest (surface) content and its latent content." I then quoted from a chatty e-mail from Christopher Bush that ends up comparing asparaguses to penises. I discussed the asparagus/penis comparison (the point was to ask how you would account for the resemblance between the manifest and the latent content; though technically anything can be a symbol, asparaguses or sausages tend to symbolize penises more often than, say, eggs) for another few sentences. At the end of that discussion, still in the middle of the paragraph, I wrote, "What is it about the shape of China that has made it a likely candidate for Western dreams about science, translation, writing, politics? It seems to me that sinography must attempt to answer this question if it is to be honest about the 'material and historical conditions' of the West's 'China.'" Sinography's return at that moment, I thought, would come as a relief. Readers, having expected more on the concept, would have been alarmed, I imagined, by the rapid switch in topics (Freudian dream analysis) and registers (e-mail, asparagus, penises). They would have wondered where they were in the text, whether they had fully grasped what was happening. And then, in the middle of the paragraph, the sentence "what is it about the shape of China . . . ," with the word "shape" shifting from the literal (asparaguses) to the metaphorical (China), would bring the seeming digression back into the main line of the argument. The subsequent sentence reveals that we have been talking about sinography all along. I wrote the paragraph both to create the anxiety that we had switched topics without properly finishing out the subject under discussion, and to relieve that anxiety in a surprising way. My sense was that the intensity of those two emotions—the anxiety and the relief—would heighten the emotional impact of this section, especially by comparison to a version in which I simply met readers' expectations for continuous, sustained, clear explanation. And I thought that this emotional intensity would make sinography more memorable and richer, both effects stemming from the emotional and stylistic range within which the concept first appears.

I'm not saying that this was the greatest move of all time. I'm not even sure it worked. I provide the example to illustrate the kinds of things you *might* think about and manage, were you to make the reader's psychological state a lever of your argument. And also to suggest that clarity, like any other feature of prose, has no value outside of the circumstances of a particular writing situation. Be clear when clarity will maximize the reader's overall experience of your work.

I'll have more to say about how to manage the reader's experience in the next part of the book. For now I simply want to assert the general principle: that if you understand the difference between your relationship to the text and your reader's, and if you begin to imagine the reader as

Is Manipulating the Reader Wrong?

We all think it's completely normal for any other work of art to engage its audience rhetorically, to adjust its emotions, making it laugh, startle, grimace, or cry in the name of its total experience. And we know, when it comes to things like the Shakespearean comic interlude, that the modes of such engagement and management can be codified, formalized, taught, and used by artists and critics alike. So why exclude those modes from literary criticism? Well, because—someone could say—manipulating the reader is wrong. When it comes to scientific research, we owe it to the reader to write as clearly as we can, to present plainly and with no ornament a straight line to the truth. This plain presentation reflects the solidity of our conclusions; it guarantees the emotionless, objective, impersonal quality of our statements of fact.

This is an odd position for anyone in the humanities to hold, though many people hold it anyway (mostly unconsciously). Reading books on the history or rhetoric of science should set such folks straight: language has never been a neutral screen for the truth. If we recognize that the power and beauty of literature as a social force stems from its (sometimes hostile) engagement with language, then we ought to *live up to*, rather than deny, that power and beauty and their capacity for truth-making in our own prose. Thinking about the reader's psychological journey is a natural consequence of asking academic writing to embrace what we know is best and most exciting about the power of the written word: its greatness as a medium for social and intellectual life.

the site of the performative action of your work—the place that inhabits it with meaning—then thinking well about what readers like, how they read, or the ways writing can make them feel will improve your ability to write work that matters. Your goal is to build, synchronically, a winning diachronic experience.

Part II
Strategy

So here's what we've covered so far:

1. How to think of writing as a dynamic practice that includes its behavioral, emotional, and institutional parameters
2. How to build habits that help you get work done and stay happy
3. How to match your writing to its institutional, generic, and national contexts
4. How to orient your work toward the unique experience of its reader.

The rest of it is just work: strategy for the big concepts, tactics for the small ones. Let's move forward.

Eight

The Uneven U

Imagine a system or a continuum that, across five levels, divides one major function of a piece of literary critical prose: its proximity to a piece of evidence. Call level 5 the most abstract, theoretical kind of statement an essay might make and level 1 something like pure or raw evidence: a quotation, a paraphrase, plot summary, descriptions of art objects or historical events—anything that approximates the objective or the neutral. In between you have the three other levels: level 4, for general theoretical statements that govern a specific subtopic; level 3, for statements that balance between the evidentiary and the conceptual; and level 2, for sentences that shape, describe, or otherwise locate evidentiary material in an abstract context. We can see the difference between the levels in a sentence like this one:

> The conflict's final resolution comes only in the poem's fourth stanza, when the poem's habitually enjambed lines give way to a sudden series of end-stopped, fragmentary, thoughts: "he didn't see me there in flames / the going rate annunciates / I clasp Marconi's radio / still waters of the Thames."

The part in quotes, relatively unmediated evidence from the object at hand, is thus level 1. The sentence that precedes the quotation combines two levels: the sentence's first component, which is conceptual and argumentative (it makes a *claim* about what happens to the resolution of a conflict), is level 3 or perhaps even 4, while the second part, which *describes* the evidence that's about to appear, is level 2.

Here is a list of the levels, and what they indicate:

5   abstract, general; oriented toward a solution or a conclusion
4   less general; oriented toward a problem; pulls ideas together
3   conceptual summary; draws together two or more pieces of evidence, or introduces a broad example
2   description; plain or interpretive summary; establishing shot
1   concrete; evidentiary; raw, unmediated data or information

You can work through these levels for an entire paragraph (example 8.1). See how the paragraph opens with general statements, moves down to provide evidence for its claim, and then summarizes and extends that evidence before moving to an abstract conclusion? You should also notice how some sentences operate at two levels, usually broken by punctuation. This is most obvious in the last sentence, which moves after the long dash from a general summary of the work of *this* paragraph to an argument that connects to the larger goals of the article from which it is drawn (which is one way to think about the difference between 4 and 5). But you can also see it happening in the sentence immediately before it, where the comma after "minority" seems to split the sentence into a slightly less abstract front half and a slightly more abstract back half. If you wanted to, you could call the first part level 3 and the second level 3.5, but the point here is not so much to get the numbers just right as it is to use the numbers as a shorthand for pinpointing and discussing *relative* differences in the function of academic prose.

Now, once you begin using a system like this one, you will find that a basic shape exists that can describe a very effective structure for any given paragraph, sub-section, section, essay, or book in literary criticism: the Uneven U (figure 8.1). I will be using the Uneven U to give you diagnostic and prescriptive advice about structure from here on out. I don't claim that it describes all academic writing, though it does describe much of it. I also don't claim that the U is the only surefire way to write, just that it is one useful way to do so. Because the U visually represents a calcification of the general principles about writing elaborated in this book, it is not so

---

We begin with the problem of character. (lv. 4) That the reader understands that the novel is populated by "minor" characters—that these seeming protagonists have come detached from their usual narrative position—depends heavily on intertextual references to a number of other works. (lv. 3) These range from the popular to the highbrow. (lv. 2) Belvedere and Nestor, for instance, are the names of the butlers in the 1980s American television sitcom *Mr. Belvedere* and the Tintin graphic novels, respectively; Clopin and Yorick hail from Hugo's *Hunchback of Notre Dame* and, of course, *Hamlet*. (lv. 1) All together these characters amount to a cavalcade of conspicuous minority, an exemplification of the notion that quantity has a quality all its own. (lv. 3) To understand the novel thus requires us to understand how that characterological quality emerges from onomastic proliferation (lv. 4)—and in turn understanding what the novel might mean by *quality* at all. (lv. 5)

The first sentence establishes a general theme; sentence 2 provides specifics about the argument of *this* paragraph (thus moving conceptually "down" from the general to the specific).

This sentence introduces the evidence (level 2) . . .

. . . and this sentence presents it (level 1).

Beginning with "All together," which signals a move "up" toward summary and interpretation, these two sentences interpret the evidence given in level 1, thus operating at levels 3 and, as the ideas get bigger, 4.

The paragraph concludes with its biggest, most abstract idea, which appears after the em dash in the final sentence

---

EXAMPLE 8.1

much a guide or ideal that exists outside of or prior to those structures, as it is a memorable distillation of the way those structures can be made to work in practice. Once the language of the U becomes part of how you think about literary criticism, you will also be able to use it not only to understand and describe types of writing that do not follow its patterns at all but to *write* them.

So what does the U describe? A pattern of development. A classic U body paragraph will begin with a sentence that locates readers inside an existing argument and prepares them for the thematic, evidentiary, or argumentative developments that follow. The typical U paragraph opening often operates at level 4. This situates the reader inside the essay and makes a set of promises about the content to come. It does not—and this is the importance of the 4 (as opposed to a 5)—tell the reader exactly what will happen in the paragraph. It is not in this sense—and in a way that contradicts what most U.S. students will have learned in high school—a *thesis* statement. The 4 *opens* the paragraph; it makes thematic, argumentative, and structural promises.

A classic U paragraph will follow the level-4 sentence by moving toward a piece of evidence or an argument that is closer to the "ground." The second and/or third sentences might contextualize the evidence historically or thematically (level 3); the next one(s) after that might tell the reader where the evidence appears by, for instance, describing where or when in a novel someone says something (level 2). Finally we arrive at level 1, direct evidence. (What this direct evidence will be depends on what you're talking about: for a novel, it could be a citation or the description of a scene; for a film, a description of a shot sequence or montage; for historical material, it might be a firsthand report of an event; for an argument, it would be the central ground for the larger claims

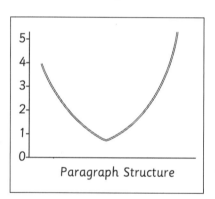

FIGURE 8.1 The Uneven U.

of the paragraph; and so on). Most direct evidence will be followed by contextualization and interpretation of gradually increasing complexity (moving from level 1 up to level 2, then 3). The next-to-last sentence(s) of the paragraph will further contextualize the larger argument (level 4). The final sentence articulates the major claim or contribution of the paragraph to the essay as a whole (level 5). It summarizes but, like all good conclusions, it does more than that: it draws together the material of the paragraph in a way that establishes new knowledge, a new concept or a step forward in the argument.

The key to this developmental pattern is that the final sentence (level 5) is *higher* than the one you started with (level 4). This gives the paragraph a progressive structure. Unlike paragraphs that begin with a sentence that gives everything away ("In this paragraph I show that the Reagan presidency had three major features . . . "), the best kinds of level-4 beginnings open up an entire field of meaning, essentially giving the reader an interesting problem to think about, while also promising that the problem will be at least partially be resolved by the end of the paragraph ("How did the Reagan presidency work?"). If you go back to the paragraph about minor characters, you will see that it follows exactly the pattern I have laid out here: 4 – 3 – 2 – 1 – 3 – 4 – 5. It starts with a general statement of the problem, introduces evidence, provides evidence more fully, summarizes and interprets that evidence, and finally connects to a new idea whose endpoint lies beyond the paragraph itself.

But of course that's because I wrote it as an example of the Uneven U. What happens when we look at paragraphs written by other people? Does the Uneven U describe their work?

Let's start with a couple introductory sentences:

As with ethnography before it, so today the nature film both charts and carries through the ultimate receding of nature. (Pick 168)

"Ithaca" neither mocks nor glorifies the meeting between Stephen and Bloom; it employs and exploits it. (McCrea 142)

Each of them sets up the reader for a paragraph that will develop toward a conclusion. We get themes (for Pick, nature film; for McCrea, the "Ithaca" chapter of Joyce's *Ulysses*) and we get argument (that nature film manages the receding of nature in a particular way; that "Ithaca" handles Stephen and Bloom in a particular way). But neither sentence gives everything completely away. We don't know how nature film charts and carries through nature's receding; we don't know how "Ithaca" employs and exploits the meeting. So we keep reading.

Let's see how McCrea's paragraph fulfills the promises made by its opening sentence. I have numbered the units of movement, some of which break inside longer sentences (and are hence labeled 3.5 and 5.5).

[Sentence 1] "Ithaca" neither mocks nor glorifies the meeting between Stephen and Bloom; it employs and exploits it. [2] It is important not for what it is or what it means but for what it generates, what relationship to existing, concrete reality it produces. [3] The long lists in "Ithaca" do not—as some have suggested—serve to mock or obscure the supposedly mythical meeting of father and son; [3.5] the meaning of the meeting for the characters is a matter for them, or for the reader's own sensibility. [4] Whether it fails or succeeds, whether it is a spiritual revelation or an absurd disappointment is an open question, a variable. [5] But for *Ulysses* itself, a sprawling, unruly work, what matters is not its spiritual function but its narrative one, its role as a system, not an event: [5.5] it is this meeting that produces and structures the particular account of reality the novel gives us. (McCrea 142)

Now, this is an interesting paragraph, because what we might think of as a level-1 clause or sentence, a pure piece of evidence, never really appears. Nonetheless you can watch McCrea move down and in relative to his major claim in the shift from the first to the second sentence, where he uses a repeating "not/but" structure to emphasize the parallelisms. He moves from level 4 (a general abstract claim) to level 3 (less abstract, because it serves as an extension and argument for the initial claim). The third sentence repeats the "not/but" structure, as McCrea adds more evidence. Notice that the evidence is progressively more detailed and precise here; we have moved "down" again, to something like level 2. The opening of that sentence seems to be the trough of the U in this paragraph. We never get a citation; the mention of the "long lists" is the closest to pure evidence we see. By the second half of that sentence (after the semicolon) we are already moving up and into interpretation of the evidence (levels 2 and 3). Sentence 4 now begins to move back up and out, a shift signaled by the "Whether it fails or succeeds," which opens the possibility of *judgment* of the evidence, and is thus "higher" than sentence 3. That entire sentence in fact moves upward from level 3 to level 4—it begins with "whether," repeats the "whether," and withholds its own judgment till the sentence's last few words; judgment is "higher" than the possibility of judgment (but note: the judgment is that judgment is "an open question"!). The last sentence now gives us what McCrea really thinks: in *Ulysses* the meeting matters by virtue of its relation to novelistic structure and pattern; the novel is essentially indifferent to its moral or emotional weight. This is what McCrea meant, back in the first sentence, when he

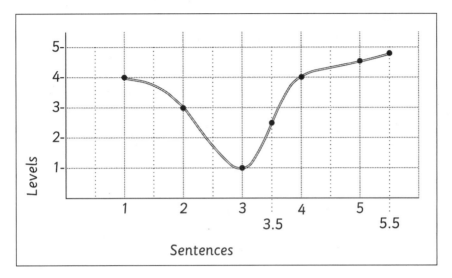

FIGURE 8.2 The Uneven U in a paragraph from Barry McCrea's *In the Company of Strangers*.

said that the novel "employs and exploits" the meeting. But we couldn't have known that then. We could only be engaged by the promise of an explanation for those terms, which the paragraph gives us in its final sentence (level 5). You can see the rough shape of the Uneven U when we graph the level movement of the paragraph (figure 8.2).

We find a far more classic U structure in McCrea's next paragraph, which includes a long block quotation from the novel:

[1] The parallel between Stephen and Bloom allows for extensive extrapolations, which move and stretch backward and forward across the generations. [2] The chapter showcases this idea in its exposition of the ration of their ages, creating a supposedly consistent relationship between the two men that spans the period from 81396 B.C. to 3072 A.D.

[Here McCrea gives a very long block quote from the novel]

[3] As Patrick McCarthy and others have shown, the math in the passage above is "either confused or flat wrong." [4] If the errors are deliberate, the idea is perhaps all the more forceful, and not because the "fusion" of Stephen and Bloom is a failure; the passage showcases how their meeting could *theoretically* be a point of view for all of human history.

[5] *Ulysses* as a whole does not push it this far, and the passage is designed to highlight that the novel must keep the idea within limits. [6] The world is neither perfectible nor fully describable, and the mistaken calculations serve as a reminder that this is a novel and that no account of the relationship between Bloom and Stephen, or of reality itself, is sufficient, universal, or precise, that nothing, queer or straight, can ever be wholly all-encompassing (Stephen's inexplicable decision to sing an anti-Semitic ballad to his host underlines this). [7] This key recognition about genealogy—that it is but one contingent mode of structuring time and relations—applies equally well to any queer alternatives to it. (McCrea 142–43)

Again, the first sentence sets up a promise and a thematic context for the rest of the work (the reader will ask, "What are these extrapolations? How do they work across generations?" and can expect those questions to be answered). Skipping from the first to the final sentence will allow you to see how McCrea gets from level 4 to level 5 over the course of the paragraph, giving you the "extensive extrapolations" he promised in the first lines in the last ones. The appearance of the word "genealogy" in the final sentence, which picks up on the word "generations" from the first, binds the two sentences together with sound as well as sense.

Overall the paragraph is a classic example of the Uneven U. As he proceeds through the paragraph, McCrea approaches the block quotation with a level-2 sentence that brings us down toward level 1 by beginning with "the chapter" (signaling specificity), the word "showcases" (pointing to the imminent arrival of evidence), and a brief contextual paraphrase of the citation. Coming out of the block quotation (pure evidence, level 1), he recontextualizes the evidentiary material in the context of contemporary criticism, focusing on largely factual features of the paragraph in sentence 3 (level 2). Sentence 4 abstracts the factual matter, especially in the material after the semicolon (level 3). Sentence 5 moves us up again, this time using the name of the novel, *Ulysses,* to tell us we've gotten from the smaller unit (the chapter, the quotation) to the larger one (the novel as a whole) (level 4). The long sixth sentence—you will find that often in scholarly writing the penultimate sentence of a paragraph is its longest—pulls together the various abstracting threads; we might think of it as coming between levels 4 and 5, a grammatically complex fulfillment of the promise of the first sentence. The final sentence consolidates and confirms the most important aspects of sentence 6, bringing the reader fully into level 5—the paragraph's payoff, its take-home idea. It tells us as much with the words "This key recognition," which begin it.

As you can see, the Uneven U (which, as far as I know, Barry McCrea has never heard of) does a pretty good job describing his paragraph. We get an opening promise, a move toward detail, and then a building up from the detail outward to a conclusion that supersedes the first sentence. In the two paragraphs of McCrea's that we looked at, we also saw something of the difference between a paragraph with a "true" level 1 (that is, a piece of direct, objective, or completely evidentiary material, namely the block quotation) and a paragraph without one. In the first paragraph we get the same general movement and shape, from a general premise/promise down to a more detailed and subsidiary development of the premise (the detail is essentially argumentative and paraphrasal, not citational), and back upwards to a consolidation of detail and a conclusion. But despite these differences both paragraphs look structurally like an Uneven U.

Once you've seen the basic structure of the Uneven U, you can amend and complicate the principles that govern it. First, you will have noticed, in the analysis of McCrea's sentences, that a level-2 sentence that follows the bottom of the trough is not the same as a level-2 sentence that precedes it (one usually sets up the evidence; the other contextualizes and moves toward abstraction). The levels are *relative*: a level-4 sentence before a level-3 sentence is not the same as a 4 after a 3; likewise a sentence that functions as a 2 in one paragraph could function as a 4 or a 5 in a different paragraph. Because they are relative, they are also *flexible*: in the first paragraph we see how McCrea moves from level 4 down to something between 2 and 3 in the course of the first three sentences, then moves all the way back out in two longer ones (the longer sentences make up about 44 percent of the words in the paragraph altogether); in the second paragraph, by contrast, he takes 114 words, three very long sentences (5–7), to get out and close, after having spent two sentences (2 and 3) just getting into and out of the level-1 block quotation (itself longer than the rest of the paragraph).

Despite these differences, the simple structure of both paragraphs is the same. The capacity of the Uneven U to manage difference inside pattern—its combination of structural and rhythmic flexibility with narrative power and drive—makes it the default structure for the vast majority of U.S. academic writing about literature today. It is this basic arrangement, this rhetoric of argumentation and persuasion, that I recommend you use in your own work. I also suggest that you learn to see and identify it in the work of others, since it will help you understand how and why certain writers whose tone or style differs from the quasi-normative version of the structure McCrea uses here actually *produce*, via shifts in structure, their differences.

I have been calling the Uneven U a "structure" or "arrangement" because it is more than simply just a way to build paragraphs. It is an essentially fractal or scalable model for any unit of argumentative or narrative prose larger than a paragraph: a sub-section, a section, an essay, or a book as a whole. So long as the levels remain relative to one another, what happens is that the level 5 at which one closes a paragraph or a section becomes or leads into, the level 4 of the following one (figure 8.3).

Note what happens in figure 8.3. We have two paragraphs, one following the other, in which the conclusion of the first paragraph (a level-5 sentence) transitions into the beginning of the next one, becoming in effect a new level 4 for that paragraph. That paragraph in turn closes at its own 5. Underneath that—or more accurately, parallel to it—we have the larger structure of the section that both these paragraphs belong to. This section may have its *own* paragraphs—the parts labeled "4" at the beginning and "5" at the end, that is, could actually be paragraphs of their own (and not simply reflections of the section-level structural work being done inside the two units labeled with the ¶ symbol). A paragraph, for instance, at the beginning of the section as a whole (where the "4" is), would essentially function as a 4 for that

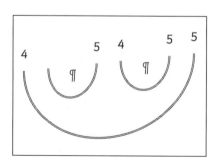

FIGURE 8.3 A two-paragraph section.

entire section, even as *inside that paragraph* it has its own U-shaped structure. Following the two "body" paragraphs, you could close with a final paragraph (where the last "5" is in the figure), which would function as a 5 relative to the initial level 4 paragraph, fulfilling the promise of the section as a whole even as it, once again, had its own structural rhythm relative to its own labor as a paragraph. In other words you would have four paragraphs: a paragraph to open the section, two paragraphs of evidence, and a paragraph to close it.

Alternatively, you could imagine a short two-paragraph section in which the sectional functions (the major promise of the section, the 4, and the close, the 5) appear *inside* the two paragraphs themselves: the 4 at the beginning of the first paragraph, which would close with a 5 for that paragraph, which would then lead into a 4 for the second paragraph, whose penultimate sentence would close the paragraph (5 relative to the paragraph) and whose final sentence would close the whole section (5 relative to the section). When integrated into paragraphs this way, section-level (or subsection level) 4s and 5s stay "smaller" than they would if they were constructed as entire paragraphs; the U stays relatively proportional to the parts that made it up.

The fractal structure can get quite complicated, as can be seen in figure 8.4. Here you have two sections, A and B, each composed of subsections, named a and b, which are in turn composed of paragraphs. Each large section will need its own opening and closing structure, for which the subsections will function as level-2, 3, or 4 building blocks. For instance, let's say that section A is an argument about the impact of oil painting techniques on the historical relation between persons and backgrounds in eighteenth-century Italy. The two smaller sections, a and b, might each be on different techniques or artists. They would thus function as level-1/2 (evidentiary) units in relation to the larger claims made by the section as a whole, even as they might—over the course of their paragraphs—begin their paragraphs with level-4 sentences, move down to give direct evidence (an image or a description of a painting, for example), interpret that evidence, and draw theoretical conclusions from it. The movement from a to b inside the larger section would have to be carefully considered, so that it too moved "up" as it progressed, helping set up the close of the section as a whole. More work has to be

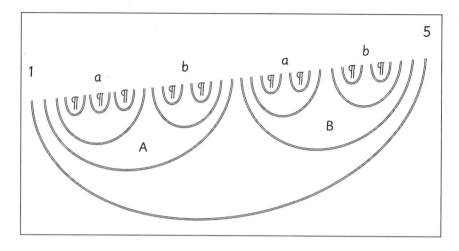

FIGURE 8.4 Fractal madness: two large sections, *A* and *B*, with subsections, *a* and *b*, inside a larger section.

done, therefore, at the end of subsection b than at the end of subsection a, since subsection b is contiguous with the close of section A as a whole, and needs to lead into it.

At any given moment, then, a sentence may be serving as a 4 in relation to its own paragraph, but a 1 or 3 in relation to its subsection, and something else again in relation to its larger section. If you imagine this same structure (but larger in scope) for an entire book, you can see how the conclusion would be the 5 to the introduction's 4, and how each of the chapters would, ideally, help build a structure that would lead to the level-5 work of the conclusion doing for the book as a whole what Barry McCrea's seventh sentence did for his long paragraph: giving readers a clear, exciting explanation of why what they have just read matters and what it's worth. (I will have more to say later about why this structure may not work for some books.)

Let's look at one more example, from a work in progress by Andrea Bachner (example 8.2). Here the U appears across three paragraphs, rather than in a single paragraph. I've annotated the structure in-line and drawn out the U after that (figure 8.5).

First Paragraph

Nolan's *Memento* is trauma made film, on two different levels.

A classic level 4 opening, this sentence sets up the promise of a conclusion that draws those levels together.

On a first level, the presentation of Leonard's amnesia and compulsion to repeat not only narrativizes the consequences of trauma—both physical and psychological.

We move down and in. This sentence combines elements of levels 3 and 2.

Mirrored in the film's reverse structure, it also links the protagonist's suffering and the viewer's visual experience.

The "also" signals that we are staying on the same level.

On a second level *Memento*'s translation of memory traces from the psyche to other material surfaces, such as paper and body, reflect on a situation of interrupted storage of information as well as a change in medium: from analog to digital film.

"On a second level" creates a slight conceptual move up. The rest of the sentence moves us down and explains what author means by "second level."

By analogy, the protagonist's posttraumatic condition parallels film's plight after the impact of digitality.

The last sentence of the paragraph is a 4, if a very weak 4. It gathers the two levels and moves up conceptually, via the word "analogy," but it does not present us with a strong closure, for which you'd need *another* sentence at level 5.

Second Paragraph

And yet, several moments in *Memento* resist such a reading.

The "and yet" is a very light transition, signals disagreement inside continuity; we are here at a level 4 again but a light one. The word "moments" tells us that we are moving toward evidence, and thus levels 2/1.

True, Leonard's psychic state fits the label of trauma. But his condition effectively doubles trauma by way of amnesia.

These two sentences continue the level 4, since they articulate the paragraph's major claim.

Leonard's amnesia is not only a side effect of trauma (of the attack on his wife, of his head injury), but lies at the core of the traumatic experience itself: it caused the death of his wife, because, oblivious to prior injections, Leonard administered her an overdose of insulin.

After the colon in this sentence, we're moving down and in toward filmic evidence; this is probably level 2, a plot summary. The insulin episode is the trough of the overall U, the closest we come to the direct description of a filmic moment.

EXAMPLE 8.2

Paradoxically, then, Leonard's reduplication of oblivion, his effort to forget by rewriting reality, by redacting information for the benefit of his future self who will have erased all recent psychic impact and can start anew, is at once a way of keeping trauma at bay and a traumatic return of the repressed.

Now we are moving up and out, but slowly— this sentence closes this paragraph, but in relation to the section, it's more of a level 3, summarizing evidence and beginning to conceptualize.

Third Paragraph

This also means that inscription and amnesia work together rather than being at odds.

"This also means" is a classic light, consecutivizing transition; the rest of the sentence previews the final thesis.

Ultimately the protagonist's production of material reminders, his notes, photographs, and tattoos, do not counteract his loss of memory. They aid and abet it instead. Erasure and inscription collude as Leonard produces his own reality.

With "ultimately" we head toward 4/5 space, but this is the conclusion to the *reading* of the film, not the paragraph. Together these three sentences conclude the reading of the film proper. We're about to move to level 5, the theoretical and conceptual payoff of the reading, for which the coming word "meta-filmic" serves as a signal; here, however, we're still in level 3 or 4, relative to the close reading.

On a meta-filmic level, this gives the lie to a facile dichotomy of digital amnesia and analog traces.

This begins of a very short, four-sentence U inside the larger structure: in the larger unit, it's part of level 5; in this paragraph, it's part of a closing 4; in this unit, it serves as an opening 4.

Such a binary, as a media politics, reflects the ideologically charged debates about digital and computation media, rather than accounting for their material reality.

This smaller unit is a level 3, since it's part of the evidence/argument for the previous sentence.

The creation of inscriptive supplements in the filmic diegesis does not remedy the supposed superficiality and blankness of the digital medium.

More level 3 for this short unit.

Rather, the absence of memory traces, inscriptive media, and the process of active erasure together enable Leonard's willful manipulation of his own past, present, and future, as well as *Memento*'s filmic creation.

And now the small unit, which is both the 5 of the whole section and the 5 of this paragraph, closes with a final sentence that is also the 5 of the small unit proper. As a whole the close explains why *Memento* is "trauma made film," the promise of the first sentence of this whole section.

EXAMPLE 8.2 (CONTINUED)

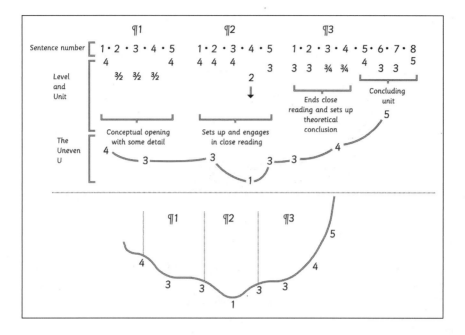

FIGURE 8.5 Paragraphs from Andrea Bachner's *Ethics of Inscription: Poststructuralist Prehistories*, mapped out.

Nine

Structure and Subordination

During the Q&A of a talk I participated in a little while ago, I wrote a note to a colleague saying that I couldn't figure out why I didn't like the talk, since there wasn't anything technically *wrong* with what the speaker had said. "2 – 2 – 2 – 2 – 2," she wrote back. And that was, in fact, the problem: the evidence accumulated but didn't aggregate, and the whole presentation, after an exciting opening, felt empty as a result.

When I said earlier that you should understand your writing synchronically, this is what I was talking about. If you work within the Uneven U structure, you will know at any given moment where your prose is going and what it aims to do, and you will begin to vary your structure so that the reader follows a developmental rhythm and trajectory that communicates the overall goals of your work. Especially for longer pieces of writing, you need to manage the U to allow your reader to keep up with your big ideas, to understand how the various pieces of your work relate to one another, and to grasp how they come together as a whole.

The U makes this easier by asking you, whenever possible, to order and hierarchize your ideas. Organizing your work into paragraphs and sections means at a minimum subordinating the evidence to the arguments — the 1s and 2s to the 3s and 4s. The reader understands, much as we did in McCrea's paragraphs in the previous chapter, that some information should be carried forward to the next paragraph, whereas other information, having served its evidentiary function, can be left behind. (This does not mean that evidence does not matter, or matters less, than abstract thought; it is its bedrock.) What's true in the paragraph stays true in the subsection and in the section; at the end of each structural unit the reader should be taught what mattered about what he or she read and, ideally, how what mattered fits within the larger structure or argument of the book. That is, the subordinating function of the close (level 5) to any given unit ought not only to close the section as such but also relate the unit to a larger unit of which it forms a part.

You can do that structurally or thematically. Thematically is the easier option: it's just then a question of reconnecting to certain key terms or concepts established in the introductory material. At its simplest this involves repeating key words. You see McCrea doing this with the words "queer" and "genealogy" in the second example; both words figure heavily in the major arguments of his work. But you could also imagine a few sentences that would more explicitly rejoin the parts to the whole, asserting, for instance, that in the novel's relation to the encounter between Stephen and Bloom we see once again the kind of queer genealogy that we have observed in the previous chapters before going on to compare or typologize the genealogy we see in Joyce to the ones in other chapters, figuring the genealogies as relations to the boundaries of the family unit, or to various kinds of family unit.

Here we approach, naturally, a structural subordination, in which the 5 of the entire Joyce section would not only close the section as such, but also put us back in touch with the major thematic and argumentative body of the book as a whole and set up, ideally, the final bringing together of all these 5s in the conclusion, which would make something new from their gathering. This allows us to understand how everything we just read *fits* into the larger book; this *fitting* is itself a kind of subordination, one that makes it possible for us to draw a mental map of the chapter or book in which we grasp the various relations among its parts. Producing that subordination is just what 5s, or closes, should do. As always, because the structure is relative, closes for larger units like sections or chapters will take longer, and require more rhetorical pop, than closes for a paragraph or a subsection. You can't close a chapter with a single sentence; it's a matter of weight and balance, allowing the time you spend on something to communicate its import and place to the reader.

In general, you will find that readers get annoyed, or stop paying attention, when confronted with three or more consecutive units of the same level. A series of quotations with no reading or a series of examples that don't seem to amount to anything larger than themselves will lose readers along the way. Likewise a series of heavily theoretical or abstracted paragraphs will eventually begin to feel empty if you don't stop occasionally to ground them in some kind of closer (evidentiary or argumentative) work. To manage that potential boredom, you will either (if you're down in the evidentiary weeds) need to pop up for air, bringing the prose back up to the higher levels, even briefly, to reconnect the reader to the big ideas (of the section, of the essay, of the book—depending on where you are), or to push down and in so that the abstract work you're doing becomes concrete and real. When that doesn't happen, readers get anxious, and will begin wondering if there will be any payoff to the work they're doing.

Figure 9.1 is an example of how to structure and subordinate multiple Uneven U's in individual paragraphs while together forming a multiple U's across the section. So, after doing two paragraphs that operate at roughly levels 1–3 (for instance, paragraphs giving two extensive examples of the way Toni Morrison stages moral conflict), you will need a short paragraph (or sentences at the end of a paragraph) that brings those two paragraphs

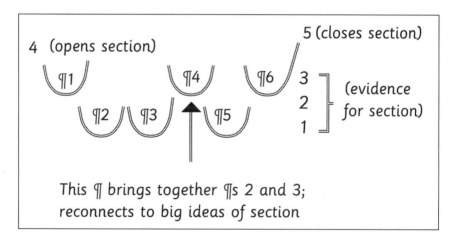

FIGURE 9.1 Subordination inside a section: this paragraph brings together paragraphs 2 and 3, and reconnects to the big ideas of the section.

up and pulls them together, as shown by paragraph 4. You can then follow that with a third example at level 2, if you have one, and then close all three examples together (again, arranging them in some kind of relationship, so that the reader understands why we needed three examples in the first place) in a final paragraph that serves as the close, or 5, for the section as a whole (paragraph 6).

Subordination and structure become increasingly important as writing projects grow longer. The longer something is, the more likely it is that your readers will forget what has happened earlier, if only because they will not read your book in one sitting or because the brain's capacity to retain information and logic while processing new ideas can only stretch so far.

Beyond the principles encoded in the U, you can understand why communicating structure matters by considering the concept known as "chunking." First used by cognitive psychologist George Miller, chunking helps explain why complex thought is not limited despite the fact that most humans can only hold seven objects or concepts (plus or minus two) in short-term memory. Chunking refers to the ways in which our minds organize information in order to increase the amount of material we hold in working memory; essentially the mind groups or "chunks" smaller pieces of information into larger ones. For example, if I ask you to memorize the following shape — 国 — you will have an easy time if you have studied Chinese (in which case it's a chunk meaning "country"); otherwise, you'll be stuck trying to memorize an arrangement of arbitrary, individual lines. If you try to help yourself by imaging the four outside lines as a "box," you will also be chunking. For similar reasons a random series of seven words is harder to remember than a grammatical sentence of seven words; grammar functions as a chunking device, allowing us to hold more information in working memory by putting that information into relationships, thus reducing the effective number of units we keep in mind. (This also happens when you break a memorized phone number into three pieces.)

Asking readers to hold in mind a series of unstructured or unsubordinated paragraphs is like asking them to memorize seven random words. At some point, if the lack of structure goes on long enough, readers simply cannot remember what happened before. Any conclusions you draw at that point will feel unsubstantiated and thin—not because they technically are, since the evidence may be there in print, but because the reader cannot reasonably be expected to remember what the evidence was. Level-5 sentences or paragraphs chunk the sections they close, drawing together the major ideas and putting them in a neat package, further associating them with key words or phrases. Building these associations will help you later on, as you can use them to signal or recall the entire chunk you've subordinated to them. This kind of chunked recall—which may be a matter of a single word or could involve a sentence or two—allows you build strong conclusions to chapters and books. You use them to pull together the large pieces of your argument in the reader's working memory, and to build further conclusions from it, stepping up the ladder from a series of 5s drawn from sections or chapters to a brand new, larger 5 that closes the entire chapter or the entire book.

Chunking also allows you to establish over time a privileged vocabulary of themes and concepts that will serve as the skeleton of your prose. You will want to consider the relation between this kind of thematic chunking and the titles of your essay, sections, or book chapters. You can let your chapter titles and introduction do one thing—establish certain privileged terms—while developing in an unmarked and implicit way over the course of two hundred pages another piece of the skeleton, about which you do not speak until the conclusion, when its long ossification and sudden appearance can surprise the reader and motivate a dramatic finish to the work.

Beyond Subordination

Not all structural relations are subordinating or subordinatable. But what works for subordination also works for other kinds of structural relationships. What if, for example, you have two passages to read, both of which contribute to a larger whole, but their relationship is oscillative, or dialectical, or serial? What if they illustrate a chronological development? What if the ideas ramify, extending an origin into many directions? That's fine—but then you need to make that clear in the openings and closes, and you will want to think about the ways in which your metalanguage (including the titles of your chapters or your sections) communicate those relationships to the reader. Some books, for instance, give a series of chapters that present different points of view on a single conceptual field of play. The chapters do not subordinate or succeed one another; they do not present us with chronological or conceptual development. They fan out perspectives that collectively produce a whole. At their worst, such books resemble the bad dissertations William Germano describes: theoretical introductions that contain the whole argument followed by a series of examples that each repeat the main idea (5 – 2 – 2 – 2 – 2). But books that take a variety of "core samples" from a broader field of play can still be structured and organized, if the points of view can be justified in relation to the content of the project and if their presentation (even if not itself successive or subordinatable in some conceptual sense) can be, both at the end of the chapters and at the end of the book, organized into a conceptual whole bigger than the sum of the parts. That is, you need to communicate to readers *how* exactly the various chapters relate to one another, so that they can build a mental picture of the entire book. Readers should in general understand *why* your book is structured the way it is, and should understand how that structure both reflects and contributes to its arguments.

That said, I do want to warn you against writing a book for which the chapter order does not matter at all. This is true even if, say, you are writing about thirteen ways of looking at blackbirds, and part of your argument is that those thirteen ways operate in a nonhierarchical system whose total logic eschews any kind of subordinative or developmental pattern. At that point you might want simply to assert that these are thirteen ways and that none of them is more important than any other. If you could manage to publish such a work online, you might illustrate this by having thirteen lines branch off of a center, inviting readers to pick and choose the order in which they read the book. (Or you could try this in print, as B. S. Johnson does with the chapters in *The Unfortunates*.) But if you are going to put this kind of book into print, you must recognize that—short of encouraging readers to flip among the chapters, and even then—*most readers will read the book in order*. This is the effect of the book as a medium, a function of the codex format. Though it is, when it comes to flipping back and forth, more flexible than something like a scroll or a series of stone tablets, a book nonetheless comes with a normative set of

Descriptions and Norms

So is all this advice descriptive or normative? Both, but differently for each. I hope to have convinced you that the various rhetorical patterns and strategies I describe here actually happen out there in the world, that they represent descriptions of activities that writing undertakes, and that as a result they will allow you to more deeply understand scholarly writing, even if you never want to do any yourself. On the other hand, any act of abstraction from examples will necessarily disrespect the integrity of the vast field of singularities and differences that make up the arena from which the examples are drawn. There are more things in heaven and earth than are dreamt of by the Uneven U.

That said, the purpose of abstraction is to eliminate clutter—every definition is a negation, as Spinoza once wrote. The somewhat violent clarifications here aim to make the process of academic writing easier to understand. You should feel free to follow these lessons and rules as they were, for now, norms of some kind. But the final rule is . . . break the rules! The best writing is the best because it upends standards in some way, either by enacting them with an opalescent, devastating skill (at the limit, the truest violation) or by carving new paths through the shady woods that separate what the reader understands from what the writer means. This is a book that wants you to surpass and destroy it. After which someone will write us all a new primer.

readerly practices attached to it. So I say again: readers will in general read your book in order. If you are writing a *book*—if, that is, you are writing something designed to appear in a specific medium and not just a piece of text that has no mediatic home—then being responsible to the format of your project means thinking about chapter order. How should you order the thirteen ways of looking at birds? I don't know. But—whether or not you ever say so explicitly in the text—*you* should know, and you should write for a reader who might one day wonder about the logic of your book, read it seriously, and make interpretive claims about your work on the basis of the chapter order, just as critics do for the Stevens poem.

Ten

Structural Rhythm

I do not think, I should say, that you have to know about your structure before you begin; nor do I think that your writing needs to be fundamentally structure-driven. The Uneven U helps you think about how your writing could or should work; it helps you chunk your own work, so that you can consider the ways you want it to fit together. I often start with a loose structure in mind (certainly with an idea about the number of sections or chapters), but the final structure of a piece only emerges in the process of rewriting and development that happens as my ideas become clear to me. I say all this because I know some people feel oppressed or intimidated by structure, like it means that they have to know everything in advance or that their writing must conform to a rigid set of parameters whose function it is to make them feel inadequate. Please don't take this that way—this is all supposed to help you, to increase your sense that you can control your prose and your writing practice, so that you can be ambitious on its behalf and use it to imagine and write the projects that matter to you.

So.

Structural rhythm: once you start building the book or essay, you will inevitably have to make some decisions about the relation of the parts to the whole. Whether you want long sections or short ones, long chapters or short ones, how the sections will be balanced relative to one another, what types of relations they will have—all these choices determine how structure shapes the overall rhythm of your work. A thirty-page essay can have three sections, or it can have ten; which decision you make will make a big difference to the reader's experience of the work.

Let's look at one very common structure for an academic essay:

Introduction	Section A	Section B	Conclusion
	Usually longer	Usually shorter	

In general, but not always, sections A and B will focus on different texts or authors, or they will cover instances within the same text or author; they may also focus on different theoretical problems, partly as a function of the change in text or topic. The second section tends to be shorter partly because some of the preliminary or theoretical work that it needs has been done by the first one.

The structure has a couple major variations. In one you'll find a third section, C, which will either be significantly shorter than A and B, or will split the body of the essay evenly with A and B; in another you'll find a shorter A and a longer B. In a third the conclusion contains a third major primary document, which extends that section, allowing it to function as a counterpoint to the work in A and B. And, in a structure more common in book chapters than articles (because it often requires more time), you will start with an introduction, then have a second section (A) that provides background material (and hence also counts as introductory), before moving into the longer section B, which contains the reading and analysis, and finally to a conclusion. In that model B is often split into two major sections, like so:

Introduction	A	B1	B2	Conclusion
3–5 pp	10 pp	10–15 pp	10–20 pp	3–5 pp

. . . or

Introduction	A	B1	B2	C	Conclusion
1–3 pp	5–8 pp	10 pp	10+ pp	4–6 pp	2 pp, or fold into C

In the second variation, the decision to create a section C will usually stem from some kind of break in the conclusion, after which the conclusion ends up working as a kind of coda. In both cases the A section will actually extend and expand the introductory material, often with historical or theoretical context that sets up the readings in B1 and B2. (I call them B1 and B2 because often book chapters focus on single authors, so the B section therefore considers two movements in a single work, or two works by the same person; for chapters that deal with two authors, you might think of B1 and B2 as B and C [and then section C as D].)

Essays and chapters that follow these structural patterns propose, implicitly or explicitly, a series of relationships among their parts. Essays that have two major sections will have to manage and describe the relationship between A and B (i.e., what does B do that A didn't? what does B add to the analysis in A?), and these in turn can be managed or related to a possible section C. If we structure the sections *oppositionally,* we compose relationships of balanced pairs: A vs. B, then (A/B) vs. C, in which the C section adds nuance to what might otherwise feel like too reductive a binary (this or that . . . but actually a third way!). Alternatively, we can put sections A, B, and C in a triangular relation. Or, finally, we could structure the sections *developmentally,* giving us something like A + B (that is, the insights in A are tested and improved by the example of B), which gives a preliminary result that is then tested in turn (and boosted, twisted, ironized, or extended) by C.

The point is that there are really only so many ways that two or three things relate to one another, and that you should know which ones you're choosing and why. You want to think about both development and balance. In terms of development: How do the structures organize the reader's experience of the argument? Do they reflect any claims about the actual relationships among your subjects? (Imagine an essay in which the sections on Isherwood and Wilde are oppositional in terms of their relation to the argument, even though they do not together argue that Isherwood and Wilde were somehow opposed; you can also imagine an essay in which the argumentative structure aligns with the representational one.) For balance, consider not only length (long vs. short sections) but also referential weight and discursive type. By "referential weight" I mean the relative importance of your subjects, either relative to the discipline at large or to your project. It's not uncommon in an essay that has two large sections on relatively unknown authors to put a highly canonical figure in section C or in the conclusion, allowing the weight of the famous person to balance out (and rhetorically justify) the inclusion of the other two. If your essay has one very famous subject and one unknown one, you will want to think about which one to discuss first and about section length devoted to each, since an essay mainly about Shakespeare but a only little bit about someone else is not the same as an essay mostly about someone else with a little bit on Shakespeare. As for "discursive type," I refer to the different kinds of functions a section can have—historical background, review of critical debates, theoretical context, close reading. Especially in chapters, where you may end up devoting whole sections to different types of critical discourse, you will want to consider what order to put those in, and to vary the order so that you don't end up with a series of sections all doing the same thing. In articles this is less of a problem since the restriction of twenty-five to thirty-five pages means that most sections will include a number of different types of discourse.

As for books, we're really talking about the balance of chapters to one another. For dissertations and first books, you will almost certainly be doing something that's three to six chapters long, focusing on one or two authors per chapter. With that in mind you need to think about geographic, historical, and thematic balance. Three chapters tend be balanced around the middle (that is, you usually can't, say, write three chapters that primarily address the years 1830, 1840, and 1950; instead you should probably end up with something like 1830, 1890–1900, 1950). Four chapters must have rough parity, either four ways or two (ex. 1830 and 1840, 1930 and 1940; or 1830, 1880, 1920, 1970). The same rules apply to geography, so that in general you can't do three chapters from one place and one from another.

Some exceptions: some books follow a one/three pattern, where the one will be from another place or from a substantially earlier time than the other three, allowing the author to open the book with a canonical or classic version of a problem. The latter three chapters, grouped thematically or historically, follow with a more recent time or a different place. The crossing of the one to the three thereby splits the book in two—unevenly in terms of page numbers, but evenly from a conceptual point of view. (For example: "Here's how the Greeks handled metaphor; *now* let's see what happens to that problem in the eighteenth century.") Much rarer is the three/one structure, in which the outlier appears last; when outliers appear at the end of books, they almost always do so in conclusions.

All this goes out the window when you have more than four or five chapters. In a book with ten chapters, structure matters less because the relative weight of any given chapter or example diminishes as it participates in a larger whole. Such books will sometimes be attempts to completely cover some topic (a book on the entire canon of Léopold Senghor, for example). More often they are a series of successive, developmentally organized meditations structured by varying degrees of nearly aphoristic intensity, or they are a series of geological "core samples," in which a

Why Are Book Chapters Longer Than Articles?

A comparison of the article and chapter versions of the same piece of work will show that though the chapter includes more information, it rarely includes more argument. Chapters are usually longer than articles (many chapters are forty to sixty pages in manuscript, compared to thirty or so for articles) because they move elements of the iceberg from the footnotes or the deep, unpublished background into the main text. As a result chapters tend to cover more examples than articles, which usually results in the appearance of a third or fourth major section in the latter half of the chapter, there where the article will have closed out its major claims and started moving toward a conclusion.

This relationship may affect your writing practice. It would seem to make sense to do the article before the chapter, since it's shorter (you can imagine laddering up the scale with a project, from conference paper to article to chapter). But in fact that tends not to work for me. Since articles function best if they present a series of strong arguments and their minimum necessary exemplification, it is actually easier (for me) to get to the article from a chapter. By the time I've written the chapter I have a clear sense of the biggest and best arguments, because all the examples and background I've worked through have had their effect on the overall piece. As a result the article that comes from the chapter has a better chance of being the *best* version of the project; if the article comes first, the chapter will suffer because the arguments in the original article will tend to normalize themselves, meaning that the new material will feel extra or tacked-on. That's a bad model for chapter writing, since even if chapters are longer, you still want every piece of them to have a significant and meaningful relation to the conclusions the chapter reaches. Otherwise you're just wasting your reader's time.

variety of approaches to a single conceptual problem illuminate and alter it by degrees. Some books with many chapters also divide themselves into units of two or three or more, using these sections to reduce the chaos and returning to themselves the basic decisions involving smaller, more obvious numbers.

Understanding how the arrangement of the book constitutes a fundamental aspect of its logic and its implicit argument will help you in two ways: it will undergird the various decisions you make about length, metalanguage, and rhythm, and it will allow you to use those decisions to communicate, implicitly or explicitly, rhythm and pattern to the reader.

To put some of this information in context, I want to show you some numbers from an analysis my research assistant, Darwin Tsen, did of one hundred recently published books in literature and cultural studies (he looked at ten books each from ten major university presses). The first thing we tried to confirm was my sense that first books tend to have fewer chapters than other books. The sample had 41 first books and 59 non-first books: the first books averaged 5.6 chapters, not counting introductions and conclusions; the others averaged 6.9 apiece. The first books clustered very strongly around five or six chapters, with a small few at three, and some at four or (more rarely) eight. A heavy clustering around five or six chapters was largely true of the non-first books as well, where the mean was dragged upward by a small number of books with nine, ten, or more chapters (including books with fourteen or even twenty). This seems to suggest that the academic norm for all books is for something between three and eight chapters, with a strong central grouping around five or six. These rules seem to loosen for second books and beyond, when the top of the range opens out substantially, even though the central norm remains roughly the same.

The other thing Darwin and I looked at had to do with structural rhythm as it affects the presence of introductions and conclusions. Of the books in the sample, 51 (of 100) had both a labeled introduction and a labeled conclusion; 37 had a labeled introduction only, and folded their conclusive material into a final chapter; six had a labeled conclusion only; and six had neither, folding both introductory and conclusive material into named and numbered chapters. This confirms my general impression that labeled or marked introductions are close to normative (88 of the one hundred books in the sample) and that labeled conclusions are not (57 of one hundred books had them). This general balance of the relationship between introduction (almost necessary) and conclusion (optional) reappears when we note that introductory material took up, on average, 8.8 percent of the available pages of the books in our sample (that is, roughly seventeen pages of a 200-page book), whereas conclusive material took up 3.7 percent (eight pages of a 200-page book). We'll talk about why that is, and how it might affect your own work, in the chapters on introductions and conclusions. For now I simply want you to observe that the pattern exists, and to think about how such a pattern expresses, at a large scale, some general sense of the *rhetoric* of literary and cultural studies as fields, and thus teaches us all, mostly unconsciously, about the nature and modalities of research, scholarship, and argument.

Chronology and Development in Books

One effect of the dominance of historical approaches to literature (in the last couple decades) is that almost all books in literary studies will order their chapters according to the chronological appearance of their primary examples. But that creates a problem: unless the biggest argument of the book itself is about chronological development—in which case it will us how what happened in 1055 affected what happened in 1155, which in turn changed 1255, and so on—then the chapters will be ordered according to a logic that does not necessarily match the argumentative or theoretical rhythm of the book itself. If you're comparing, for instance, the interaction between literature and urbanization in ancient Babylon, early modern Chang'an, and Victorian London, you will almost certainly have the chapters in that order, but what you discover will not lead successively via a historical logic from one to the next.

How, then, do you manage the relationship between the order in which things appear to the reader in the book and the order in which they appeared historically? If you're not saying that this relation is the same (first one then the next), then you are faced with a situation in which you are almost obliged—if you want your book to develop and to have a sense of self that exceeds its parts—to choose one of two paths: either shape your argument to the examples, so that the development of your argument actually does parallel (*parallel*, mind you! not reflect!) the chronology of your examples; or, layer over the chapters another, non-ordered logic that happens simultaneously as the chronological, developmental one. Either way you'll probably need some metalanguage to keep the reader settled.

I tried the first of these in *Chinese Dreams*, where, quite explicitly, the lessons learned in the first chapter on Pound became the subject of the chapter on Brecht, and the questions that came out of the work on Brecht opened the chapter on *Tel quel*. In a secondary key, the Brecht chapter began, following Pound, with a discussion of his poetry before passing over, late, to his theater and his politics; and the *Tel quel* chapter then began with politics. In this way the thematic shifts also paralleled, for neatness, the chronologies. I tried the second approach in *The Hypothetical Mandarin*, where the chronological ordering felt genuinely arbitrary, and so as I wrote I had to discover another structure that would supersede it. I ended up organizing the entire book around the structural possibilities of a Greimasian semiotic square. I located the chapters within a simpler version of that square in both the intro and the beginning of the conclusion; on the book's final page I reproduced the square, which then retroactively produced (or reproduced) for the reader the full logic of the book. (As always, I'm not saying that these strategies worked; I'm just saying that they're what I did.)

One final option, which would be a variant on the one I tried in *The Hypothetical Mandarin*, would be to drop the chronological ordering of your examples altogether, subjecting the entire project to the demands of some other pattern or structure that would be its dominant logic. You see something like this in the twenty-one chapters of Daniel Heller-Roazen's *Echolalias: On the Forgetting of Language*, whose ordering logic belongs solely to their appearance in that book or, more arbitrarily, in the alphabetical organization of the chapters in Roland Barthes's *A Lover's Discourse*. Less extravagantly, you can imagine a series of chapters on different affective stances (Sianne Ngai's *Ugly Feelings*) or a sequence like this one, from Laura U. Marks's *Touch: Sensuous Theory and Multisensory Media:* "The Haptic Subject," "Haptics and Erotics," "Olfactory Haptics," and "Haptics and Electronics." None of these imply or require chronology at all.

Eleven

Introductions

How long is the introduction for the average twenty-five-page seminar paper?

If you answered somewhere between one and three pages, you get a prize. Now ask yourself: how long is the introduction for the average twenty-five-page published article?

I asked Darwin to look over five years' worth of essays published in *PMLA* (2007–2011) to answer that question. The results were surprising: on average, 25 percent of a *PMLA* article in those years was devoted to introductory material. In other words, some six to seven pages of a twenty-five-page piece were devoted to introducing the essay and the argument. (This judgment is subjective. Darwin counted material he deemed to be introductory in nature, even if it was not labeled as an introduction; you might think of it as including the sections labeled "Intro" and "A" in the model of the chapter structure.) The difference between published articles and seminar papers at least partially explains why graduate students who spend years getting really good at writing seminar papers have a hard time when it comes to transforming those papers into articles: the article is simply a different genre.

What accounts for the greater amount of room taken up by introductory material in the article? And how can we use that habit to understand how an article differs from a seminar paper, a book chapter (where the proportion given over to the intro is, in my experience, relatively smaller), or an entire book (where it occupies more like 9 percent of the whole, as we saw a moment ago)?

 Let's begin by talking about what introductions ought to do. First, they have to bring readers into the piece; second, they have to give readers the information they need to understand why the work matters; third, they have to prepare the reader for the argumentative labor of the rest of the work. We can think of these three related goals as, in order, *engaging* the reader, *locating* the essay in a disciplinary context, and *teaching* the reader what s/he needs to know to understand the critical activity that's coming up.

The work of engagement happens in two phases and in two modes. The most intense moments of the first phase, which involve drawing the reader into both the *topic* (one mode) and the *style* (another mode) of the essay, appear at the end of the first sentence, the end of the first paragraph, and the end of the first section. (Sections can be marked explicitly or implicitly; see chapter 16 on metalanguage.) All these are moments of significant rhetorical intensity, places where the reader can be grabbed and not let go.

Consider one of my favorite introductory sentences ever, which comes from a 1969 article by Associated Press writer Jules Loh (I saw it first in a journalism textbook):

> His work done, his children grown, his age past 80, his days of toil to get ahead well behind, George Oakes nonetheless sat down one day and built a better mousetrap. (1)

The whole thing hinges on the surprising appearance of the word "mousetrap" at the end of the sentence, whose importance Loh emphasizes by making you wait through a number of dependent clauses. You can imagine extending and revising the sentence to increase that sense of suspense: ·

> His work done, his children grown, his parents buried in the hardscrabble ground, his age past 80, his mortgage paid for, his days of toil to get ahead well behind, his body a shadow of its former self, his memories of the Iowa farm where he spent the first decades of his life

before becoming, as three of his brothers did too, a small-town realtor, fully faded and disappeared, George Oakes sat down one day—he was always tinkering, his wife Lois told me one afternoon over iced tea— and built a better mousetrap.

Now a sentence like that wouldn't work in journalism, but it could begin a short story. The extension shows you the operations of suspense. The variable lengths of the clauses—that third one, about his parents, breaks up the short-short-short rhythm that it would otherwise leave behind, though I follow Loh in making the final clause the longest one—are there to show you how rhythm works in the construction of a unit like this one, and the piece between long dashes is there to give you a sense of what it feels like to have a final break or pause appear just when you're expecting to get to the surprise. (I also removed the word "nonetheless" from Loh's sentence; it seems more or less implied by the structure, and its slightly elevated tone doesn't fit with the rest of the piece.)

You can see in the basic structure of this sentence all the qualities of an excellent anecdotal introduction, used in literary criticism to especially great effect by Stephen Greenblatt, whose habit of opening essays with the narration of a surprising and delightfully detailed historical circumstance or event became one of the major stylistic markers of new historicist criticism. In those introductions, the relative weight of engagement rarely lay in the first sentence alone; rather it came from the slow build-up of story, the quality of the details (thematic mode), the pleasure of Greenblatt's sentences (stylistic mode), which ended up placing a great deal of weight on the last paragraph of the story, and the last paragraph of the interpretive section (a section that almost always began with a variation on, "What are we to make of the story of I have just told?") that followed the initial act of storytelling.

Narrative, anecdotal introductions are far from the only way to engage a reader. You can also start with a strong question or argumentative claim. "What kind of work is writing?" is the first sentence of Walter Benn Michaels's *The Gold Standard and the Logic of Naturalism* (1). Susan Stewart starts the fourth chapter of *On Longing* with this statement: "The body presents the paradox of contained and container at once" (104). Daniel Tiffany begins the first chapter of *Toy Medium* with a strong, nearly aphoristic declaration that calls out for explanation—"Only a fool reads poetry for facts"—before going on to show exactly how and why the reader should want to be such a fool (11). And Ian Watt opens *The Rise of the Novel* with an almost classically expansive series of arguments and questions that lay out the framework for the rest of the book:

> There are still no wholly satisfactory answers to many of the general questions which anyone interested in the early eighteenth-century novelists and their works is likely to ask: Is the novel a new literary form? And if we assume, as is commonly done, that it is, and that it was begun by Defoe, Richardson, and Fielding, how does it differ from the prose fiction of the past, from that of Greece, for example, or that of the Middle Ages, or of seventeenth-century France? And is there any reason why these differences appeared when and where they did? (9)

In that first paragraph, technically all a single sentence, lies the germ and the promise of Watt's entire book. Though not seductive stylistically, this opening makes promises so large and asks questions so important that I feel compelled to keep reading.

What the anecdotal, argumentative, or question-asking introductions have in common is that they truncate the Uneven U, lopping off its first half to begin *in medias res*, in the middle of the thing. Anecdotal openings start with material from level 1 of the U—a piece of evidence like a story or a quotation—while you might think of the argumentative or question-asking ones as beginning from level 3 or 4 and then rising directly to 5. Such introductions move from an intense and uncontextualized beginning up through the levels of abstraction to close with a promise to teach us what and how that initial story, question, or claim means and matters. You see this especially in anecdotal openings of the "mousetrap" type, but you can observe it equally well in Michaels's opening question, or even in Watt, which precedes, in the material before the colon, the question-asking 4 with a hint of level-2 throat-clearing. The sheer speed with which he launches us into the major topics at hand—when you consider that he's just begun a 300-page book—is what qualifies Watt's opening, nonetheless, as "truncated."

There are of course other ways to begin, ones that bring readers into thematic and argumentative space. Such openings can put metalanguage (language *about* the work the author is doing) to good use. Let's look at a long example, the introduction to Melissa E. Sanchez's recent article for *PMLA*:

This essay explores two interrelated questions about the way that we read representations of early modern female sexuality. Are depictions of female rivalry, masochism, promiscuity, and zoophilia ever feminist? And are those of female heteroeroticism ever either feminist or queer? In general, scholars of early modern literature have implicitly answered no to both questions, an answer that I will argue registers a persistent tension in the articulation of queer and feminist thought. One reason that scholars turn to the early modern period is that its representations of sexual desire and practice can upset narratives that assume a transhistorical heteronormativity. What Valerie Traub has described as the "simultaneously feminist and queer goal" to "render adequately the complexity and alterity of early modern sexuality" has produced groundbreaking and sophisticated studies of early modern women who resist the imperative to marry and reproduce: nuns, virgins, Amazons, lesbians, and female friends ("Sonnets" 285). However, in focusing almost exclusively on nurturing and egalitarian same-sex relations, this work has overlooked a range of alternative sexual fantasies and practices. In the pages below, I argue that the prevalent, limited definition of queerness derives from an unspoken adherence to a particular strain of feminism, one that sees not only heterosexuality but also any eroticization of power as incompatible with feminist aims—and one that some early formulations of queer theory sought to contest in the debates within feminism known as the sex wars. By tracing the legacy of the sex wars in early modern studies, I propose to make available a mode of reading that reintegrates some of the foundational work of queer theory—much of which was done before such theory was called queer—into understandings of female sexuality. The theoretical frameworks offered by what we might call queer feminism, I argue, allow us to reassess past and present views of what counts as good sex for women. (493)

This paragraph doesn't really *engage* the reader with style. Instead it shifts the burden of engagement over to two other introductory tasks: *locating* the reader inside critical discourse, and *teaching* the reader what s/he needs to know about the material that's about to appear. In so doing, it illustrates the second "phase" of the engaging work introductions perform. Rather than appearing in certain high-pressure rhetorical moments—sentence, paragraph, section—this second phase spreads out over the entire course of your introductory material. Less punctual and stylistic than the first phase, the second phase relies on content, on argument, on clarity, and on your capacity to make the reader—to say this in the least dramatic way possible—want to keep reading your work.

Locating and teaching share a number of features. Teaching locates and locating teaches; it's just that they do so about different kinds of things. Together they elaborate the critical parameters of the essay. We might distinguish them by thinking of "locating" as that which orients us toward the article's place in professional discourse—how it fits into existing criticism—while teaching points us toward, and educates us about, the background material—some of it critical but some of it potentially argumentative or historical as well—connected to the article's primary sources. You might also think about locating as having a strong differentiating function, what Gerald Graff and Cathy Birkenstein teach as the "they say, I say" method, in which spelling out exactly how what you're doing differs from what other people have done helps you develop, and demonstrate clearly to the reader, your basic argument. By contrast, teaching is less antagonistic, more oriented toward the internal work of your essay than toward its external context.

Sanchez's first paragraph is a locating paragraph. It allows any reasonable professional reader, even one who knows almost nothing about the history of work on queer theory or early modern sexuality, to understand what position this essay will take in relation to existing criticism. It answers the question "what is original in this essay?" by showing us how it takes up a position—that readings of early modern sexuality have borrowed too heavily from one strain of feminism—in relation to existing scholarship. As we might expect, the work of the introduction, still devoted almost entirely to locating Sanchez and the reader within the

Introductions to Books

What about introductions to books? As we've seen from the statistics, most books in literary and cultural studies have some kind of introduction, often around ten to thirty pages long. (Anything shorter is usually called a preface, and that's fine too.) If you are thinking of the book as a coherent whole, then it must have an introduction, as that will be the only place where you can easily gather the thematic strands, locate the discussion, and frame the ideas for the project as a complete work. From the perspective of the Uneven U, the book's introduction is the 4 to the conclusion's 5. (This is the case even though, inside the introduction, you may start *in medias res*, with an anecdotal 1 or 2, before leading up to the close of its first section, which will function as the introduction [level 4] to the whole introduction, which then concludes with its own section or paragraph at level 5.) The introduction to the book asks, therefore, the fundamental questions that motivate the line of research undertaken in the book—What are they? Why do the matter? How do they fit into existing professional debates? It also tells the reader why the chapters that follow are the best (or at least a very good) way to pursue that line of research. At best, it remains open both to the possibility that this is the perfect book, but also, because you want to leave some sense of mystery in any 4-level structure, to the chance that the book will turn in interesting and possibly unexpected ways for the reader.

parameters of this argument, continues after this paragraph for more than three pages. The whole of the introductory material thus occupies four of fourteen pages, about 28 percent, of Sanchez's essay.

Sanchez does not need to do much "teaching" in her introduction, since the texts she deals with—Spenser's *The Faerie Queene* and Shakespeare's *A Midsummer Night's Dream*—require little or no introduction for professional readers. For an introduction that combines locating with teaching, we can page back in that same *PMLA* issue (May 2012) to Eleanor Johnson's essay, "The Poetics of Waste: Medieval English Ecocriticism" (figure 11.1). Her essay begins with several locating paragraphs. The first quotes four scholars on the question of waste and ecosystems to establish a general critical framework ("waste" is a serious topic); the second connects this framework to the Middle Ages, and the third opens with an almost-classic expression of the locating gesture we saw a moment ago in

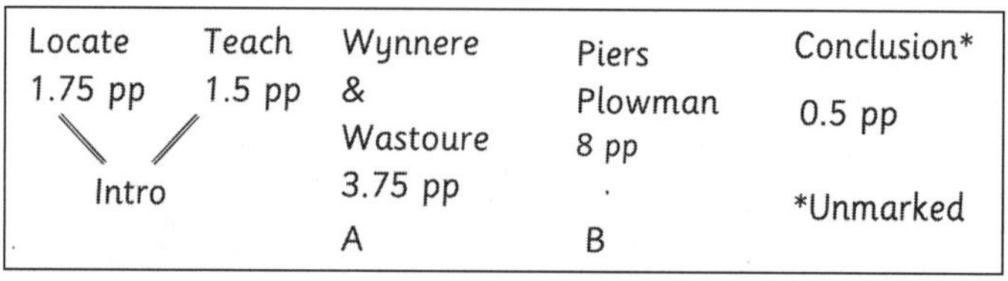

Locate 1.75 pp	Teach 1.5 pp	Wynnere & Wastoure 3.75 pp	Piers Plowman 8 pp	Conclusion* 0.5 pp
	Intro			
		A	B	*Unmarked

FIGURE 11.1 The structure of Eleanor Johnson's "The Poetics of Waste: Medieval English Ecocriticism."

Sanchez: "Although waste appears frequently in medieval discourses, current criticism has largely ignored its presence there, for two reasons" (461). But in the sixth paragraph we see a dramatic switch in registers: "Three historical circumstances help to contextualize the intensive poetic focus on waste in the fourteenth century: real-estate contractions, population decline, and wartime taxation" (461). From here we are in teaching mode, which continues through that paragraph and into the next short section, titled "Legal and Penitential Waste." This entire section is devoted to historical background that aims to contextualize the upcoming reading of the fragmentary Middle English poem, *Wynnere and Wastoure*. We can see Johnson begin to transition away from the historical material (and thus, from teaching mode) in the final paragraph of that section with a sentence that connects the background specifically to the primary material: "The slippage of waste—its shuttling between physical land and the abstract resources of the soul—proves generative for *Wynnere and Wastoure* and *Piers Plowman*" (463). From here we get a brief rundown of the coming argument regarding both those texts, and then the section closes. All together, the two opening sections of Johnson's article—the first mainly devoted to locating, the second to teaching, both belonging specifically to the world of the introduction—take up 3.25 pages of a fourteen-page article (about 23 percent of the total).

Let's summarize. A good introduction will create emotional high points via style and structure that help anchor the reader to the piece. It will also use the time, trust, and *engagement* generated by those high points to perform the more content-oriented functions of introductory material: *locating* readers in a disciplinary context, telling them why and how your work matters, *teaching* them what they need to understand what follows, and preparing them, via the introduction's close, for the material to come.

Of these three tasks the most important is locating, because that is where you will establish the fundamental rationale for writing and publishing your work, that its argument makes a difference to the disciplinary conversation it joins. Here's Wendy Belcher on the absolute importance of the argument to publication: "Editors or reviewers may not mention the lack of an argument as a reason for rejection. They may instead state that the article is not original or significant, that it is disorganized, that it suffers from poor analysis, or that it 'reads like a student paper.' But the solution for all these problems lies in having an argument, stating it early and clearly, and then structuring your article around that argument" (82). I'm going to quibble in the next chapter with the phrase "early and clearly," since I've managed to get away with not doing both (for the right reasons, I hope). But Belcher's is otherwise truly excellent advice.

And it helps explain, I think, why introductions to published articles tend to take up a quarter of the available space. Seminar papers—which are written in the context of a specific course, syllabus, and set of research questions—don't need to explain why their work matters or show how and why it is that the research topic at hand has come to be important to the field, since those questions are answered implicitly by the writing context, namely the course itself. Seminar papers are written—even when we try to avoid it—mainly for the professor who assigned them. The shift in readership when you try to write an article means that you simply need to spend more time on the fundamental tasks of engaging, locating, and teaching the reader—and suggests, also, that we ought to revise our understanding of the role those tasks play in the elaboration and expression of scholarly knowledge. Which is why I've spent so much time on introductions here.

Introductions Happen Everywhere

Consider the opening to the fifth chapter of Jing Tsu's *Failure, Nationalism, and Literature*:

> The indispensability of defect in the narrative of nation building enabled nationalism to tap into the anxieties of everyday life. Yet the notion of faulty character did not belong to nationalistic discourse alone. It carried a greater versatility than the proliferation of racial anxieties. Instead of defining the discourse of failure, nationalism shared in its appeal. In this web of diversity, notions of racial ruination existed alongside those of beauty and ideal femininity. The question of the national character extended into a quest for the "New Woman" as well. (128)

It will not surprise you to discover that this paragraph comes at the beginning of a chapter called "The Quest for Beauty and Notions of Femininity," which follows a chapter called "Loving the Nation, Preserving the Race." The entire work of this paragraph is to get you from the latter to the former. The key turn is the "yet" that begins the second sentence (the first sentence, meanwhile, summarizes the argument of the previous chapter). The "yet" tells us that the story hasn't finished being told, and its work carries over to the third sentence as well. The fourth sentence begins to open us toward the major concept of the new chapter, though it remains vague about what exactly that concept is (something is "shared" but we don't know what yet); the fifth tells us what occupied that shared space (notions of racial ruination, from the previous chapter, exist *alongside* those of beauty, which are the topic of this particular chapter); the sixth specifies the particular arena of discussion within the general field of beauty and femininity, namely the concept of the "New Woman."

In an introduction like this—which is, as you can imagine, far more likely to appear in a later chapter than at the opening of a whole article or book—you see how an author will handle, further along in a piece of larger work, the relations among sections. This reminds us that *introductions happen everywhere*: that when we think about what introductions say or do, we need not only to consider the first sentence, paragraph, or section of a chapter, but the first sentence of any paragraph that takes on an introductory role in relation to a chapter, to a section within an article or a chapter, or to a subsection inside a section. Most of what I've written here applies to introductions conceived as opening entire articles or books; but when you introduce a second chapter or a third section, your intro will need also to handle the relation between what it introduces and the material the reader has just left behind. See chapter 14, which covers transitions, for more on how to handle that challenge.

Twelve

Don't Say It All Early

The idea that you must say it all early—that you should somewhere in the first section, ideally in the first paragraph, lay out the exact structure of what you're going to do in an article or a book—feels like a real mistake to me. Here I recognize that I am somewhat idiosyncratic, slightly more European in style and temperament than your average American academic. Nonetheless I want to insist that scholarly writers ought to take advantage of the tremendous resources of anticipation, surprise, and suspense—to draw on the affective lessons of fiction and our knowledge of the pleasures of mystery and discovery to organize our writing and our thought. Giving up on those possibilities in the name of saying everything up front—especially in the format, "In this essay I will make three arguments"—means abandoning the opportunities given you by the fact of the reader's diachronism (i.e., the simple fact that he or she will read your essay from start to finish).

Taking advantage of that diachronism is one of the guiding principles behind the Uneven U structure as it applies to paragraphs, sections, chapters, or whole books. It's precisely the unevenness of the pattern, the transition from the opening 4 to the closing 5, that aims to guarantee a minimum level of development and growth, thereby integrating the possibility of surprise into the very framework of your prose.

Of course this doesn't mean that you should totally obscure your argument so that the reader has no idea what's coming or where you're going at any moment. The point is to use obscurity and clarity strategically as ways to maximize the reader's understanding of, and pleasure in, your work. Part of this means that the work of the all-important level-4 sections—which is how I think of introductions—is to *lay out interesting problems* and not to give away the solutions. You truly engage readers in the introduction when you convince them that it's worth their time to keep reading, which means making a variety of credible promises (implicit and explicit) about

Should You Describe the Chapters?

Often left over or copied straight from the author's book proposal, the highly conventional introductory section that describes the upcoming chapters at length is usually one of the most boring things in the universe. I almost always skip it.

Part of the reason why that section bores me is that I have no way of evaluating it. I'm going to read the chapters anyway, but at this point I haven't understood them, so I can't evaluate any of the claims made in the summaries. The chapters will also each have introductions of their own, which will presumably do the work being done by the summaries. So it just feels like a waste of time.

That said, I think that at some level you *must* say something about the chapters to come—you have to prepare the reader for the book. You can start, however, by radically shortening the descriptions. There's no need to subject the reader to a long paragraph per chapter. Sarah Cole in *At the Violent Hour* emphasizes (in a section labeled "Chapters") the *relations* among and between the chapters rather than their contents; the former strikes me as the kind of thing that the reader might find very useful at that point. Susan Stewart's *On Longing* manages the work of describing her chapters in two paragraphs that describe *their main ideas*, only mentioning in passing that these ideas happen to have whole sections of the book devoted to them. In any case there are several better and worse ways to do this necessary job. The worst way of all will be to simply reproduce the unexciting, conventional structure without asking how you might alter it for the better.

One place to describe the chapters that almost no one takes advantage of, by the way, is one where the reader might actually need it, namely the conclusion. Part of the work of summing-up may actually require you to remind the reader of what has happened over the last hours or days of reading, using the chunking and other structural mechanisms you've developed over the course of a work to help make this a relatively brief procedure. That summation—which should not just recite what happened, but frame it in new ways—will help set up the conclusion's final task, which is also the book's: to draw the curtains on a scintillating, sunlit 5.

both the value of the problem you will solve (usually explicit: "We have an inadequate or limited theory of early modern sexuality"), your professional credibility for addressing that problem (both explicit and implicit: you show the reader that you understand and know the field in which the problem takes place), and, ideally, by writing sentences or laying out ideas in ways that are rhetorically, rhythmically, or lexically appealing (always implicit). By having, in other words, some kind of *style*.

Thirteen

Paragraphing

The paragraph is the unit of a single idea.

This principle follows naturally from the Uneven U concept since the whole point of the structure is that the opening 4 is closed by the final 5, so that the paragraph functions as a total coherent unit with its own logic of occurrence and development. This theory of the paragraph suggests, in turn, that the paragraph break is a crucial feature of what I will later discuss as unvoiced metalanguage. Simply put, the paragraph break *means something*. It communicates with your reader as much as any other punctuation mark, word, or sentence in your work. And what it communicates is: this is a single idea.

How long should paragraphs be? As long as a single idea. Paragraphs can't really be too long or too short; in general if the idea is contained within the framework of the paragraph unit, then the length is just fine. That said, any quick look over a journal issue in your field will reveal that paragraphs are rarely shorter than half a manuscript page, and rarely longer than one and a half pages. Somewhere in that range (probably between three-quarters of a page and a full page, or 225 to 300 words) is the normative length. Knowing this will help you develop a sense of how to use paragraph length to create rhythm, such as putting a short paragraph after a series of long ones or dragging out a long paragraph to create a feeling of development or suspense.

How can you tell if your paragraph structure works? The easiest way is to look at the first and last sentences and ask yourself if the later one is the 5 to the first one's 4. In other words: do you keep promises you make—promises about the theme, topic, or argument of the paragraph, either on its own or as it relates to the paragraph before it— in the paragraph's first sentence?

The second thing to look for is subordination within the paragraph. Most paragraphs are long enough to have one or two kinds of material in them. Is that material arranged in a structure that helps the reader grasp the paragraph's most important idea, so that the paragraph functions as a single unit? Let's look at a paragraph of Susan Stewart's *On Longing*:

[1] The souvenir reconstitutes the scene of acquisition as a merging with the other and thus promises the preimaginary paradise of the self-as-world even as it must use the symbolic, the narrative, as a device to arrive at that reunion. [2] But the collection takes this movement even further. [3] In its erasure of labor, the collection is prelapsarian. [4] One "finds" the elements of the collection much as the prelapsarian Adam and Eve could find the satisfaction of their needs without a necessary articulation of desire. [5] The collector constructs a narrative of luck which replaces the narrative of production. [6] Thus the collection is not only far removed from contexts of material production; [6.5] it is also the most abstract of all forms of consumption. [7] And in its translation back into the particular cycle of exchange which characterizes the universe of the "collectable," [7.5] the collected object represents quite simply the ultimate self-referentiality and seriality of money at the same time that it declares its independence from "mere" money. [8] We might remember that of all invisible workers, those who actually make money are the least visible. [9] All collected objects are thereby *objets de lux*,[9.5] objects abstracted from use value and materiality within a magic cycle of self-referential exchange. (165)

The first sentence summarizes (and extends) some of the work done in the previous paragraphs; the key word is "thus," which signals the summative function. The level-4 introduction of the paragraph appears in sentence 2; you can pair it with the ninth and final sentence to see in germ the structure of the entire paragraph.

How does Stewart get from sentence 2 to sentence 9? Sentence 3 moves down by making an assertion that dovetails with sentence 2's, but is more specific. Sentence 4 then explains and extends sentence 3—it clarifies what Stewart meant by "prelapsarian" in that sentence and is thus strongly subordinated to it. Sentence 5 happens at roughly the same level as sentence 3—it *extends* it forward into another phase, introducting a new concept (luck replacing production). Sentence 6 moves back upward; beginning with "Thus," it summarizes and pulls together the work of sentences 3 and 5. It adds new material after the semicolon (what I have labeled 6.5). Sentence 7, whose beginning with "And" indicates an extension of the function of sentence 6, has two major pieces—the first, which repeats and reframes material from 6.5, appears before the comma, and the second (labeled 7.5) abstracts and conceptualizes the argument of the first half of the sentence. Sentence 8 is fully subordinated to the conceptual work of 7.5; it gives us an example of the conceptual practice in action (what workers do), and signals that subordination through the use of "we might remember," where both "might" and "remember" mitigate the polemical force and necessity of what is to come. Sentence 9 presents us with the argumentative conclusion to the paragraph, with 9.5 functioning as a necessary explanandum for the phrase *objets de lux*.

Let's chart the paragraph (figure 13.1). The paragraph's movement is largely horizontal and developmental. The closest we come to level-1 "evidence" comes in sentence 8, which is the paragraph's most heavily subordinated sentence. (You can very easily imagine the paragraph without it, as all the other sentences are more crucial.) The subordination in

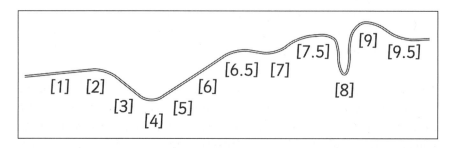

FIGURE 13.1 Movement in a paragraph from Susan Stewart's *On Longing*.

8 is one of five subordinative moments. Of these, two are major: what happens in 8, and the transition from sentence 3 to 4 and back to 5, which constitutes the heart of the paragraph's argument (in U terms, its "lowest" moment). But three other minor subordinations, these happening *inside* rather than *between* sentences, also help guide us through the paragraph. These occur in sentences 6, 7, and 9. In the first two cases we have two-part sentences that help us transition from one sentence to the other by pointing backwards to the material that came immediately before (as 6 does in summarizing 5, or 7 in summarizing 6.5), and then extending us forwards into new material (in 6.5 and 7.5, respectively). Sentence 9 does something quite different, since there the second part of the sentence (9.5) does not move us forward but rather repeats and explains material from 9. You can imagine a paragraph without 9.5, or a paragraph that replaced *objets de lux* with the longer, explanatory phrase ("All collected objects are thereby objects abstracted from use value and materiality within a magic cycle of self-referential exchange"). In both cases the generally summative function of a level-5 close to a strong paragraph is retained. But we would lose, as you can see from the *objets de lux*-less sentence, the strong, quasi-aphoristic quality of the first part of 9 or, if we cut 9.5, the necessary explanation and extension of that aphorism ("All collected objects are . . . *objets de lux*"), which gives us time to come to terms with its complex layers of meaning. (I can't tell, by the way, if *lux* is a typo for *luxe* or if Stewart is punning on the translation of *lux* as "light," thus asking us to imagine "objects of light," with an extra bilingual pun giving us objects *de*light.)

Stewart's paragraph works, then, because it is full of grammatical and lexical structures that signal to the reader how its various parts relate to one another. Over and over, Stewart communicates—using words like "and," "but," "thus," and "thereby," with punctuation marks and with syntax—the paragraph's status as a *process*, as a living, developing thing characterized by leaps forward, pauses for repetition, and asides (sentence 8). All of this holds together because the fundamental promise of the paragraph, made in two parts—that this will relate to what came before it (in sentence 1) and that it will present us with a new idea (in sentence 2)—is kept in the final sentence, which expresses clearly and forcefully the concept only vaguely gestured toward in the second sentence. Another way to think of this is that the final sentence solves the mystery presented to the reader in sentence 2, as though the paragraph were pulling off the silver dome, after a pause for drama, from a platter featuring the head of John the Baptist.

A–A–B, not A–B–A

One of the really common mistakes in paragraph structure comes when you want to present three pieces of evidence, two of which contrast with the third. My students will often want to set this up in an A–B–A structure, in which we start with one piece of evidence, find it contradicted by a second, but *nonetheless* return to a third piece which allows us to come back to the first proposition. If done too quickly, for instance in the space of three sentences, the effect is jarring. The reader has no time to get used to A before B comes in and upends it, and then, just as the reader's getting used to B, A (or some new C) comes in and changes everything back around.

Part of understanding how to write means developing a better sense of how readers actually read. You will want to give readers time to take in and adjust to new information; one sentence is *never* enough to communicate a significant new idea. Especially if you are later going to make an idea more complex, extending it in a surprising direction or upending it in some way, you will do so more successfully if you give the reader time to inhabit the idea seriously. Then, when your extension or upending finally appears, it will have a more serious rhetorical and emotional impact, since the reader will have developed an attachment (to idea A) that will be extended or upended by the new information in B. For that reason—especially inside a paragraph, but even in a sequence of paragraphs or sections—you will usually want to go A–A–B, not A–B–A.

Fourteen

Three Types of Transitions

Stewart's paragraph in the last chapter actually shows us one other major subordination. It happens outside, not inside, the paragraph because it is oriented toward the paragraph that immediately precedes it. Together sentences 1 and 2 place this paragraph into a hierarchical or developmental pattern happening at the paragraph level: "The souvenir reconstitutes the scene of acquisition as a merging with the other and thus promises the preimaginary paradise of the self-as-world even as it must use the symbolic, the narrative, as a device to arrive at that reunion. But the collection takes this movement even further" (Stewart 165). These sentences locate the reader inside the larger structure created by the paragraphs around it, much as the various syntactical and lexical movements inside the paragraph places the reader inside a series of sentences (and just as a section opening or closing orients the reader toward a series of sections, or a chapter toward a series of chapters).

All of these gestures might be thought of as "transitions," if by the term we designate any words, marks, or sentences that aim to move the reader between units of argument. In this way we can recognize that transitions happen at every level of the text—inside paragraphs or sentences (using a "but," an "and," or even a semicolon to signal relationships among units, as we see in Stewart's paragraph) as well as, of course, between paragraphs, sections, or chapters in any larger unit. Indeed the only sentence that can truly said to be nontransitional, in any given text, is the first one.

Everything else is getting us from somewhere to somewhere else. Transitions, therefore, are pieces of text (including punctuation) that *communicate relationships between units.*

The most obvious transitions happen between paragraphs, partly because the paragraph is in itself the signal of a transition (from one idea to the next). The first question that comes up is, then, whether you should transition at the end of a paragraph or at the beginning of one. My answer: almost always at the beginning.

That's because I conceive the job of the end of a paragraph to be to close out and reframe the action of the paragraph itself. Replacing that closure with transitions that point us forward, though it looks and feels natural to many writers, often produces paragraphs that never quite take responsibility for their own work. It's a strange form of writerly impatience, in which the promise of a paragraph ends up deferred to the next, and then to the next . . . so that the *value* of any given paragraph unit becomes that it sets us up for the next unit. This tends, in my experience, to substantially reduce the pressure on the writer to think about and argue forcefully for the meaning of the work. It gives the illusion of linking and subordination when in fact what you often have is a series of purely horizontal relationships that don't communicate what they amount to.

(This position is therefore part of my general theory that writing should be hierarchical and subordinated, with the various parts should articulating themselves with some regularity into a coherent whole. I recognize that the metaphorics of this position—for hierarchy, against metonymic, paratactic, or horizontal relationships—will feel somewhat constraining, even "totalizing" or [as we might have had it, back when I was in graduate school] "fascist." What can I say? I love Mussolini! No, but really, this emphasis on hierarchy is a strategic response to the ethos of writing and the theory of the reader I laid out in the first part of this book. Its impulses are essentially democratic. I'm all for more parataxis and a wide variety of styles, but I'm not for end-of-paragraph transitions when they, as they so often do, obviate the writer's responsibility to think and express the parameters of thought.)

So, I think you should transition at the beginning of paragraphs. How? I teach students three major types of paragraph-level transition:

transition-word, x / y, and lexical. They can be used alone or in combination. Most **transition words** communicate quite clearly the relationship between what's coming and what came before, like so:

Extend, same level	and (mild), similarly, likewise, in the same way that, moreover, also
Extend, summative	then (mild), thus, therefore (strong), as a result, accordingly, in sum, in short
Exemplify/explain	for example, for instance, because, that is why, for
Contradict	but, however, although, in spite of, despite, nonetheless, even as, even so, that said, while, whereas, at the same time
Restatement	in other words, that is, in short
Conclude	in conclusion (please never use!), in the final analysis (avoid), given these claims, when it comes down to it, finally, ultimately, so
Temporal/narrative	after, before, until, eventually, in the long run (also conceptual), meanwhile
Deictic/logical	here, now, then, at this time

A quick internet search will reveal any number of longer lists, but this gives you the overall idea. You see how in each case the transition word (or phrase) communicates not only the fact of the transition but also the specific type of relationship between units. We can add to this list the various punctuation marks; differentiating between the force of a period and a semicolon (the latter is smoother); noting the use of commas or parentheses to mark subordination, exemplification, or asides; and seeing how the colon functions as a predecessor to examples (as in a list: this, that, and the other) or explanations (the problem is this:). (A colon can also be used non-transitionally, as a strong substitute for the copula; "Michael Dukakis: Wrong for America," for example.)

Transition words and phrases tend to set up certain very common grammatical structures at the sentence level. Hence the **x / y transition**, in which the first part of the sentence points backward to the previous material and the second part forward to the new paragraph. If the parts are long enough, the x / y can split into two separate sentences (as we saw in Stewart's paragraph); more often, however, the x and y are two clauses in a single sentence, separated by a comma. The first clause is usually the dependent one, whether the transition word appears between clauses or at the beginning of a sentence:

> By the fifth year of his term [x], **however** [t-w], Mitterand was battling an ever-more fractious electorate [y].

> **Despite** the successes of the early 1980s [x], Alphaville never managed to break out of its mainly European reputation [y].

> **Because** the novel never resolves this question [x], readers must answer it for themselves [y].

You can get a sense of how x/y transitions work if you compare them to versions that simply give us the y, leaving the x unstated or implied. These can involve dependent clauses containing only the transition-word or they can be simple independent sentences.

> **At the same time,** the novel's treatment of its minor characters radically changes.

> The community **nonetheless** could not resolve the problem.

> **Until** 1968.

> **But** not for long.

Notice that in all these cases you can reconstruct some version of x—getting some sense of what the preceding paragraph must have been talking about—even though you have no direct evidence of what it said. Any good transition will allow you do that, since the transition's basic function is to communicate to the reader the relationship between the previous paragraph and the next one.

The possibility of relating a paragraph to the previous one without commenting on it, which we have seen in the examples just above, takes on a special feeling in the case of deictic markers. Deictics are words like "here" or "there," "now" and "then," or the various pronouns, whose referent depends on the situation of their use ("deictic" comes from the Greek for "to show"; it shares a root with the *dex* in *index*, the pointing finger). "Now" means something different when I say it now than when you say it five minutes from now; likewise "I" means me when I say it, you when you say it, and so on. Deictic markers are used transitionally to locate the reader in the argument—we are *now*, at this moment in the reading, going to look at something new—as in these sentences from Fredric Jameson's *Postmodernism*:

> **Now** we need to complete this exploratory account of postmodernist space and time with a final analysis of that euphoria or those intensities which seem so often to characterize the newer cultural experience. (32)

> What we must **now** ask ourselves is whether it is not precisely this semi-autonomy of the cultural sphere which has been destroyed by the logic of late capitalism. (48)

I confess to a deep love for Jameson's stylistic tics, one of which is the use of *now* to draw attention to the reading process. When done well deictics collapse, for a moment, the normal sense of distance between writer and reader, producing a sense of immediacy and discovery that reinforces the idea that the book is *happening* to, with, and through the reader's engagement with it in the present.

Lexical transitions tend not to use transition words (although they can). At their most simple they involve using or reusing key words from the previous paragraph (often the last sentence of the previous paragraph) in order to help the reader understand how the new paragraph relates to the old one. You'll find some that use cognates of the key words, obvious opposites, or other words from the same general field; in all cases the goal is to establish thematic connections between units.

Let's look at an example. A paragraph from Irene Ramhalo Santos's *Atlantic Poets* ends like this:

> In other words, interruption is detrimental to "the poetical." (222)

The sentence has some obvious key words: *interruption, detrimental,* and *poetical*. Any of these might be a good candidate for a lexical transition since they are all relatively strong words, but of the three *detrimental* is least likely, simply because it's an adjective. Here are two very simple possible first sentences that simply repeat the key words:

1. By "the **poetical**" I mean that within poetry that resists the call to interpretation, the thing whose ineffabilty presents the readers of its moment with the greatest difficulty in understanding.
2. At this point [t-w] we need a theory of **interruption**.

And now let's turn to two examples that showcase the use of cognates or opposites—though I had to be careful with *poetical* since its most obvious cognate is *poetry*, a word whose frequent use in the text has robbed it of some of its normal lexical weight.

3. From this point of view [t-w] Pessoa's acts of poesis—of creative making—present their readers with a theory of **unbroken** language.
4. We can now reread Whitman's language games as **disruptions** inside the poem, **eruptions** of the prosaic worldedness that he understands as history taking apart, willfully, the carefully outlined parameters of the aesthetic.

Note in the first example how *unbroken* echoes, via opposition, *interruption* in the earlier sentence; in the second example I've taken the –rupt suffix and used it twice, in the hopes that such a doubling will be caught (consciously or not) by most readers.

And now here's Santos's actual next sentence:

> In this chapter, I argue that, without the forceful, *interruptive* calling of attention to an utterance . . . what we call "poetry," that is to say, the imagined self-enclosed perfection of an utterance, would not exist. (222)

She picks up on both our major keywords, using cognates both times and italicizing one of them to emphasize its force in the argument.

One more example, this time from the last line of a Jameson paragraph:

I will therefore provisionally define the aesthetic of this new (and hypo-thetical) cultural form as an aesthetic of cognitive mapping. (51)

And the first line of the paragraph immediately following it:

In a classic work, *The Image of the City*, Kevin Lynch taught us that the alienated city is above all a space in which people are unable to map (in their minds) either their own positions or the urban totality in which they find themselves. (51)

Though the beginning of the sentence seems to suggest a radical shift in topic, by the middle of it (especially thanks to "in their minds," which makes absolutely sure you see the connection) readers return to comfortable and familiar ground. *Cognitive* becomes "in their minds"; *mapping* becomes "map," and all of a sudden they understand how where they're going relates to where they've been. You can get some sense of how Jameson creates and then releases anxiety by imagining a friendlier version of this transition, which could go something like this: "This aesthetic, which figures the capac-ity to manage mental images of social and geographic space, appears to us most forcefully when that capacity is violated, as it is in what Kevin Lynch calls the 'alienated city.' In *The Image of the City*, Lynch argues that . . . " That friendlier version would remove some of the emotional tension around Jameson's new phrase, which would diminish its rhetorical impact.

Three more short lessons on lexical transitions. Lesson one shows you how you can use grammatical structure to create the feeling of summation. I learned this particular trick from reading Franco Moretti, who frequently uses sentence fragments that restate key phrases as elements in a summa-tive transition, as in these examples from *Graphs, Maps, Trees*:

The rise of the novel, then; or, better, *one* rise in a history that . . . [he goes on] (5)

A—multiple—rise of the novel. (9)

An antipathy between politics and the novel . . . (12)

The whole pattern; or, as some historians would say, the whole cycle: [followed by quote] (13)

From individual cases to series; from series to cycles, and then to genres as their morphological embodiment. (17)

Forty-four genres over 160 years; but instead of finding . . . [he goes on] (18)

Two brief theoretical conclusions. (26)

A rounded pattern in Helpston before the enclosure; and a rounded pattern in *Our Village*. But with a difference: [he then proceeds to explain]. (39)

In some cases Moretti piles two or three fragments upon one another, creating a listing effect; in a number of others he uses semicolons or colons to mitigate the force of the fragment, even when what follows the punctuation mark turns out to be a second fragment.

Lesson two: lexical transitions can happen across multiple paragraphs. Look the following, the first sentences of three consecutive paragraphs by Paul Saint-Amour:

1. Copyright is stranger than we know, and its strangeness becomes more visible as modernism draws near.
2. Even less well understood is copyright's equally complex influence on modernist studies.
3. Perhaps the strangest place to which modernism and copyright jointly lead us is the graveyard. ("Modernism and the Lives of Copyright" 34–36)

The double use of "strange" in the first sentence emphasizes the arrival of an important new term. The word appears in shadow form in the second instance ("less well understood"; "understood" repeats "understand," which also appears at the end of the second paragraph). It then returns in the third to draw the string together. At some level this is uncomplicated: Saint-Amour is using the word and the concept because that's what he's talking about. Yes. That's exactly right. Much of the work of lexical transitions comes naturally, but it's important to understand *how* and *why* it does so in order to more fully understand the work done by what you write.

Lesson three: though most lexical transitioning works semantically, by repeating the meaning of a term, you can also at the far end try for transitions that aim to create connectedness via sound. For something like this you'd be looking for words that repeat or rhyme across the paragraph boundary, as in the example below:

[end of paragraph] The observer is subjected to manipulation and misunderstanding, just as Gulliver is condescended to by the king. (Stewart 87)

[next paragraph] If this Manichean pattern is to last through the remainder of the text, it will be because Gulliver himself cannot bear the manifold operations of the observer's ill-starred attention.

Here I'm just using "Manichean" and "manifold" to repeat the first sound of "manipulation," smoothing the flow across the paragraph jump. But you might try for something weirder:

[next paragraph] If this pattern is to last through the remainder of the text, it will be because Lilliput folds, like a maniple, over Gulliver's outstretched arms, vesting in him the power to remake the dwarf nation's vision of itself.

If you ever ended up writing something like this, it would be because you had a chance to use the word "maniple" (from the OED: a strip of material suspended from the left arm near the wrist, worn as one of the Eucharistic vestments) and reverse-engineered the previous sentence to fit (adding "vesting" to get a slight pun on clothing, via "vestments" in the definition). Poetic effects, like poetry, often get done easiest if you start with the rhyme you will finish with, and work backwards to set it up. The fact that the reader reads left to right doesn't mean that you have to write in that order.

Fifteen

Showing Your Iceberg

Every piece of scholarly writing results from a good deal of hard work that never makes it onto the page. This work can be defined and sorted into a number of general types, which I list below. The examples of how they work in practice are from two imaginary projects, one on Henry James and queerness, the other on Qing dynasty real estate.

Archival: You spent six months digging through boxes of records or historical documents.

- You looked at documents of land sales in the Qing dynasty.
- You read drafts of an early novel by Henry James and looked at his journals or personal documents.

Critical: You mastered the scholarly discourse about a topic.

- You read other books on the Qing economy and on the study of Chinese real estate.
- You know the general state of criticism on James and are especially familiar with scholarship involving your focus, James and sexuality.

Theoretical: You read the major work governing your big concepts.

- You are familiar with other work in Chinese economic history and in economic history outside China; you also know the major theoretical

work governing models of historiography and those that involve thinking about the economy.

- You have a sense of the history of critical thinking on sexuality; you
know the big names in the field (Foucault, Butler); you know the history
of literary criticism and understand where and how you fit into it.

Biographical or Historical: You intimately know the period you're working
in plus, though less well, the periods that precede it or surround it; or
you know the personal histories of your major figures.

- You have a general sense of the entire history of the Qing dynasty,
as well as the Ming; you can locate each record in relation to local,
regional, national, or global historical contexts.
- You know Henry James's biography well; you know the biographies of
other major figures in his life; you understand the general history of his
period locally, regionally, nationally, and globally.

Aesthetic: You grasp the history of aesthetic figures that make up the work
you're looking at; you know the styles or schools to which your work
belongs.

- You have a sense of who wrote the documents; you also know the style
(elevated or vernacular) of the documents and can spot unusual stylistic
moments. You know whether authors of these documents were likely to
be writing anything else and have a sense of what kind of general stylistic
or formal interactions might happen between your genre and others.
- You know where and how James fits into the history of the novel; you
also have a more general understanding of how novels work, and are
familiar with the modes of reading novels (narratology, for example),
even the ones you don't use. You know what was happening in other
aesthetic fields when your author was writing.

Documentary: You know the social and formal rules governing the objects
you discuss.

- You know how real estate records have looked over the course of Chinese
history; you understand the standard format of these documents.

- You understand the history of the development of the novel as a whole; you know what it meant to be a writer of James's type in his period, and you understand how he fit into that period (early, late, high, marginal).

Linguistic: You have mastered the languages of your source materials.

- You can read and translate from the Chinese, and/or have special training focused on the vocabulary used in discussions of real estate during the Qing dynasty.
- You not only read English, but are attuned to the particular modes of its literary style, which you can use to perform critical and intellectual work.

Some of this you will know before you start a project; some of it comes only after beginning it; and some of it may finally make a difference in the last drafts, as you become more surefooted about where you're going. But all of it needs to be done. Beneath every piece of scholarly work lie years of patient learning and accumulation, as well as torrid months or years of focused thinking, research, and reading. From below the waterline, the labor and investment done in these dark, underwater seas sustains the small portion of the work that appears above it: a finished article or book.

It goes without saying, then, that one of your major tasks in graduate school and beyond is to build the iceberg that will sustain the early parts of your career. In an unfocused way, this has been happening since grade school and has continued through your undergraduate years, whether or not you were actively paying attention. In graduate school you begin building a more disciplinary (literature) and field-specific (medieval studies) iceberg; you also start filling in theoretical and critical gaps, which did not get covered as much early on. By the time you're on your dissertation and for every project beyond that, you will be building, on top of that generalist iceberg, specific fields of knowledge for specific intellectual projects. The work you do in the first years after starting graduate school—including the languages you learn—determine, in almost every case, the first decade or so of your life as a publishing scholar.

Most of this learning never makes it into the actual piece of work, which focuses on some tiny percentage of the material you know. You don't need to go over the entire history of the world since Mesopotamia in an essay on *The Jeffersons*; if you're publishing in a journal devoted to television studies you probably don't even have to talk about the history of television (and in *The Journal of The Jeffersons Studies*, you don't have to give background on the show). You also don't need to say, somewhere in your essay on Qing real estate, that you read Chinese. Part of deciding how much iceberg to show depends, then, on what your audience knows about your work and recognizing that much of the communication you do will happen implicitly rather than explicitly. Even your assumptions about what your audience knows will testify to your general trustworthiness as a source of knowledge, since they indicate how well you understand your discipline or field.

Iceberg is communicated at every moment of the work. Consider for instance the following sentence from a book called *Grammatology and Literary Modernity in Turkey*: "Fazhoğlu shows how Ottoman scholars of the classical period regarded Arabic as both the medium of divine revelation, as materialized in the Quran, and the medium of divine will, as materialized in Being; Arabic was understood as the 'house of Divine Logos" [*kelâm-t ilâhî*],' and was formalized and studied as a 'half-symbolic language.' (153–54)" (Ertürk 7). Now ask yourself, what does Nergis Ertürk have to know to write that sentence? Arabic; something about the relationships among languages; something of Ottoman history (enough to judge, for instance, whether Fazhoğlu is a reliable source); the history of the Quran; the history of Turkey more generally; and the philosophical and theoretical work necessary to make confident claims about social perceptions of language. More generally you might guess (on the basis of this sentence and the book's title) that Ertürk reads Turkish; that she knows her Derrida (that's what "grammatology" refers to) and that, consequently, she has a grasp on the field of French theory; that she has a general sense not only of modernity but of literary modernity (and knows the theory, philosophy, and history associated with them); that she's familiar with theories and histories of language use and language reform, not only in Turkey but more generally (which may include, for instance, a strong understanding of language modernization movements in nineteenth- and twentieth-century Eurasia, and a weaker understanding of similar movements in places outside Europe [East Asia, for example] or in earlier centuries [Dante on Italian, for example]).

Neither the title of the book nor the sentence I just cited were written for the express purpose of demonstrating Ertürk's iceberg to the reader. They show it nonetheless. Practically every sentence of a book, as well as every one of its paratexts, communicates at some level the iceberg that sustains its claims. This is always true. Everything you write implies a history of work that justifies it.

The writing question before us is, then, how and when should you show your iceberg. That is, how can you use icebergs to create rhetorical or thematic effects that improve your work? Here are three simple rules:

1. *Use notes to maintain flow and establish bona fides.* Look at these sentences . . .

With the development of banking in the eighteenth century, checks began to be addressed to and drawn on a bank and required the banker to pay the sum named on the check to its bearer on demand. The form of the instrument then remained relatively constant through the next century and a half, but, sometime in the middle of the nineteenth century, banks began to print uniform books of blank checks for their depositors to use as payment. (Poovey 51–52)

. . . to which were attached the following footnote:

McCulloch notes that, for a brief period in the nineteenth century, between 1853 and 1859, two kinds of checks were issued. The first, unstamped checks on plain paper, had to contain a date of issue and to be drawn on a bank at no greater distance than fifteen miles. Checks on stamped paper did not have to contain their date or place of issue, they could be drawn on anyone, they could be issued at any distance from where they were to be paid, and they could be made out to bearer or to order. 21 Vict., c. 20, extended the stamp duty to all checks. McCulloch also describes the innovation of the printed checkbook, which he says originated "within the last twenty years"—i.e., in the 1840s (McCulloch, *Dictionary,* 290). Jevons notes that checks came in several forms, including bankers' checks (drawn from one banker on another) and certified checks (equivalent to promissory notes of the banker) (*Money,* 242–43). Like nineteenth-century commentators, I focus on personal checks drawn on a bank. (Poovey 526n49)

Notice that the footnote is longer than the sentence to which it refers. Iceberging like this is especially common for work done in a historicist style, which tends to be more heavily footnoted than formalist or theoretical reading. It allows you to maintain an even through line for your *own* story, while gesturing to an immense array of resources that undergirds the relatively larger claims made above the waterline. If you imagine a paragraph that brought most of the footnote up into the main text, you can see, first, that the footnote material itself would have to expand in order to cover all its ground (for instance, if it were up top we would need something to move from McCulloch to Jevons); and second, that laying all this out would essentially create a significant new subsection.

2. *Less is more.* In math class in grade school we lost points for not showing our work. You have to give the reader what s/he needs to follow along, right? No. Somewhat counterintuitively, showing too much iceberg often weakens your argument. It does this both by distracting the reader from the main argumentative or narrative line (thereby disrupting force and flow) and—more dangerously—by suggesting that you lack confidence in your own process or methods. My undergraduates, for instance, will often write sentences like, "analyses of poems can use scansion to discover new things about how a poem is built." You could imagine someone footnoting such a claim. But if you're a scholar of poetry, you already know this; in fact that basic presumption is central to the field. Including it in the body of the text—rather than simply exemplifying it in your reading practice—indicates that the claim is new enough to you that it has not yet become part of your iceberg. This is a sign of weakness. You want to *show* that you know the professional

iceberg without ever actually talking about it, which means communicating implicitly what you know. Explicit conversation about method should only appear when the method is new or complicated. A classic example of how to get this wrong involves oversharing theoretical material that professional readers already know because it happens to be new to you. (Part of what this means is that writing well requires knowing what other people know.)

What goes for method goes for references as well. Look at the following three sentence fragments:

the French philosopher Michel Foucault's *Discipline and Punish: The Birth of the Prison* is one possible example

Foucault's *Surveiller et punir* is one obvious example

the Foucault of the prisons book is the obvious example

Which of these communicates the deepest iceberg? For me, it's the third one (which is from the fifth page of Jameson's *Postmodernism*). Jameson suggests the most by doing the least—the phrase "the Foucault of the prisons book," like a casual mention in conversation of "the early Hegel," suggests that the author not only knows the named figure, but actually knows of that figure's multiple versions (meanwhile, the reader's still struggling with one). The move is especially powerful (and/or obnoxious) because Jameson refers to *Discipline and Punish* by a keyword in its subtitle, leaving the less-well-informed reader struggling to catch up. By comparison, the first example tells too much. The second tells less and shows more (points for indicating that the author reads French). Neither has the casual strength of Jameson's aside.

This kind of implicit indication of the iceberg happens constantly. Like transitioning, iceberging is everywhere. Once you see that almost every sentence implicitly communicates information about the background of an article, you can grasp iceberging as an information management strategy: a set of ways in which you communicate what you know, lay out what you expect readers to know, and indicate what is genuinely novel and interesting in your own work.

3. *Iceberg according to your needs.* Let's read a paragraph of Christopher Bush's:

> The Japanese thing would thus seem to go against Marx's classic account of the commodity in that far from presenting itself as *sui generis*, its value is produced precisely by its signifying that it is a product of human labor, specifically of a localizable source and mode of production. If the classic commodity form is said to disguise social relations among persons as objective relations among things, the japoniste commodity would present as some sort of human encounter what are in fact market relations. These aren't mutually exclusive, of course—just a question of how many dialectical whacks one gives the piñata of the commodity form. Indeed, already in Marx's account the commodity's lies, analyzed, are its truth.[27] The aesthetic valorization of the Japanese thing therefore implies a critique, however flawed, of the commodity. While Marxian anticapitalism of course focuses on the social relations that are understood to precipitate in the commodity, japoniste anticapitalism's attention remains far more focused on the commodity itself.[28] The specificity of this "Japanese" thing resides in the way its and/or, neither/nor character is expressed: unlike the mere commodity, which is rootless and trivial, the Japanese thing is bound to and expresses a historically deep and essentially integral national culture; yet unlike the art object, the Japanese thing is useful and likes to travel. Or so the story goes. The Japanese thing answers the false universality of quantitative, global, monetary exchange value with its own, differently false, universality: that of the qualitative values of the national and the aesthetic. Japonisme would disavow the dissolving, homogenizing effects of capital—the universal solvent—while retaining the dream of global exchange based on a common standard—a universal currency of mind.[29] (84)

Look at the way Bush handles Marx. Already in the first sentence the decision to not use Karl's first name signals something about the role Marx will play here: Bush expects his reader to know which Marx he's talking about, and he wants to remind the reader—gently, in that same sentence— that the account of the commodity is "classic" and therefore need not be described. At the same time, he *does* describe it, both by negation in the second (dependent) clause of the first sentence, then affirmatively in the first dependent clause of the second sentence. This double move is a really good (dare I say, classic) way to handle certain kinds of background—you both assert that it does not need to be repeated and you simultaneously, but in a grammatical form that reduces the information's effective weight, repeat it anyway. The best of both worlds: you've indicated your iceberg, shown that you know the current professional status of knowledge of Marx on the commodity form, and helped teach readers what they need to know to understand your work.

Not one of the three footnotes in that paragraph icebergs Marx or anything else—the first and third add theoretical explanation, and the second historical and theoretical detail. Relatively speaking, because the focus of the paragraph is not Marx, Bush has done only a little iceberging; he's managed this partly with rhetoric (the function of the word "classic" is duplicated by an "of course" later on) and partly by inserting necessary information—but only the minimal necessary information—into dependent clauses. All this happens because Marx is not the focus of the paragraph. It is in fact what *makes* Marx not the center of the paragraph.

Part of what I'm suggesting then is that iceberging gestures depend partially on the kind of work a paragraph or section does. Writing that covers background information will tend to iceberg through general statements supported by footnotes; writing focused on conceptual or theoretical claims will, as in the Bush example, iceberg lightly, perhaps in the dependent clauses. And writing that does philological, formal, or theoretical close reading will show *almost all* its work above the waterline, so that the reader can follow along, as in a math problem, every painstakingly ratiocinated step of the reading process. At the limit of a certain deconstructive slow reading, even the process whereby the author stumbled across a quote or came up with a thought (in a dream, for example), which we would normally consider deep background, will appear above the waterline, where it will wreak its subtle effects on the unfolding prose. How and what you iceberg, how you show your work, is both an effect of the kind of work you're doing (historical or polemical, close analysis or general claim) and a way for you to communicate to the reader what kind of work is going on.

Handling Theory

Handling what you might think of as "theory"—using the term to mean any large-scale concept, usually connected with a master term or two—remains a major writing challenge even for experienced writers. Say you want to use the Freudian notions of condensation and displacement, Best and Marcus on "surface reading," or Sloterdijk on cynical reason. When you move into the discussion of the concept—and here let's assume that it's a relatively unfamiliar concept that must be explained—you end up with two problems: first, you push yourself into relatively unmotivated summary or description, disrupting the energy and flow of your argument; second, you put yourself in the position of a student or an inferior in relation to the theorist (or school of theory) you're citing. It's very common to end up with about two paragraphs describing the theorist and his or her idea, a return to your reading, and a finish that more or less says, "You know that idea from the big theorist I just told you about? Well, it applies here." Which is, let's be frank, no one's idea of a good time.

The best solution is almost always to do less, or more, with the theory you use. If more, then you need to make the theory a genuine interlocutor—to make it primary rather than secondary, so that you deal with it in an engaged way, modifying it as you move through it. This will break apart any static, descriptive paragraphs by allowing your argument and voice to stay alive throughout the discussion. This kind of dynamic engagement with theory cannot happen fully outside your primary text. You won't, or shouldn't, end up with two paragraphs that give "background" on the theory; instead the theory will be right in the foreground and will stay in place even as you focus your discussion more on your primary text. You don't want to be "applying" some theoretical concept X to text Y, but rather to put both X and Y in a relationship with one another, and having both of them come out the other side of that relationship changed in some way.

The other option is to do less. Here you'd handle the theory in a sentence or two (maybe three), while putting the necessary background (or even some of the citations) in the footnotes. If you do something like this, you can begin a paragraph with a reference to the theoretical work ("In the Lacanian model of the unconscious, . . . ") before shifting in the second sentence to its relation to your ideas ("We see something like Lacan in the novel's arrangement of . . . "); this basically splits the introduction/transition work into two. Or you can try to subordinate the theory inside one of your own paragraphs, making it part of a level 3–4 section that interprets a piece of evidence, for instance.

What the "less" and "more" strategies have in common is getting you out of a negative or helpless position in relation to the theory you want to engage with. You don't want to ever feel like you're "using" or "describing" theory. (You might be explaining it; but as we know the gap between an explanation and the thing it explains is the gap of living thought.)

Sixteen

Metalanguage

By now I hope it's clear that any serious theory of metalanguage—language that communicates *about* the writing that it's in—begins with the recognition that every sentence communicates metalinguistically. If you consider the implicit transitional work done, for instance, by the paragraph break or the long dash, or the iceberging done in those sentences of Bush's or Jameson's, you will see that at every moment of a good essay the reader is being located inside the apparatus of an argument and a process of development.

With that in mind we can stop thinking of metalanguage as identical to what some people call "signposting," making, that is, highly explicit, usually structural remarks of the following type: "This essay reads Milton's poetry in order to argue that," or, "I have three main points," or, "In what follows I suggest." Metalanguage does include explicit, signposting statements like those, but it also involves the nearly invisible action of grammar, rhythm, tone, and punctuation marks, all of which can serve as structural signals to the reader. Somewhere in between those elements you will find x/y or transition-word transitions, which combine metalanguage with words and phrases that belong quite clearly to the prose's argument. And even such transitions can be more or less explicit, ranging from something like "we now see how Adorno's politics reflect the experiential drama of the postwar" (more explicit) to "by the end of the nineteenth century these structures had almost entirely collapsed," where the only real metalinguistic pointer is the marker of chronological

development encapsulated in "by." Recognizing that metalanguage operates along a continuum that includes a wide variety of signaling mechanisms will help you understand how to fulfill your responsibility to locate
and engage readers within a piece of work.

That's not to say that the implicit–explicit continuum is the only way to
think about metalanguage. We can also describe it by looking at its major
functions:

• *Anticipation.* Metalanguage can set the reader up for what's to come,
like "In what follows I consider," "this essay argues," and so on. Here's a
less explicit instance, from Derrida's *Of Grammatology*: "Then we glimpse
the germ of a profound but indirect explanation of the usurpation and the
traps condemned in [Ferdinand de Saussure's] Chapter VI. This explanation
will overthrow even the form of the question to which it was a premature
reply" (44). All the work here is done by the "will" of the second sentence.

• *Summary.* Implicitly, we see this in all kinds of transitional structures,
including the sentence fragment summations of the Morretian type. More
explicitly: "Let's review," "To sum up," "As we saw earlier," "As I mentioned above," and so on. Jamesonian deictics like "now" and "here" can
summarize or anticipate, depending on context.

• *Ordering.* Either by anticipation or summation, such as "In what
follows I consider three major events of the 1890s"; "we have seen that
three features of the novel emerge at roughly the same time in southern
England." Much ordering metalanguage belongs to the general category
of signposting. But ordering also happens implicitly in a sentence like
Bachner's "Nolan's *Memento* is trauma made film, on two different levels,"
where "two" tells the reader pretty clearly to expect two units of analysis.

• *Logic.* We include under this category the various transitional words
and phrases that communicate logical structure (rather than explicitly
essayistic structure). "On one hand" prepares the reader for the other
one, "as a result" sets up a cause-effect conclusion, and phrases like "ultimately," "in the final analysis," or "in conclusion" (of which the third is the
most explicit) announce an upcoming close.

These functions, and indeed the entire apparatus of the metalinguistic
continuum, do not take place exclusively within what you might think of

as the "body" of an essay or book. If we think of the work as a whole that includes everything in it (including the medium that makes it up), then we recognize at once that properly metalinguistic communication happens the minute someone looks at a page of writing or the form of a book.

• *Paratextual metalanguage.* Paratextual metalanguage tends to be anticipatory and/or ordering. It includes sections, chapters, or book titles or subtitles—whether naturally, explicitly ("Three Women's Texts and a Critique of Imperialism"), thematically ("Jorge Amado: Exile and Literature"), or in a weird combination of anticipation and retrospection (aka the future perfect), as when a title will only make sense *after* you read the work (Lee Edelman's *Homographesis* comes to mind). Frequently titles will also be the subject of some discussion in the work, often explicitly, as in the first sentence of Lauren Berlant's *Cruel Optimism* ("A relation of cruel optimism exists when something you desire is actually an obstacle to your flourishing"), which leads unsurprisingly into a discussion of the major themes of the book. This allows the paratext to reappear in the main text and can, if you wait some time to produce the title's textual return, produce a nice rhetorical surprise. (My favorite instance of this type comes from the movie *You Got Served* in which, about a third of the way through, a member of the winning dance crew, having been accused of dance plagiarism, tells his accusers that they're just mad because "You got served." Kapow!!)

Another major form of paratextual metalanguage is the epigraph, which will tend to signal—when not used immediately as the opening subject of a work, where it will function as the 1 in a classic truncated U introduction—upcoming concerns, whether thematic or theoretical.

• *Unvoiced metalanguage.* I have mentioned punctuation marks and the work done by a paragraph break. But under this category we must also include section breaks, especially when numbered (where they have a strong ordering function) or when denoted by asterisms (* * *) or other ornamental symbols, line breaks (blank lines inserted between paragraphs), as well as, of course, chapter breaks in books. This information, which would be entirely lost when reading aloud, communicates order and relation nonetheless (you can, for instance, use line breaks or asterisms to divide subsections inside numbered sections). To this I add, as a mediatic interloper to the party, the fact of a reader's location in a book (or, for that matter, its length). Just as, when approaching the last few pages of a mystery novel, we anticipate the unmasking of a murderer, so in the final pages of a scholarly work we await the fructifying, final revelation.

I leave aside, as subjects for someone else's discussion, the many other facts governing the reader's metalinguistic experience of a piece of work, including the design of a book (and its cover) and the name and/or affiliation of its author. All these constitute the *mise-en-scène* of the work; just as the appearance of Arnold Schwarzenegger on screen signals that we are in the presence of a certain kind of film, so too does the name of the scholar or the press that published it sometimes prepare us for a certain kind of communication.

Seventeen

Ending Well

More than any other aspect of a piece of writing, I feel, endings, like unhappy families, should each happen in their own particular way. But such a dream is impossible for endings (and, *pace* Tolstoy, for families), which are subject to the same processes of structuration and habituation as any other feature of scholarly writing. Nonetheless the pressure to end well, to have the ending mark in both formal and thematic terms the final value of the essay as a whole, wreaks its merry havoc on my own sense of confidence and comfort; I find endings absolutely the hardest thing to write and advice for other writers of endings difficult to produce.

Let's begin with some general principles. The one thing endings should *not* do is summarize the argument. Summary as the very end of a piece violates the principle of the Uneven U, which is that your close should be bigger, better, newer, and more interesting than your open. A good ending is also a beginning—the coming together of everything that has happened, yes, but so that it leads into *novel* thought. A good ending is a triumph, a pulling together of various threads and strands, figures and themes, that shows us a new picture made out of the same puzzle pieces we have had all along. It's not that endings shouldn't include summary at all—in fact the *opening* of an ending can often summarize the work so far, pulling together the things you've done and setting up for the new conclusion (thus they serve as 4s in relation to the final 5s). But they should not end with it.

All this means that endings bear an immense amount of rhetorical and argumentative pressure. That is, of course, why they're hard, and also why so many books simply forgo them—almost half the books in our review sample, you will recall from chapter 10, simply had no labeled conclusion at all. The best endings not only engage the reader in the final moments of actual reading, but leave the reader *pensive*, like Balzac's unhappy Marquise, producing a pause for reflection and consideration whose silence accompanies the turning over of the work's final page.

One way to think about a good ending is that it first closes all the things you've opened and then

FIGURE 17.1 The Matryoshka doll: this machine kills fascists.

does something more. This is why so many conclusions will begin by turning back to an example from early in the article or the book. This simple rhetorical gesture, like putting the top back on the largest Matryoshka doll, signals the enclosure of the work's near-final arc (figure 17.1). So if you're stuck with the ending, begin by asking yourself: Have I closed all my "dolls"? Can I go back to the beginning of the essay (or book) and pull something back in, to show how it looks different now that we've done all this work?

In other words, your final close has to bring together every single other close at the next level "down"—sections for an article, chapters for a book, and so on. A good ending puts that series of closes together in some way that allows them to illuminate each other, that fulfills the promises made in the introduction, and extends beyond those promises to something else. In articles, this is easier because you're likely dealing with only two or three major sections; your conclusion will likely just put A and B into some new relation with C. Books, with their multiple chapters, make this kind of gesture (A + B + C + D + E = F!) more difficult. One way to manage it all is to imagine that the first chapters of the book set up a structure or pattern of reading that is violated or altered in some way by the later chapters, so that you have a grouping (A + B + C) that produces X, and another grouping (D + E) that produces Y. The conclusion might then open by summarizing and even placing the A–E sequence into these two new groups and then close by bringing X and Y together into some final argument, Z (which might be just that X and Y are in a dialectical relation with one another).

I want to list some common mistakes or weaknesses in endings, but before I do, I want to tell you that I have more sympathy for these problems than for any of the others I describe in this book. The pressure of the ending makes it really hard to avoid falling into bad versions of these formal clichés. The difference between a really good and a really bad ending is often *not* that the good one has foregone a bad habit, but rather that it has figured out a way to make that habit and its logic fresh and believable.

That said, try to avoid falling into any of these patterns or, if you're doing them, make sure you're doing them really well and on purpose:

1. *Be careful not to wax lyrical as a substitute for ideas.* One way writers react to the pressure of the close is to radically elevate their prose style, using a wide variety of fancy words (or unusually long and lyrical sentences) to give the reader the impression that something is happening. This obviously works at some level—look at political speeches—but in scholarly writing too often the sudden shift in style stands in for the incapacity to generate new ideas, to really make something that not only *sounds like* a 5, but actually *is* one. Be careful especially of dragging out of nowhere some big-sounding words (global, modernity, humanity) that have had nothing to do with your topic so far, or of suddenly moving to a strong, non-rhetorical "we" that you have not used anywhere else. At the same time you must recognize that the biggest Matryoshka will almost always involve precisely a set of concepts that are larger, more abstract,

and more broadly general than the rest of the work, since the level-5 ending is also where we tend to highlight the most expansive possibilities and impacts of the work.

(Kwame Anthony Appiah tells a story about walking in on the end of a René Wellek lecture: "As I pushed gently on the swing doors at the end of the hall, I heard—or, at least, I think I heard—a voice that sounded Mittel Europaïsch pronouncing a dozen or so words. These words have stuck with me since, even though I can no longer be sure that I really heard them. What I heard was: ' . . . the life of reason, which is the life of the spirit.' That was it. The last words of the peroration. Tumultuous applause followed" [51]. This is the dream version of the rhetorically devastating ending.)

2. *Avoid making vague claims of radicalism or political import that are out of proportion with the work.* We all want our work to matter, and we know that we have to say it matters. One of the most common ways to do this is to assert that your conclusions—or the work of the writer under consideration—ought to radically reshape the way we think about everything. At some other level it *is* important to show how the work might change the way everyone thinks; making the reader aware of this possibility is not unreasonable. But be careful! Not everything needs to make us radically rethink everything we know, nor can it. So before you do this, think hard about whether a conclusion more modestly connected to the actual work you've done is possible. If it's not, then something may be wrong with your work. The tiger's leap to radical possibility is often a signal of a fundamental emptiness at the origin of the jump.

3. *Be careful saying that this work gives us new work to do, or demonstrates the continued relevance of the questions with which you began.* The danger here is that you end up simply ending by saying something like, "and so the work I have done is important," which is pretty flat considering that you've just asked someone to read thirty or more pages of your writing. Here especially the membrane separating a bad and a good version is very thin.

But now we need to look at some short examples—just a few final sentences—to clarify what the options are and to realize the ways in which these cautions, too, are inadequate to the mysterious task of concluding well.

> Although some current versions of the posthuman point toward the anti-human and the apocalyptic, we can craft others that will be conducive to the long-range survival of humans and of the other life-forms, biological and artificial, with whom we share the planet and ourselves. (Hayles 291)

> Perhaps it will require nothing less than another major convulsion of the capitalist world-system, and some radical shake-up or reorganization of the current literary world-system to boot, to compel us to revisit our overfamiliar histories of realism and modernism with fresh eyes or to create the conditions that might allow for new modes of narration with ambitions to realize promises that neither realism nor modernism could ever realize separately. (Cleary 268)

> These are the words that prevent [Benjamin's] writings and readings from being crystallized and frozen into a merely negative method. Words of light, they correspond to the cremation of his work, a cremation in which the form of the work—its suicidal character—reaches its most brilliant illumination, immolated in the flame of its own criticism. (Cadava 130)

All three endings feature heavy lyricism and big concepts. To judge them successful or unsuccessful would require knowing how they grow out of their context. I can tell you that of the three I prefer Eduardo Cadava's, even though it is in many ways the most overtly lyrical, because it manages to repeat the title and key concept of the book ("words of light") and because its tone and structure absolutely resembles that of the rest of the work (though I don't, for whatever reason, like too much the quasi-rhyme of "illumination" and "immolated").

N. Katherine Hayles's I love least at the level of the rhythm. I think it might have been better to split "ourselves" into two words, to highlight the actual argument being made (about sharing our *selves* with the planet and its creatures); otherwise "ourselves" feels flat, too ordinary. (One of the things you'll notice is that both Hayles and Cadava interrupt their final sentence with a late dependent clause; we'll talk more about that later on, but for now you want to notice the way the late interruption creates a strong sense of upcoming finality and closure.)

Joe Cleary's is tricky. It's a very long sentence made longer by the lack of pauses for breath after "to compel"; he also has a pretty ugly repetition with "conditions" and "ambitions," though I love and find hilarious and great the use of "to boot." Having read the essay, which is really amazingly good and inspiring, I will say that in this case I nonetheless feel like the distance from the big concepts of the close and the rest of the piece is a little too far—that though this ending in and of itself is strong and interesting, it could have been written for many more articles than this particular one and sounded equally as good. This is not a disaster, just a reminder that even a strong ending can fall slightly short of the mark.

Let's look at a few more:

Would such a world involve a radical reorganisation of time and space? It seems likely. With these sorts of reflections, however, we start to dissolve the connection between utopian speculation and realism. And that is further than a study of this type ought to go. (Giddens 178)

These observations from another discipline confirm the view that modern literature has been engaged in transmuting the time world of history into the timeless world of myth. And it is this timeless world of myth, forming the content of so much of modern literature, that finds its appropriate aesthetic expression in spatial form. (Frank 64)

Lyric poetry and materialist criticism in its most authentic form thus both maintain a realism without authority, based on the powers of persuasion and divination inherent in pictures. A body composed of pictures is little more than the substance of history and the imagination. As long as things appear to us in this way, and as long as matter remains a problem, poetry will be an indispensable guide to reality. (Tiffany 294)

The rhetorical strategy of the preceding pages has involved an experiment, namely, the attempt to see whether by systematizing something that is resolutely unsystematic, and historicizing something that is resolutely ahistorical, one couldn't outflank it and force a historical way at least of thinking about that. "We have to name the system": this high point of the sixties finds an unexpected revival in the postmodernism debate. (Jameson 418)

Each of these four closes ends by pairing some reflection on the preceding material with metalanguage about the value of the project immediately before the reader; in this way each plays with the third habit I identify above, of restating and asserting the value of the already-known qualities of the work. Their differences illustrate a variety of strategies for managing this gesture, some (of course) more appealing than others.

Anthony Giddens shows us restatement by negation: my book has done this and no more. As a result his conclusion feels more like an abdication than an ending. You could improve it, I think, by flipping the order of the sentences, so that the reader ended with speculation about ideas beyond this work, some vision of another project made possible by this one, rather than with a thin and unsubstantiated assertion about what a work of this type should or shouldn't do. But then it wouldn't be this kind of ending.

Joseph Frank's close exactly reproduces the thesis of his essay: "this timeless world of myth . . . finds its appropriate aesthetic expression in spatial form." This is an older model of closure, where a brief swerve at the end (you can guess at it from Frank's "these observations from another discipline") serves merely to confirm the analysis at hand. Points to Frank for using "spatial form," the essay's key concept, but otherwise . . . meh. You might think of this as a kind of zero degree of the restating ending: fine, but nothing more than fine.

Daniel Tiffany's is better because the prose has more verve and rhythm. The final sentence, like Frank's, restates the book's major argument, though the "as long as" at the beginning allows us to begin to imagine some scope beyond the work, in which poetry's relation to matter would change (here compare to Cleary, who opens that beyond quite explicitly). I very much like Tiffany's second, simple sentence, whose clean grammar allows its message to feel novel. Though it reprises arguments from the book, stating them in this bald and somewhat dramatic way (the "is" is really forceful here, almost aphoristic) gives the reader a fresh view of the work of the whole. (By contrast I don't love Tiffany's first sentence, where the "both" is ambiguous: it's a pronoun [referring to both "lyric poetry" and "materialist criticism in its most authentic form"] but it feels like it might be a conjunction [setting up a both/and structure]; this disrupts the reader at a crucial moment in terms of pace and flow.)

Jameson, finally, both summarizes and extends the argument. The first sentence is pure metalinguistic summary, though summary that also gives us something new since Jameson has not told us so explicitly about the nature of his experiment. The final sentence, with the citation, is almost too complicated—you have to read it at least twice, since while you're looking at the quotation, you have no idea why it's going to matter, so you have to go back afterwards and reread it. But as a close it's interesting because it recontextualizes the preceding pages in a new historical frame: a slogan from the 1960s, meaningful in one context and in relation to one social sphere, returns in the 1990s, where it both connects us to the recent history of political dispute and marks our distance from it. This is a *new* argument for the book, but it emerges naturally and thematically from what came before. It thus opens up new horizons of thought while closing and reframing the earlier material.

Let's close this discussion of endings with two more examples, each of which includes significant metacommentary on closure. Each of these belongs purely to the book it closes. You could not copy exactly the rhythm, the rhetorical gestures, or the sentences, but you can learn, I think, from the concepts behind them.

As I close my book on Lacan I feel that he and I are neither properly dead nor properly married (the only true endings for books). Desire is not yet calmed. I do not possess him, to either marry or bury. He is still fading, not faded yet. But my eyes are open. If I have not perfectly mastered Lacan, at least I can read the d in perfectly, the letter of desire which spoils the perfect mastery of the dead author. (Gallop 185)

Mink Snopes stopped waiting after thirty-eight years. He set out down a straight road to impose his notion of a good ending upon his story: a pistol shot and then rest, his vital energy not wasted but reabsorbed into earth and universe. There are surely other endings more appropriate for us than the one Mink chooses. That is the point: *my good ending may be your bad one.* The thing is, at the very least, to question the manager's dearly held belief that there is "one best way" for us all. (Banta 326–27)

These two allow us to contrast explicit first-person metalanguage with its third-person counterpart. While you could imagine anyone ending a book like Martha Banta's in the way that she does, Jane Gallop's ending on Lacan could probably only end Jane Gallop's book on Lacan. It draws heavily on the emotionally open readings that have preceded it and sustains the book's general interest in the ways that conceptual claims emerge from highly personal acts of criticism. It is, in this way, completely hers.

Banta's conclusion comes at the end of a final chapter called "Ways Out." The chapter's basic question—what were the ways out of the heavily ideological force of new patterns of thinking about bodies and machines in the American twentieth century?—is answered partly in Banta's readings of Faulkner, whose character Mink Snopes appears at the beginning of this last paragraph. This reading of Mink's position on endings and stories allows Banta to produce a final conclusion about the history of Taylorism *as a theory of endings,* even as she ends her own book. The re-citation of the manager's line, chunked and highlighted earlier, neatly slots that puzzle piece into Banta's final conceptual claim.

Mapping the problem of concluding the book onto the thematic concerns that govern it is, when all is said and done, also formalizable as a rhetorical strategy for ending-making, one whose potential pitfalls would become apparent the minute it began to be used on a regular basis. That's the problem with endings: we want them to be different from one another, because that uniqueness will shore up—against the fear of repetition or codification—some vision of the work as having been made entirely from scratch, happening this time and this time only, in perfect synchronicity with its own becoming. Banta's and Gallop's endings reflect back to us that desire, which is why I like them so much and why, as I've suggested, they both can and cannot be imitated.

The ending's desire for uniqueness, the drive to find the "one best way" for a single project, is itself a refracted version of the dream of a democratic distribution of the right to end in one's own unique way. Coupling it with our knowledge that in any piece of writing we will be walking down formal paths laid out for us by the countless decisions and preferences of a world of others, thus repeating and reworking patterns and habits that have for a long time been used and known, allows us to recognize the ending as also—and therefore—a microcosm of the problem of making, of originality and repetition, in general.

Eighteen
Titles and Subtitles

The interplay between the writer's synchronic experience of the text and the reader's diachronic one rarely feels more intense than when you start a piece of writing, when the curious and discovery-oriented writer is in the odd position of not knowing exactly how the whole thing will turn out. Because the earlier the material is, the more it needs to "know" about what comes next, titles and introductions are especially difficult if you tackle them at the beginning of a writing project.

Some people deal with that problem by writing the project out of order. For whatever weird reason, I can do this for books but not for articles. I write books like this: chapter I'm least afraid of; chapter I'm next least afraid of; so on until the chapter I'm most afraid of; then the introduction; then finally the conclusion. But *inside* each chapter, or for articles, I write an introduction first, and I can't really work without some kind of tentative title adorning the first page. I just can't make myself write evidentiary or argumentative paragraphs if I don't have something ahead of them that pretends to know what the essay (my generic term, going forward, for a chapter or an article) will be about.

Titles are probably best written at or near the end of a project, unless something really spectacular comes to you earlier on. I usually start with a provisional title, just to get going. But I have changed the titles of most of my chapters, essays, and books multiple times over the course of the writing. Part of this reflects the growing sense of the project as it comes clear;

it also reflects, for book chapters, a growing sense of the overall integrity of the book and the chapters as a whole.

With titles for book chapters, for instance, you want to think about the balance among them, and between them and the title of the book. In general you want chapter titles to be parallel in structure and tone, and you want them to communicate information beyond what the reader gets from the title and subtitle of the book as a whole. Don't, say, make your chapter titles the same as the subtitle to your book; you lose out on the chance to convey more information to the reader about the basic ideas and structures of the project.

Let's compare the chapter titles of two books by the British historian Norman Cohn. The first is from *Europe's Inner Demons: The Demonization of Christians in Medieval Christendom*:

1. Prelude in antiquity
2. Changing views of the Devil and his power
3. The demonization of medieval heretics (1)
4. The demonization of medieval heretics (2)
5. The crushing of the Knights Templars
6. The reality of ritual magic
7. Demon-worshipping magicians that never were
8. The society of witches that never was
9. The night-witch in the popular imagination
10. How the great witch-hunt did not start
11. How the great witch-hunt really started (1)
12. How the great witch-hunt really started (2) (v)

My first thought: too many demons. Overusing a word whose force comes from its rarity undercuts what made it rhetorically powerful in the first place; the book loses energy from the minute the subtitle undercuts the title. Second thought: Why are some of the chapters in two parts? What's the logic here? The reader cannot tell from looking at the table of contents why the book divides the way it does and the repetitions (in 3 and 4; in 7 and 8; and in 10, 11, and 12) block understanding. They tell the reader, "You're going to have to read the book to figure out what it covers and why it divides its topics the way it does."

Now let's look at the chapters for Cohn's *The Pursuit of the Millennium: Revolutionary Millenarians and Mystical Anarchists of the Middle Ages:*

Introduction: The scope of this book
1. The Tradition of Apocalyptic Prophecy
     Jewish and early Christian apocalyptic
     The apocalyptic tradition in medieval Europe
2. The Tradition of Religious Dissent
     The idea of the apostolic life
     Some early messiahs
3. The Messianism of the Disoriented Poor
     The impact of rapid social change
     The poor in the first crusades
4. The Saints Against the Hosts of Antichrist
     Saviours in the Last Days
     The demonic host
     Phantasy, anxiety and social myth
5. In the Backwash of the Crusades
     The pseudo-Baldwin and the 'Master of Hungary'
     The last crusades of the poor
6. The Emperor Frederick as Messiah
     Joachite prophecy and Frederick II
     The resurrection of Frederick
     Manifestoes for a future Frederick (vii–viii)

The book goes on (it has thirteen chapters, some of which [8 and 9; 11, 12, and 13] reproduce the bifurcated structure Cohn employed in his other book). Nonetheless you see pretty clearly here how these titles communicate much more about the style, scope, and direction of the work than the ones in *Europe's Inner Demons*. Even if you ignore the subchapter headings (though again, it's worth noticing how much they help the reader), these chapters feel stronger, clearer, and more progressive; the inclusion of temporal markers (the crusades, Frederick II) in particular makes the whole thing feel like it must be developing in a certain direction. Note also that the chapter titles are more grammatically parallel; you don't bounce back and forth between common structures like "The reality of ritual magic" and weird verbal phrases like "Demon-worshipping magicians that never were." Overall *Pursuit of the Millennium* feels like a more coherent and structured book; it locates the reader intellectually and historically inside its own project.

This at least gives you some sense of how to think about your chapter titles. But what about the titles of articles or whole books? As you almost certainly have noticed, the current standard format for most work in literature, history, or cultural studies is:

EVOCATIVE, OPAQUE TITLE: DESCRIPTIVE, THEMATIC SUBTITLE

Some examples: *Telling It Slant: Avant Garde Poetics of the 1990s* (Mark Wallace, Steven Marks, eds.); *Animal, Vegetable, Mineral: Ethics and Objects* (Jeffrey Jerome Cohen); *Our Aesthetic Categories: Zany, Cute, Interesting* (Sianne Ngai); *Beautiful Circuits: Modernism and the Mediated Life* (Mark Goble); *Pluralist Universalism: An Asian Americanist Critique of U.S. and Chinese Multiculturalisms* (Wen Jin); or *Cosmopolitan Style: Modernism Beyond the Nation* (Rebecca L. Walkowitz).

If for whatever reason you're committed to avoiding this format, you will find another major cluster of titles that follow the following pattern.

A CONCRETE NOUN AND AN ABSTRACT NOUN

This structure is more common for article titles than for books. It gives you things like "Elizabeth Bishop and the Ethics of Correspondence" (Siobhan Phillips) or "Working-Class Writing and the Use Value of the Literary" (Sonali Perera). It also has variations that involve three nouns ("Hannah Arendt, the Jews, and the Labor of Superfluity" [Dorian Bell]) or that replace the last noun with a time and place ("Obscenity and Work in Early-Eighteenth-Century British Fiction" [Laura J. Rosenthal]). At some point all of these begin to resemble the descriptive, thematic subtitles that follow the colon in the more conventional form.

You see how this works. But there are better and worse ways to go about following these patterns. Basically what you want to think about is the balance of evocation and content. In the list above, for instance, something like "Animal, Vegetable, Mineral" sounds like it could be anything, and isn't clarified much by the subtitle. "Telling It Slant" acquires a nice new meaning once you read the subtitle since the title now refers (in the context of poetics more generally) quite obviously to the Emily Dickinson line, giving you a sense that the book itself will focus on the ways the avant-garde tells it slant when it can. Something like "Beautiful Circuits" works pretty well too, and has a nice ring; if you compare the structure of Goble's title to Walkowitz's, you will see classic uses of the subtitle to locate the project within two major contexts, a literary one ("modernism") and a theoretical one ("media" for Goble, "nation" for Walkowitz).   .

Another common option for titles, the quotation used as the first half, I don't like: it tends to be almost immediately forgettable, since the reader has no way of understanding what the quotation signifies within the intellectual context of the article. If you do something like " 'Use Me But as Your Spaniel': Feminism, Queer Theory, and Early Modern Sexualities" (from Melissa Sanchez's *PMLA* essay), the only thing you can hope for is that the reader will think, "I wonder what the hell that means? I guess I'll keep reading . . . " My impression is that academic readers almost never keep reading for that kind of reason. At best, it feels like a cheap trick (if the quotation does in fact turn out to be racy enough, as here, where we're titillated by the possibility of bestiality); at worst, the first half of the title is completely unmemorable and communicates no information at all.

Of all these titles the most efficient and professional one is, for me, Walkowitz's—not necessarily the most beautiful or evocative one, but the one that most clearly communicates every single one of its major affiliations. That's because "Cosmopolitan Style," unlike "Beautiful Circuits," refers to something outside the book proper, since the word "cosmopolitan" will naturally lead the reader to imagine a connection between the book's content and the broader debates about cosmopolitanism, a suspicion the introduction immediately confirms. "Cosmopolitan Style" also has the advantage of being highly quotable; you can imagine (and can find) people saying things like, "and this is another example of what Rebecca Walkowitz has called 'cosmopolitan style.'" That wouldn't work for "Beautiful Circuits," or not nearly as well; the book includes examples of beautiful circuits, but it does not develop a portable concept of the beautiful circuit that readers can carry away from the book. (Similarly: consider the way that Jacques Derrida's *Archive Fever* or *The Monolingualism of the Other* have become the name of something, symptoms or structures that we all have a shorthand for, whereas one almost never sees this kind of encapsulating reference to "what Derrida calls writing and difference" or "limited inc." or a "margin of philosophy.") Even as it marks all its affiliations, the title of *Cosmopolitan Style* sets itself up as a powerful rhetorical structure for grasping and talking about the ideas in the book.

Now let's look at the subtitles: I've already said I'm not a huge fan of "Ethics and Objects," which feels too much like it could be a title. In general you want to be careful not to put two titles together since in that case the evocative structure gets doubled. I actually think Sianne Ngai's title has this problem. *Our Aesthetic Categories: Zany, Cute, Interesting* starts out strongly; the "our," a very unusual use of a first-person pronoun for a title, suggests a dramatic sweep of the "way we think now" type, recalling the American literary critical era of the 1950s and 1960s. But the subtitle has some of the problems that the one for *Chinese Dreams* had: it names the chapter topics and, with respect to the title, gives the surprise away too soon ("What *are* our aesthetic categories? Oh, they're the zany, the cute, and the interesting"). Given the ambition and rhetorical sweep of the title, I wonder if that book would have been better off without a subtitle. As for the subtitle to Wen Jin's *Pluralist Universalism: An Asian Americanist Critique of U.S. and Chinese Multiculturalisms*, it locates itself well in the field, but the word "critique" feels awkward to me, like the book is trying too hard to announce its polemic. I might have tried something like "U.S. and Chinese Multiculturalisms After Asian America," or "After Asian American Studies," which would have gotten you the sense of critique (via "After") without having to say so. My sense is that the subtitles for *Thinking It Slant* and the two modernism books both exemplify what a good subtitle should do in this format. (I should say here, by the way, that I don't like the subtitle to my book, *The Hypothetical Mandarin: Sympathy, Modernity, and Chinese Pain*, very much at all either. So I'm no genius. But you might be, and even if you're not, you might as well try to have a good title.)

What makes for a strikingly original title? Usually it ignores the expected formulas, or finds a way to turn them on their head. If you're a young scholar, I would actually recommend you not worry much about having an incredible title. Especially when your list of publications is small, when you're unknown, or when you're on the job market, the titles of your published work set in standard format can do a huge amount of work on your behalf. They will signal your theoretical and formal affiliations; locate your work within national, linguistic, generic, or historical frames; or showcase the range of your knowledge and the reach of your critical interests. You're therefore best off with titles that communicate well and clearly what your work does and who you are as a thinker and critic. Think about the effect on a CV of a title like *The Stelliferous Fold: Toward a Virtual Law of Literature's Self-Formation,* which doesn't really tell anyone anything (except that you're probably interested in theory), as opposed to something like *Reading Fiction in Antebellum America: Informed Response and Reception Histories, 1820–1865,* which clearly establishes an area of interest and expertise. You can get away with the first title if your reputation precedes you (as it does for Rodolphe Gasché). Otherwise, you will want to tell people what you do.

Isn't this all formulaic? Yes, it is. Title/subtitle, like the Pythagorean theorem, becomes a formula for a discipline that values the work it does, and for which it produces reasonably predictable and socially functional results. The standard model's combination of evocation and description lets academic writers appeal simultaneously to originality and creativity (beautiful circuits!) and to humanistic narrowness and rigor (not *all* beautiful circuits, just the ones involving modernism and media theory). The other major advantage of clear, coherent titles (for books but also for chapters and articles) is that they're easy to find with internet searches. Now that most scholars do not read paper journals, having your work be findable is a way of helping make sure that it has a chance to be read.

If you want to distance yourself from the herd, then you'll have to break the rules. But break them well! You will find that others do not have much tolerance for that kind of fooling around, so if you do it, you have to be good. Here are four ways to play with the standard format:

1. *Change the evocation/description balance.* You see this in James L. Machor's *Reading Fiction in Antebellum America: Informed Response and Reception Histories, 1820–1865,* for which you could have just as easily switched title and subtitle as long as you left the dates in place. Machor's decision to be descriptive in both halves of the title allows him to communicate a great deal of information about the book in relatively few words. You can also go evocative/evocative, as in *Animal, Vegetable, Mineral: Ethics and Objects,* but my feeling is that this makes it difficult for readers to know what they're getting into.

2. *Drop the subtitle.* Sianne Ngai did it for *Ugly Feelings,* a book whose complexity and originality would have been diminished by any subtitle; the title has the advantage of being eminently quotable. See also Lauren Berlant's *Cruel Optimism* or Northrop Frye's *Anatomy of Criticism.* In general this is a power move, more common among established critics than younger ones (partly because the younger critics need to teach people what they're up to, though *Ugly Feelings* was Ngai's first book). You might also drop the title, making the subtitle the effective title: "Three Women's Texts and a Critique of Imperialism" (Spivak 1985).

3. *Consider older structures for title-building.* The semicolon/or structure remains pretty unusual; you can see it in Jameson's *Postmodernism; or, The Cultural Logic of Late Capitalism.* Semicolon/or allows you to pack two titles into one. It asserts a strong, non-surbordinated relationship between the two concepts it separates. You can also try the classic "On [blank]," which connects you to an essayistic, speculative tradition. I kind of love Carolyn Steedman's title, "On a Horse," a great and hilarious twist on this convention.

4. *Alter length.* In the standard account, evocation is short, description long. You can try shortening the title to one word (the only place left to go, since most titles are two words long); lengthening it to four or five; altering the balance so that the subtitle is shorter than the title; or getting rid of the subtitle entirely and having a strangely long (more than six- or seven-word) title (Fiona Apple is one possible model here).

5. *Play with grammar.* Many evocative titles are two-word, adjective-noun combinations, or, if three words, then noun phrases (Birgit Mara Kaiser's *Figures of Simplicity*, for example); longer titles, on the other hand, tend to be adjectival or noun phrases (Ken Seigneurie's *Standing by the Ruins* or Barry McCrea's *In the Company of Strangers*). Try a sentence, as David Rollo does in *Kiss My Relics*; or a question (Judith Butler's *Frames of War: When is Life Grievable?* or Leo Bersani's classic, "Is the Rectum a Grave?"). Or experiment with a fuller, imperative sentence, with a stronger implied or actual pronoun (James Kincaid's "Resist Me, You Sweet Resistible You," or Jonathan Goldman's *Modernism Is the Literature of Celebrity*). Or borrow from another genre entirely, following our cousins in fiction or poetry, and surprise us all.

Part III
Tactics

Within the larger frames that govern the structure of a piece of work, you will at any moment be making tens if not hundreds of decisions about smaller units of meaning. These range from the specifically prosaic—having to do with rhythm in and between sentences, figural language, rhetorical questions, and so on—to the formal and the disciplinary—handling examples, quotations, footnotes, and the like. This part of the book focuses on those subsidiary choices. Subsidiary, yes, but still important: in the long run, the style you build will depend as much on these, which amount to a kind of signature, as it does on the way you manage larger structural units.

These tactical decisions occur throughout the writing process, so the chapters in this section appear in alphabetical order.

Nineteen
Citational Practice

In a book focused primarily on the analysis of academic style in the humanities (and not, as here, on its production), I would spend more time than I'm about to teaching you how to read citational practice as a central feature of epistemological and rhetorical activity. By "citational practice" I mean something like the sum total of the ways in which an author or a piece of writing marshals information, manages critics, handles notes and footnotes, and refers to or cites the work of primary and secondary sources.

A quick comparison of the citational practice of two writers like Jacques Derrida and Michel Foucault will, for instance, reveal a vast series of differences in their patterns of citation and reference: Derrida will often partially cite upcoming primary material in advance of its appearance; Foucault tends to refer and paraphrase more than he cites; Derrida tends to have longer footnotes, and will cite and recite himself; Foucault not so much; and so on.

This amounts to little more than a brief description of the difference between deconstructive and new historicist styles, you say. Yes, but it's understanding how those styles produce knowledge differently at least partly through patterns of citation and reference that will help you grasp the ways in which critics or schools put their preferred modes of intellection and analysis into play, or rather, the ways in which that putting into play—citation, reference, mention, the distinction drawn between primary and secondary—itself constitutes a mode of thought and analysis.

Which is to say, your citational practice will depend at least partly on how you read, and will reflect in a conscious or unconscious way your belonging to a school or schools of thought. Knowing this is the first step in taking control of your intellectual and writerly process, not only as a matter of rhetoric but as a matter of understanding (and being able to justify) the epistemological presumptions, advantages, and blind spots that result from your chosen practice.

Chicago vs. MLA Style

Let's begin the discussion of citational practice with an intensely practical matter: should you use Chicago or MLA style? Usually your choice will be made for you by the press or journal that takes your work. But if you can choose I recommend Chicago, because it allows you to do one very important thing that MLA style does not: to conceal, permanently or temporarily, the source of a citation.

Why is that useful? Suppose you want to do something like this:

[Henry James's] *The American Scene* reads as a transitional text between one American generation's fascination with objects of possession and the next generation's engagement with objects as such. But its power lies in James's capacity to reenergize an obsolete trope—a trope that realism eschews, a trope we associate with the sentimental and gothic traditions—on behalf of exposing the ontological grounds on which modernity proceeds in the name of progress, and on behalf of literalizing the common sense that tells us that "an attack on architecture . . . is an attack on man."[28] At the same time, James's plea on behalf of architecture (which he hears as architecture's self-defense) cannot be reduced to a claim on behalf of the authority of merely static physical structure, for the structures are anything but static and they are rendered as something less and more than physical.[29] His animation of the world might even be said to hark back to those premodern times and places where objects were anything but inert, where "things themselves had a personality and an inherent power"—even as it anticipates modernism's capacity to vivify the physical object world by other means, means that themselves literalize the work of prosopopeia.[30] (Brown 187–88)

Now, who would you guess Bill Brown is quoting in the sentences that end with notes 28 and 30? If you answered "not Henry James," give yourself a prize. The first citation is from Georges Bataille (note 29, which follows, is entirely about Bataille); the second from Marcel Mauss.

—Oh. Hmm. I guess that means that Brown has chunked or highlighted those citations earlier, so that the reader already knows who they're from.

—Nope. Bataille appears once elsewhere, on page 3; Mauss not at all. And because the book uses endnotes, not footnotes, you have to turn to the back of the book to find out that Bataille and Mauss are involved in this paragraph at all.

So what is Brown doing? Well, this is the penultimate paragraph of the book—not a great place to be throwing around new names, which will send the reader's mind haring off in new directions; Brown wants to keep the main line of thought clear of obstructions. At the same time, though, he wants to use these quotes. It would have been easy enough to cut them, but he leaves them there. Yet what are they doing? Both quotations allow Brown to quickly and with little fanfare support large-scale, relatively vague claims: "common sense" in the first instance and "premodern times" in the second. The support these citations lend is *increased,* not diminished, by the fact that the names behind them remain off the page. Could we see them, either in footnotes or in-line parentheticals, we might be tempted to argue: Well, yes, but Mauss's position on premodern cultures has been superseded by so-and-so, or, I think Bataille is nonsense. Anonymous citation allows Brown to support these general claims, which he needs—but only a little—for his argument, without having to manage the further array of expectations or questions they would raise. He's *mentioning* these ideas, not using them.

You just can't do that when you have to put the names in parentheses, which is why I prefer using Chicago style when I can. Chicago also allows you to move page numbers up into the text when you'd like (with a note that says "further references in the text"), letting you manage far more precisely than MLA the reader's access to your citational information. In that sense it's a more writer-friendly, but less reader-friendly, way of doing things; or rather it leaves the degree of reader-friendliness up to the writer, rather than making it a professional norm.

Block Quotes, Full Quotes, Partial Quotes

Whether in Chicago or MLA, you're not always citing material for the same reasons. Sometimes you want what you quote to remain at the forefront of the reader's consciousness; sometimes you're happy to have it dissipate immediately so you can move on to the next idea. Some material is primary, some secondary; some subject to close reading, some not; some establishes that reading's contextual foreground, some its distant background.

The most obvious metalinguistic way to communicate that difference lies in how you quote. Partial quotes like the ones Bill Brown uses above, which integrate the cited material into the writer's own sentences, give the material far less weight than full ones. Compare these four examples:

> But its power lies in James's capacity to reenergize an obsolete trope on behalf of literalizing the common sense that tells us that "an attack on architecture . . . is an attack on man."

> But its power lies in James's capacity to reenergize an obsolete trope on behalf of literalizing the common sense that tells us that "an attack on architecture . . . is an attack on man," as Georges Bataille once put it.

> But its power lies in James's capacity to reenergize an obsolete trope on behalf of literalizing the common sense that tells us that, as Georges Bataille wrote in a short essay on "Architecture" published in his *Critical Dictionary*, "an attack on architecture . . . is an attack on man."

> But its power lies in James's capacity to reenergize an obsolete trope on behalf of literalizing common sense. "An attack on architecture… is an attack on man," Georges Bataille wrote.

The difference between the second and third sentences has to do with the amount of information that surrounds the citation. In the second instance the potential disruption caused by Bataille's appearance is mitigated by the phrase "once put it," which makes this rhetorical situation more casual by pretending that the enunciation of the quoted material was itself actually casual (Bataille "put it" this way; he didn't "state" or "assert" it). You can also mitigate the force of an appearance by removing, in certain cases, the quoted person's first name. As for the last sentence, if it feels incomplete—as though it needs another clause after "wrote"—it's because citation in which the quotation dominates the grammar and structure of a sentence (what I call a "full quote") establishes a metalinguistic expectation for transition. Here we would want Brown to resolve that tension by returning us to James, with something like this:

> But its power lies in James's capacity to reenergize an obsolete trope on behalf of literalizing common sense. "An attack on architecture . . . is an attack on man," Georges Bataille *once* wrote, *in a meditation that James would have loved, had he lived to read it.*

If you try to imagine diminishing that further by removing Bataille's first name, you realize that it won't work; the resulting sentence feels imbalanced. If you need to mitigate something that much, just cite it partially.

By contrast, if you want someone to pay attention to something, quote it fully. Doing so signals that you also will be paying attention to it. As with the fourth example above, a full citation, especially when coupled with a full name, will create the expectation of some kind of transition. You can use that to your advantage by beginning a new paragraph with a full name, book title, and / or partial quote from someone who hasn't been mentioned in the previous few pages:

> . . . [paragraph ends with this sentence]: These two Chinas are constructed, then, from two incompatible epistemologies: science and romance.

> [new paragraph begins]: Jonathan Spence's *The Memory Palace of Matteo Ricci* leavens its treatment of the Jesuit polymath's extraordinary adventures in the Middle Kingdom with a series of meditations on the state of neo-Confucian thought in the Ming dynasty.

Here the somewhat abrupt beginning (notice that this transition does not belong to any of the standard types, uses no transition words, etc.) actually serves as a marker of a shift in topic; it "pops" up out of the ordinary flow of the text because it breaks the expectation of continuity. You'll remember that Jameson did something like this in the cognitive mapping transition we looked at earlier. If, like Jameson, you want to bring this back around to the topic you've been covering, you would return us to the words "science" and "romance" in the second or third sentence of the paragraph as a way of signaling the resumption of continuity. Otherwise, you could simply continue along with Spence and neo-Confucian thought for a few paragraphs. In that case you would be using the somewhat jarring shift to Spence as a metalinguistic marker of a section change; essentially you would be telling the reader that the last sentence of the previous paragraph was a 5 for its section, and that the opening with Spence is the 4 for a new one.

Beginning a paragraph with someone's name or quoting someone in a full sentence is thus a way of assuring a certain prominence, either structural (you're doing it to start a new section) or thematic (you're doing it because the person's work is important to your argument). And so it would make a certain kind of sense at this point for me to say that if you *really* want someone to pay attention to something, you should put it in a block quote. But the dirty secret of block quotes, which Timothy Billings first pointed out to me, is that most readers don't actually read them. Really! That means that you *must* follow any block quotation with a short summary or reading of the material you've just quoted, while making sure that the reader doesn't notice that you're repeating yourself. In many cases you will want to re-quote material from the block, using it to draw your reader's attention to the specific passages that will matter to you, as we see Lisa Siraganian doing here:

> Due to its rigidity and its space precisions, [the typewriter] can, for a poet, indicate exactly the breath, the pauses . . . which he intends. . . . For the first time he can, without the convention of rime and meter, record the listening he has done to his own speech and by that one act indicate how he would want any reader, silently or otherwise, to voice his work. (*OPr* 245)

According to [Olson's] logic, the typewriter permits the composing poet to mark out his "breathing spaces" with a mechanical device instead of relying on the ancient literary conventions of "rime and meter" or the new and awkward convention of spelling out each phoneme as spoken by the poet. Just as . . . [she continues] (Siraganian 149)

Alternatively, you can use Franco Moretti's trick of simply repeating or reworking the last phrase of the quotation:

[a long block quote that ends like this:] The aesthetic sphere is perhaps the most appropriate to reflect overall changes of mental climate.

Overall changes of the mental climate: the five, six shifts in the British novelistic field between 1740 and 1900. [note the lovely insertion of "the" here!]

[long quote that ends with] . . . We shall therefore speak of a *generation as an actuality* only where a concrete bond is created between members of a generation by their being exposed to the social and intellectual symptoms of a process of dynamic destabilization.

A bond due to a process of dynamic destabilization; and anyone who was eighteen in 1968 understands. (Moretti 21)

Another neat trick, which I've only noticed recently, is to manage citation through extended paraphrase, as in this example from David Spurr:

Kafka often described his own writing in architectural terms. A notebook passage written in 1922, at a moment when his progress in writing *The Castle* was at a standstill, begins with the statement, "Das Schrieben versagt sich mir" (writing refuses itself to me). He then speaks of his writing as a process of construction (*aufbauen*) but in a way that also makes this a construction of the self. I want to construct myself (*will ich mich dann aufbauen*), says Kafka, like someone who has an unsafe house and who wants to build a new one next to it by using the materials of the old house. But it is bad (*schlimm*) if while he is doing so his strength gives out, so that now instead of having an unsafe but fully built house, he has one that is half destroyed and another only half built, and so nothing (*Nachgelassene* 2:373). (Spurr 87–88)

Over the course of this paragraph, Spurr moves from a general summary of the citation he's about to give (the first sentence) to direct quotation (the second sentence) to paraphrase (from sentence three onward). What's especially interesting, however, is that way that by the final sentence we have no direct reference to Kafka at all. Rather Spurr has taken over Kafka's voice and the sentence technically reads as his own, though it in fact continues to reprise what Kafka says about house-building. We might think of this sequence as showing us how to move the narratological categories of direct discourse (speech within quotation marks), indirect discourse (speech marked by phrases like "said" or "declared," as in Spurr's third and fourth sentences), and free indirect discourse (in which the voice of the character/quotee merges with that of the narrator/author) into academic prose.

You will find another instance of this kind of academic free indirect discourse in the pages of Erich Auerbach's *Mimesis*, which ventriloquizes Rabelais:

And what—Rabelais in effect goes on—did I mean to accomplish by this Prologue? That you, when you read all the pleasant titles of my writings (here follows a parade of grotesque book titles), will not suppose that there is nothing in them but jests and stuff for laughter and mockery. You must not so quickly draw conclusions from mere outward appearances. The habit does not make the monk. You must open the book and carefully consider what is in it; you will see that the contents are worth far more than the container promised, that the subjects are nowhere near so foolish as the title suggests. And even if, in the literal sense of the contents, you still find enough stuff for laughter of the sort that the title promises, you must not be satisfied with that: you must probe deeper. Have you ever seen a dog that has found a marrow bone? Then you must have observed how devoutly he guards it, how fervently he seizes it, how prudently approaches it, with what affection he breaks it open, how diligently he sucks it. (279–80)

This continues for another eleven lines. In the claim that "Rabelais in effect goes on"—placed so casually at the opening of the paragraph—Auerbach announces, and justifies, the atmospheric drama of his small, charming performance.

Citational Paratexts

I use "citational paratext" to refer to the material that surrounds and sets up the quotation—the person's name, the title of a book, the adjectival and verbal descriptors (said, wrote, noted, casually remarked) that frame the quotation at its most basic level. As the examples above make clear, full names have more weight (and imply a more serious or heavy treatment) than last names; likewise famous names have more weight than obscure ones. Giving the title of a book in the paratext ("Céline Dion's *My Life as a Party* argues that") suggests a fuller forthcoming treatment than leaving the name out. Similarly you can ladder up and down the field of expectations with verbs that feel stronger ("argues that"), more neutral ("writes"), or weaker ("notes").

The paratext's grammatical structure thus also prepares the reader for a fuller or lighter treatment. "As Feuerbach noted" is lighter than "Feuerbach's book on Christianity argues," which is lighter in turn than this example, which splits paratext and quotation into two sentences: "Ludwig Feuerbach's *Das Wesen des Christentums* (The Essence of Christianity) was the major philosophical event of that decade. There, Feuerbach's claim that 'the essential standpoint of religion is the practical or the subjective' finds its fullest form in chapter 19," and so on. The surrounding material says to the reader: pay attention; this is central to the argument.

Opening and Closing with Quotations

The danger with either one of these is that you'll forfeit your opportunity to locate the reader specifically in your project. Especially when closing, this means taking extra care to manage the quotation into a relation to your work, as in this example from *On Literary Worlds*:

> It achieves one limit in what Spinoza called the "common notions" that constitute the ground and goal of reason, which govern not only the emotions but indeed all aspects of everyday life, where they form, Gilles Deleuze notes, "a mathematics of the real or the concrete," a quasi-biological "natural geometry that allows us to comprehend the unity of composition of all of Nature and the modes of variation of that unity." (107–8)

The lines from Deleuze align perfectly with the book's argument; I've essentially outsourced the conclusion of this paragraph to Deleuze. This allows me to simultaneously close the reading of Spinoza and to provide authoritative support for it.

As for opening with quotations, what works for anecdotal introductions (where the paragraph acts as the 1 in a truncated U) or summative transitions is more complicated elsewhere, because full quotations get in the way of making promises to the reader or doing the necessary transitional work. That said, it's worth making a distinction between quotations from primary and secondary sources. Compare these two possible openings:

> Gilles Deleuze writes that Spinoza's "natural geometry . . . allows us to comprehend the unity of composition of all of Nature and the modes of variation of that unity."

> Joyce writes, "He would only make himself ridiculous by quoting poetry to them which they could not understand."

While it's easy enough to imagine the general thrust and shape of the paragraph that follows the Deleuze example, guessing at the paragraph that completes the Joyce one is a good deal harder. You could improve things by adding transitional material, at which point you turn the full quote into a partial one:

This same combination of shame and desire appears when Joyce writes, in "The Dead," that Gabriel Conroy "would only make himself ridiculous by quoting poetry to them which they could not understand."

Here you can not only imagine the rest of the paragraph; you can pretty much know the shape of the preceding one, and guess at the general place of a paragraph like this one inside a section, or an essay.

Quoting from Other Languages

Unless you're going specifically to address the syntax, grammar, or diction of the original source—really if you're doing any kind of close reading— you can leave the original-language sentences out of things entirely. If you are reading closely, however, be sure to include, via partial or full quotation, the pieces of the original you need to make your case. Know that, especially if you're working in a language that is foreign to you, doing partial close readings of original material within the context of a broader discussion is one easy way to signal your linguistic and cultural iceberg— especially crucial for graduate students and younger scholars, who have not established their bona fides.

Credit Where Credit's Due

Is it possible to quote too much? Too little? Yes on both counts. How do you strike a rhetorical balance between a forceful, original representation of your own work and the necessary work of iceberging, background-giving, and ass-covering that accompanies citational practice?

Among other things you will notice that the more famous someone is, the less he or she quotes from secondary material by contemporary critics. At the same time, the relative famousness of the primary material inclines substantially as careers increase. This kind of peer-matching allows authors to signal their own intellectual heft and worth, which is reflected by the people they engage with. In the very thin air of the very famous, this means that you will be (when you get there) quoting almost entirely from the Kants and Hegels of the world, and making references to living critics only when offering noblesse oblige acknowledgments of the "excellent" work of some younger scholar or engaging in contentious criticism of a near-peer.

Citational peer-matching also reflects and rhetorically produces (the effect of) writerly poise. Understanding how to handle the work of others means learning how to manage references to maximize the force of your own prose, avoiding too many defensive footnotes, and losing the instinct to protect yourself with references to authority figures, allowing your ideas to stand more bravely on their own. That's what makes good, convincing writerly authority: writing in full confidence that the parts of your work that belong most fully to you can stand, supported, by the set of references and arguments that you have left on the page.

What does this mean for young writers? The lesson is not, "Stop quoting other folks and start quoting Kant, so that you can pretend to be awesome." It is rather to develop rhetorical confidence when and how you can, and to write within its emotional circumference.

The crucial stage in which you develop this confidence happens between the dissertation and the first book. A long time ago Rey Chow, who had very generously read my entire dissertation (despite not being a member of my committee), wrote in response to an e-mail I sent her about turning it into a book that I should probably let it sit for a couple years, as the manuscript still showed many of the signs of my being a graduate student writer. The confidence I would develop as I furthered my career, she said, would allow me to see and get rid of those moments of excessive defensiveness, and to cut down on the various places where I showed too much iceberg, or too much work. I spent a couple weeks being offended— whatever was wrong with the dissertation, I thought, had nothing to do with my having written it as a graduate student! I was wrong, as I realized three years later when I revised the manuscript, and Rey was right.

The confidence gap between dissertation and first book, or rather, the reason that the dissertation evinces far less citational and rhetorical confidence than a good piece of professional writing, stems from the fact that the dissertation is written by someone who has never written one before, and who is therefore at some fundamental level unsure of whether s/he can do it. This is one source of the felt differences between the Dissertation (as genre) and a book. You will have to work to mitigate it as much as you can during the process of getting to that first book contract.

Ideally, you could compensate by writing the dissertation with a confidence you couldn't reasonably feel. This would entail recognizing, ideally by reading first books, what citational and rhetorical confidence *look and sound like,* and imitating them. But in practice I've found that this is really almost too much to ask from my students (as it certainly was too much to ask from me). Accordingly you will almost certainly have to go back and revise the entire work "upward" once you have finished it the first time around. Think of it as a necessary consequence of your social and emotional development as a writer, and recognize it as part of the writing process. Your revised dissertation should be the first thing you write *as someone who can write a dissertation.* Until you finish one, however, everything you write is instead written by someone who's not yet sure he or she can write a dissertation, and the difference will show.

Let me say one more thing. Though confidence is a good thing, the rhetorical performance of confidence through citational practice, when it comes to things like peer-matching or acknowledging the impact of others on your work, can be somewhat dishonest. I don't want to become someone who only quotes my amazing dead peers or whatever "lucky" young person I've decided to bestow my grace upon; I want my prose to continue to register the enormous impact communities of readers and writers, friends and strangers, have on me and my ideas. As a result I am trying in my more recent work to do a more explicit job of acknowledging where others have made a difference, either in conversation or in writing, to the sentences I put on the page, even when I know that it would be just as easy (and more conventionally confident) to leave them out. Citing generously can also be, I think, a kind of confidence, less rhetorical yet more genuinely self-assured than the alternative, because it doesn't need to assert over and over in the text my own citational worthiness, or pretend that I somehow did all this thinking or working all by myself. I didn't. My goal is to figure out how to cite in ways that acknowledge and integrate this truth into my writing while continuing to generate rhetorical strength and pleasure for the reader. I'm not necessarily advising you to try the same—as you can tell, I'm not quite sure how to do it myself—but I am telling you this because I want you to see at least one more way to think about the rhetoric of citational practice.

Twenty
Conference Talks

It is, let's be honest, rarely fun to have academic prose read aloud to you. Sometimes it's absolutely excruciating (even for the person reading it).

The mistake comes from thinking of the conference talk as a writing situation at all. Conferences are *presentation* situations. The fact of the live audience means that your text is a *script*. It ought to be designed to maximize the force of its medium, the voice, and the interest of its audience of living listeners.

This means trying one of three things:

1. *Writing your work to be heard.* Use more repetition, shorten sentences, and choose punchier phrases and clearer metalanguage. In general you should be chattier, talkier, even if you are reading straight from the page. Take advantage of the normal modulations of your own voice. Or, if you can't be chattier and plainer, try writing in genuinely beautiful writerly prose—prose so good that its very quality will hold the listener's attention, even if it is only read moderately well.

2. *Working on your performative skills.* Some people are genuinely better readers than others. Whether that's because they're uncrippled by anxiety or because they've had acting lessons, I don't know, but in any case listening to a truly good speaker will help you appreciate how inadequate most of us are. Homi Bhabha, for instance, speaks beautifully; Marjorie Garber, though she reads with her head down, has a kind of vibrating intensity

that I find very compelling. Watch what other people do that you like, practice it, and imitate it. And if it seems weird, or too much, to suggest that public speaking is the kind of thing that could be practiced, I will simply assert that practicing performance in preparation for presenting in a live medium doesn't differ all that much from practicing prose stylistics in preparation for working in a written one. Either style matters, or it doesn't. It does, and it's medium-specific.

3. *Speaking from notes.* At some point a few years ago I realized that I didn't enjoy giving talks, that most of the time I felt like they weren't very good, and that I was essentially a boring speaker. At the same time, I wondered: I was a decent classroom teacher, which seemed like it should involve many of the same skills. So why wasn't I a decent speaker? The difference, I realized, was that in teaching my mind and body were engaged in a live way with the production of ideas, and that I was responding to others; I was, in short, in an interpersonal, dynamic situation. Borrowing from my teaching habits, I started giving presentations almost entirely from notes, using what I'd learned in the classroom to write academic talks.

Practically, what I do now is to write the talk out three or four times (by hand, for whatever reason). Each version gets progressively shorter—the first will be four or five pages of notes, quotes, or examples; the second, two or three; the third a single page. I speak from that final page. The process allows me to work through structure, rearranging concepts and examples, while also focusing on distilling the talk to its tightest possible version. Keeping the notes tight matters because the biggest danger with extemporaneous speaking is that you go over the allotted time, or that the whole thing looks lazy and made-up. If you do speak from notes, you need to make it good enough that no one will worry that you're just avoiding the hard work of writing things out in full.

One of the major advantages of speaking from notes is that it allows you to present both work that you have just begun and work that is almost to publication. For new work, the exploratory quality of a live talk diminishes the pressure, inviting the audience to participate in thinking through a problem. This can be a great way to begin poking around a project. For work you know really well, on the other hand, extemporizing tends to produce (in both you and the audience) a strong sense of confidence and mastery; the pleasure and power of your work shines through your comfort and knowledge of it.

No matter how you choose to present your work at conferences, you will have to decide how to share your evidence. Doing a handout will generally result in people reading it over while you speak, which feels like a disadvantage (especially if you have multiple connected quotations, since some of your auditors will anticipate your readings, ruining the surprise). On the other hand if you're planning on close reading texts or images, making sure your audience can also see your primary evidence helps make the work of interpretation live for them too. The obvious solution is PowerPoint, which allows you usefully to control the audience's access to your material. But PowerPoint has its own dangers for presenters. These almost always involve putting too much information on slides. If you want the audience to read your talk, just hand out copies and sit silently while they do it; you'll save everyone aggravation and time. But for god's sake don't do a presentation in which you read aloud sentences that are also up on a screen.

Twenty-one

Examples

Let's say you have a piece with three major examples. And let's assume that you know that you can't just use the examples to say the same thing over and over again (a McIntosh is a kind of apple; a Fuji is a kind of apple; also a Golden Delicious is a kind of apple). What order do you put them in?

Chapter 10 discussed the advantages and disadvantages of chronological ordering for primary material as it applied to book chapters. Here I want to think about how this works within chapters or articles, and especially within single primary works, when chronology becomes less important.

So imagine that you have three scenes from a play, or three separate paragraphs from the Congressional Record, to discuss; or that you want to write an essay on architecturalism in Victorian thought and your two examples come from roughly the same period. One easy thing is to just kick the chronologism one level down, dealing with the scenes or the paragraphs in the order of their appearance, with the examples falling in relation to the strict temporal difference (let's say, April 1872 vs. May 1872). If you do that, you'll still be faced with some of the problems you have with chronology and book chapters: What if, for instance, the first chronological example is more interesting or more complicated than the second? What if the first is a metaphorical treatment of architecture, referring for instance to the city as a "memory palace," while the second is a highly literal discussion of architectural style as it refers to an actual building?

With these two questions we begin to see some non-chronological principles for the ordering of examples in series. A good rule of thumb is to arrange things from simple to complex, and from literal to metaphorical. You will want your sequence of primary evidence to move from material that clearly and in a relatively uncomplicated way illustrates your general argument, to material that illuminates and extends in complex ways those basic themes. That way the simpler material establishes two things: the reader's basic trust in your argument (this is an affective and judgmental procedure), and the historical and argumentative chunking devices and foundations that your more complex arguments require.

For these same reasons you will want to place examples and evidence that confirm your basic argument before material that extends or complicates it. This will allow you set up a framework that you can then stretch, strengthen, violate, or disrupt in subsequent examples—after which you will, in the close, refigure the relationship between those disruptions and your overall framework, so that the two emerge into a new (and subsequently disruptible) combination or structure.

All this amounts to telling you to adopt the persuasive strategy Gandalf deploys when he brings Bilbo and his companions to Beorn's: you need to get the reader engaged and on your side before you drag another few dwarves into the house. The trust you establish with simple, literal, and confirmatory examples will allow you the leeway you need to make your more subtle evidence convincing and meaningful.

Twenty-two
Figural Language

A full treatment of the uses of figural language in academic prose will have to wait for another book. For now I want to encourage you to use more of it, and to be aware of the ways in which your word choices, especially verbal ones, can activate registers of thought and feeling that make your prose come alive.

One of the easiest ways to do so is to use similes. The thing about similes is that you can always *not* use them and, since it's easier not to do so, most people don't. For my money the most elegant user of similes in scholarly writing is Fredric Jameson (again, I know). These are almost all the ones from *Postmodernism*:

> The prestige of these great streamlined shapes can be measured by their metaphorical presence in Le Corbusier's buildings, vast Utopian structures which ride **like** so many gigantic steamship liners upon the urban scenery of an older fallen earth. (36)

> It strikes one then, in that spirit, that neofigurative painting today is very much that extraordinary space through which all the images and icons of the culture spill and float, haphazard, **like** a logjam of the visual, bearing off with them everything. (176; love the echo of the last line of *Gatsby!*)

Only an old-fashioned communism and an old-fashioned psychoanalysis stood out upon the agrarian landscape **like** immense and ugly foreign bodies, history itself (equally old-fashioned in those days) being very effectively consigned to the dusty ash can of "scholarship." (183–84)

I think we now have to talk about the relief of the postmodern generally, a thunderous unblocking of logjams and a release of new productivity that was somehow tensed up and frozen, locked **like** cramped muscles, at the latter end of the modern period. (313)

Like the three wishes in the fairy tale, or the devil's promises, this prognosis has been fully realized, with only the slightest of modifications that make it unrecognizable. (320)

Media populism, however, suggests a deeper social determinant, at one and the same time more abstract and more concrete, and a feature whose essential materialism can be measured by its scandalousness for the mind, which avoids it or hides it away **like** plumbing. (356; this one especially good because it's such a surprise, and doesn't explain itself)

. . . we are led to anticipate the imminent collapse of all our inward conceptual defense mechanisms, and in particular the rationalizations of privilege and the well-nigh natural formations (**like** extraordinary crystalline structures or coral formations excreted over millennia) of narcissism and self-love. (358)

It would now seem that, far from becoming extinct, the older genres, released **like** viruses from their traditional ecosystem, have now spread out and colonized reality itself . . . (371; you could almost have left "like viruses" out, since "ecosystem" and "spread out" do the same work)

We have all those things, indeed, but we jog afterward to refresh the constitution, while by the same token computers relieve us of the terrible obligation to distend the memory **like** a swollen bladder retaining all these encyclopedia references. (383)

And here is my favorite Jamesonian simile of all, from *The Political Unconscious*:

> Only Marxism can give us an account of the essential *mystery* of the cultural past, which, **like** Tiresias drinking the blood, is momentarily returned to life and warmth and once more allowed to speak, and to deliver its long-forgotten message in surroundings utterly alien to it. (383; I love this sentence in general, but in the simile, it's the "the" that strikes me as amazing; it's what taught me the value of definite articles.)

In every single case above you could remove the simile and still be left with something pretty good. But my guess is that you would be left with far less than you'd think, because, as you can see so clearly in that last example, it is almost unimaginable to think that the prose that surrounds and sustains the simile—that explains it, I suppose—would have occurred to Jameson without the simile being there first. It is *because* of the comparison to Tiresias that the lovely extension of that sentence, and especially the last clause—"and to deliver its long-forgotten message in surroundings utterly alien to it"—becomes possible. That simile is not an ornament but a whip hand.

Figurative language expands the referential sphere of your prose. You see in each of the Jameson examples a shift in social registers. This shift tends, in scholarly prose, to concretize or physicalize abstraction, which is why it's so valuable—it increases both the possibility of readerly comprehension *in that specific moment*, and works more generally to shape the referential landscape of your work, opening up possibilities for breath, pause, or humor, as we saw in these lines of Christopher Bush's earlier:

> If the classic commodity form is said to disguise social relations among persons as objective relations among things, the japoniste commodity would present as some sort of human encounter what are in fact market relations. These aren't mutually exclusive, of course—just a question of how many dialectical whacks one gives the piñata of the commodity form. (84)

A similar opening appears in these lines of Haun Saussy's:

> What do I mean by "deconstruction"? Too much specificity at the outset will cramp the investigation (it is startling how often the comparative conversation stumbles on the question of aperture). My Barefoot Doctor's definition, not very sophisticated but at least not crucially dependent on a complex infrastructure, is that deconstruction is what happens when you set the wording of a text against its content, the means of persuasion against the persuasive agenda. (241n22)

What ices this particular cake is that barefoot doctors originated, as do the other subjects of Saussy's book, in China.

You can also use figurative language to open up an idea, giving the reader the parameters of its metaphorical expression first before coming back down into more ordinary language for an explanation, as David Porter does in the paragraph below. The heavy figuration begins with an extended metaphor (around alchemy, bolded below) and then slips into another metaphor (of walking, underlined), all this in a very long second sentence. The subsequent short sentence returns us to plain-speaking:

> If the self-consciously artful use of language that distinguishes literary writing finds its purest expression in poetry, the essence of poetry, in turn, lies in metaphor. Metaphor works its **potent alchemy** through the **explosive** combination of mismatched **elements** that, both in spite of and owing to their incongruity, generate an epiphanic insight, a **spark** of recognition that **illuminates**, however briefly, the exhilarating <u>chasms</u> between the well-worn <u>stepping stones</u> to which <u>the march</u> of everyday language is ordinarily confined. Metaphor, in other words, generates fresh meaning through comparison. Paradoxically, the less obvious or self-evident the underlying comparison appears, the more powerful is the effect. The perceived "truth" of a metaphor is purely a function of its power in this sense: it has little or nothing to do with the degree of empirical resemblance between the objects or ideas being compared. To pursue too earnestly a precise measure of similarity and difference between a metaphorical figure and its referent is entirely to miss the point. One would no more expect a poet to prove the truth of a similarity claim than one would expect a taxonomist to accept it at face value.

Porter closes the paragraph by returning to figuration (specifically personification, the taxonomist vs. the poet). The figurative rhythm of the paragraph as a whole thus moves us from a declarative opening (structured as a classic x/y transition), to a self-consciously metaphorical elaboration of the force of metaphor, to an argument about the nature of metaphor so figured. It closes with a sentence whose personification gives it a quasi-aphoristic feel (in general, aphorism is a good move for closure, as we'll see later in the section on sentence rhythm). The lesson here is that, even within a paragraph, the ebb and flow of figuration can allow you to communicate implicitly (and metalinguistically) the force and feel of an argument.

Here's another example of how to carry a metaphor along, this time from Mark McGurl, who opens a paragraph with the following:

> As we see, the textbook of creative writing can take us to the threshold of the room whose floor falls away into the abyss of unconscious physicality, but it refuses to step through the door. Instead, turning back to survey the room we always already occupy—call it the space of the institution—it sets about exploring the complex cognitive enclosure of the human point of view. (550)

What I love about the metaphor is that it's so surprising. No reason to put a room there, except that it gives you the floor falling away, the feet on the threshold, the touch and feel of a horror film, which is, as you can discover for yourself, one of the subjects of McGurl's essay.

One day you climb to the mountain top in search of the hermit master of figural prose. You will find him gone. In his place on that scaly rock however lies a copy of this amazing paragraph of Paul Saint-Amour's, whose relentless and unforgiving commitment to live language, its own and that of others, fills you with its extravagant sharpening glory.

> If, as Cynthia Koepp says, "The tree of knowledge looks more like a pile of leaves" when the alphabet is through with it, those leaves were endowed with a memory of the dismembered tree. This was the function of the parenthetical locator terms with which each entry began— (*Philosophy*), for example, in the "Encyclopédie" article—and of the *renvois* or cross-references. But these did not prevent the alphabetical

order from creating, as Diderot put it, "burlesque contrasts; an article on theology would find itself relegated to a position next to one on mechanical arts" (*DOC* 217). Some commentators have read the alphabetical burlesque as the project's most radical move, its way of scrambling the hierarchies, and particularly the disdain for manual work, incarnate in knowledge trees such as Bacon's and even d'Alembert's. Koepp again: "in the *Encyclopédie* 'mendiant' precedes 'noblesse,' and 'chaircuitier' comes before 'clerc.' One can read more about the production of iron ore than about coats of arms." But the virtues of alphabetical order—its convenience as a mode of access, its liquidation of hierarchy—precipitated out of a deeper, even more radical perception of necessity. Here I mean the encyclopedists' conviction that any tree of knowledge was perforce an arbitrary schema passed off as an authoritative one, and that instead of colluding in such a ruse it was better to embrace the more explicit arbitrariness of the alphabet. Witness this moment in d'Alembert's "Discours préliminaire," where a modesty bordering on self-abnegation meets a Borgesian turn for counterfactual inventory:

> One could construct the tree of our knowledge by dividing it into natural and revealed knowledge, or useful and pleasing knowledge, or speculative and practical knowledge, or evident, certain, probable, and sensitive knowledge, or knowledge of things and knowledge of signs, and so on into infinity. . . . We are too aware of the arbitrariness which will always prevail in such a division to believe that our system is the only one or the best. It will be sufficient for us if our work is not entirely disapproved of by men of intelligence. . . . [O]ne should not attribute more advantages to our encyclopedic tree than we claim to give it. . . . It is a kind of enumeration of the knowledge that can be acquired—a frivolous enumeration for whoever would wish to let it go at that alone, but useful for whoever desires to go further.

On the heels of a long rationale for the tree of knowledge, d'Alembert backs away, dubbing it arbitrary, provisional, useful only to the extent that it provokes its own supersession. Such passages reveal that the *Encyclopédie* was always the Chinese Encyclopedia out of Borges in its insistence that it could have been otherwise—that there are an infinite number of ways to organize order, each of them alien or even ludicrous from the perspective of the others. Even the alphabet as a solution to the problem of hierarchy is made implicitly arbitrary here. Taking d'Alembert's cue, you might well choose to abandon the twenty-six letters and parcel knowledge out, instead, into eighteen Homeric episodes, each with its own style, organ, color, and art. Or you might, if you were Musil, store the Viennese honey of the known in a vast hive of essayistic cells linked only perfunctorily by narrative. In either case, you would be presenting a picture of what a society knew, but one rooted in the view from somewhere, patterned less on the monolithic reputation of the encyclopedia and more on its actual connectivity, its miscellaneity, its eccentricity.

Twenty-three

Footnotes and Endnotes

If you get to choose, footnotes are always better. That's because, first, most people don't ever read endnotes, meaning that if you put anything thoughtful there it will never get seen, and second, because even when people do read endnotes, their location destroys any hope you have of creating *on the page* a dialogue between the two levels of your discourse. The only advantages endnotes have is that they avoid the appearance of clutter (this doesn't bother me at all, but it does some people) and that they allow you to completely, rather than temporarily, hide the source of a citation.

I have a strong preference for footnotes because I put lots of ideas there. At their best these ideas ramify the work in ways that cannot be accommodated in the world upstairs, which has to stay as committed as possible to its primary story. Plus I am suspicious, and for good reasons, I think, of the impulse against clutter—whether aesthetic or intellectual—when it seems to merge too cleanly with a concept of the work as an unblemished plane of coherence, or to a fantasy that dreams of academic writing as somehow beyond or above the footnote (Helen Sword: "In a book intended to reach a wide range of readers, endnotes and footnotes alike risk communicating at best a scholarly pretentiousness . . . and at worst a sort of fussy didacticism" [139]). I am interested always in breaking—in interesting and intellectually serious ways—the reader's or the writer's attempt to conceive the book as a perfect whole. Footnotes and other parenthetical structures help make that happen by pointing us to paths untrodden or unchosen, by adding complexity and nuance, and by establishing dialogue, either purely subterranean or between the upstairs and the downstairs, that allows the book to speak in multiple registers at once. To be sure all these modes of disrupting the alleged wholeness of the text can be recuperated, as a system, into a new and more complex vision of the whole. But I would rather have that newer and more complex version, in which the possibility of extension and the necessity of exclusion have been essentially included and marked according to the medium of their appearance—as disruptions right on the page— than I would a work that dressed its self-disruption in the same cloth as its self-assurance. The narrative footnote opens a small fold in the otherwise conservative conception of the page as pure and uninterruptible surface.

None of this interferes much with the pragmatics of writing notes, which come down to mastering these four functions:

1. *Citing.* As per Chicago style, you're just listing author(s), sources, and details about sources (location, page number, date, and so on).

2. *Giving background information.* Useful for either piling up citations that iceberg and underscore a claim made up top ("For another take on the museum as carnival, see X, Y, and Z; Z in particular shows that . . . "), or adding depth and resonance to the upstairs line ("Such a position was common in 1930s Moscow. X has argued, for instance, that . . ."). This is the most common function of the narrative footnote. It may include critical, theoretical, and historical material; sometimes it will just offer an extension of a citation appearing in the main text. Saussy's "Barefoot Doctor" note is a theoretical example of this type; Poovey's on the personal check a more classic example.

3. *Elaborating the main argument.* Useful for connecting one chapter to another ("This episode recalls Parker's insistence, in the face of his critics, on . . . "), or extending a theoretical claim ("This does not mean that Aristotelian theater, by extension, relies exclusively on a poetics of appearance. The actual plays of that theater, for instance, do not . . . ").

4. *Sending the reader beyond the text.* Here you pursue a line of thought that leads in new directions, beyond the project proper. ("A useful theory of the example as such remains to be established. One might begin the project by considering Giorgio Agamben's remark that . . . ")

Individual narrative footnotes may aim for more than one of these goals. You might begin with the citation, then offer more background information (including references to other texts); and only then elaborate some aspect of an argument.

Twenty-four

Jargon

Look, we've all had moments when we thought the emperor wore no clothes. Jargon and clichés often conceal emptiness in thought. Much of the work in the world is average, and some significant percentage of it is, by definition, worse than that.

That said, I don't find the anti-jargon arguments very compelling. Every scholarly field has its own language. Do people complain that they can't read articles published by physicists or economists, or somehow blame that incapacity on physics and economics as fields?

So though I'm not pro-jargon—and who could be? It would be like being pro-gonorrhea—I'm not anti-jargon, either. But I am anti-anti-jargon. Too often writers who complain about jargon seem to be enacting a kind of instinctive and itself somewhat clichéd version of anti-intellectual self-loathing. Years ago I remember a colleague from another university exhorting us to stop writing and talking like so many eggheads and reach out to the public. Only someone too caught up in the jargon of Fox News could, I said, use the word "public" as though it didn't include either (1) academics or (2) students. We spend most of our careers as teachers trying to help strangers—all of whom, even the rich or obnoxious ones, are members of the public—learn how to be better thinkers and writers, and somehow we're the ones who aren't reaching out to the public? Sigh.

Anyway. Whatever your official and highly theorized position on the jargon wars, you will need to master a professional discourse in order to succeed as an academic writer. That means learning, at some point, how to use "problematic" in a sentence or "stage" as a verb. Ideally it means later on deciding to stop using "problematic" (I still kind of like the admittedly shopworn "stage"). But really it's up to you to, within the broad range of professionally acceptable ways of writing, to decide on the levels of complexity, the types of syntax, and the styles of language use that will matter to you.

Let me say one more thing: being a good writer means *paying attention to your words.* You can radically change the feel of your prose by extending your conceptual and verbal vocabularies to make sure that you're thinking well about word choice.

Make growing your lexicon a matter of daily practice. Erin Carlston notes words she's been using too much and avoids them; she also keeps lists of new words to try. I do the same, stealing good words I find in the work of others (I got "vernal" from Chang-rae Lee's *Aloft,* and have over-used it ever since), or rummaging thesauruses for interesting alternatives to old favorites. I also browse dictionaries, sometimes using etymological entries to explore a single word or concept.

You can try adopting constraints to help you build your lexicon—two new words a page, for instance. Or you could grow your vocabulary of aca-demic verbs by limiting your uses of "to be." I tried this once: inspired by my teacher John Glavin, I stripped all but three instances of "to be" from my fifty-page undergraduate thesis, replacing them with other verbs (fre-quently changing sentence structure to do so). The exercise transformed what I knew of the syntactical possibilities of English, and continues to shape the ways I write today.

I am not recommending, I should say, lexical novelty for its own sake. I recommend novelty as a practice of self-awareness and self-renewal, as a resistance to habit, and as a mode of sustained engagement with the tools of your craft.

Twenty-five
Parentheticals

In case you couldn't tell, I like them. The risk is that you break the reader's concentration, that you ruin your line, and that those losses outweigh the gains.

The gains are many. You can use parentheticals to subordinate, to mitigate or complicate without breaking stride, to exemplify (like this), to add asides (especially if you're switching registers), or to elaborate on an idea. Parentheticals increase the spatial and textile volume of your prose, opening up breathing space for the reader and enlarging the referential sphere of your engagement with the material.

In keeping with the general practice here of privileging rhetorical function over grammatical rules, we will insist that parenthesizing gestures can come in a variety of punctuative, paratextual, and grammatical forms, and therefore that one ought properly to speak of a parenthetical continuum. This latter covers a set of relations to the main line ranging from the completely non-parenthetical, the absolutely central, to the totally extraneous (which by definition you should never include). Its grammatical and diacritical markers include parentheses, long dashes, subordinate clauses, and notes. Parentheticals can also be preceded by explicit parenthesizing words like "parenthetically," "incidentally," or "by the way," which tend to introduce entire sentences.

Since notes and grammatical subordination have been covered elsewhere, let's look at some examples using parentheses and long dashes.

EXEMPLIFICATION

Faced with cultural differences—indifference to famine, love of torture—Russell imagines himself as an anthropologist of the first order.

No one who has read Milloy's work can escape his odd familiarity with obscure folk synonyms for ice cream (Swedish milk, mazy-poney, churn mana, etc.).

Lu Xun never wrote directly on the subject again—"I finished with madness in 1929," he wrote to a colleague—but madness nonetheless found its way into his nonfiction prose in 1935.

ASIDES

The entire affair was resolved when Pound promised to return a few weeks later with the gramophone. (He never did.)

Late in his career, Barthes would apparently (and this is why critics love him so much) spend his days sitting by the window of his apartment, weaving tiny dolls from the loose threads of his startlingly Chinese bathrobe.

Some of the force of this decision was mitigated by the illness of his wife. She was, incidentally, also a secret member of the Party.

MITIGATION

The long lonely years of his exile in Peru—or near-exile, since he left twice for medical treatment in Cuba—saw Gonzalez publish his greatest work.

How well we understand the problem of mimesis in the Spanish age will determine our capacity to write the history of aesthetics as a whole (which is not to say that we can write such a history at all).

COMMENTARY

I do not know if he ever left the city—certainly he did not advertise his doing so and, in any case, it was the kind of city one couldn't easily leave—but in 1925 I thought I saw him standing almost naked in front of the fountain at the St. Olaf Hotel in Portsmouth. He was carrying a cane and wearing a bowler hat. With a mustache (and clothes) you would have taken him for one of Hergé's idiot sibling detectives.

My favorite user of parentheses is Roland Barthes, who—fabulously translated by Richard Miller in *S/Z*—shows you how you can use them to add voice, nuance, and rhythm to your work:

To describe is thus to place the empty frame which the realistic author always carries with him (more important than his easel) before a collection or continuum of objects which cannot be put into words without this obsessive operation (which could be laughable as a "gag"); in order to speak about it, the writer, through this initial rite, first transforms the "real" into a depicted (framed) object; having done this, he can take down this object, *remove* it from his picture: in short: de-depict it (to depict is to unroll the carpet of the codes, to refer not from a language to a referent but from one code to another). Thus, realism (badly named, at any rate often badly interpreted) consists not in copying the real but in copying a (depicted) copy of the real. . . . Once the infinite circularity of the codes is posited, the body itself cannot escape it: the real body (fictionally given as such) is the replication of a model set forth by that code of the arts, so that the most "natural" of bodies, that of Balzac's crayfish-gatherer (*La Rabouilleuse*), is always only the *promise* of the artistic code from which it has previously issued ("*The doctor, who was enough of an anatomist to recognize a delectable figure, understood all that the arts would lose, if this charming model were destroyed by working in the fields*"). (54–55)

Barthes puts the full array of parenthetical possibility into play: we move from asides (the first two instances) to the use of parentheses to double over the meaning of a single word by noting its specific connotation ("(framed)"), to a lengthy theoretical elaboration; then another aside; a specification; another specification; a specific reference; and a quotation placed into evidence. You can decide if the parentheses distract from the main line. For me, they make it.

Final warning: don't confuse the use of material between long dashes—which usually has a parenthetical function—with the use of a single long dash for emphasis. The latter replaces a comma—and highlights an upcoming clause by delaying its appearance.

Twenty-six

Pronouns

Leave alone the question of whether you should use "I"—that ship has sailed. I and his friends You and We are out on the prow of the SS *Academia* shouting that they're kings of the world. So the relevant question is, how should you use them?

Let's begin by distinguishing more and less rhetorical uses. There's a big difference between saying something like "In this essay I argue" and "I don't know why the novel is so short." In the first case the pronoun is barely a deictic. It points, at best, to the author-function of the essay. The second indicates a far more embodied being, one whose knowledge of the text has just entered into the "diegetic" or representational space of the prose. How you use pronouns will determine how much you, or the reader, or some "we" that includes both of you, becomes a character in your work. (You might go back and look at the two endings from Martha Banta and Jane Gallop in chapter 17 with this in mind.)

Most pronouns in academic writing are rhetorical, but the array of that rhetorical function is unevenly spread. "I" tends almost always to be deictically thin, pointing via phrases like "I argue" or "I show" merely to the motives of the essay itself. But in a certain strand of feminism dating from the 1980s and carrying forward through the present, you will find (one finds? we find? I find?) a strongly personal first-person pronoun coming to the fore, as in Jane Gallop's work above or in the work of others in queer and feminist theory, like Eve Sedgwick or Nancy K. Miller (this "I" finds one limit in the 1990s genre of the critical memoir;

see Alice Kaplan's *French Lessons*). Similarly, the rhetorical "we," which replaced "I" in certain contexts ("We must feel that the novel cannot adequately address these concerns") fell deeply out of fashion in the 1990s (too patriarchal). A milder version, in which the "we" refers to a real group of people, has come back into more common use, as in the stronger, more inclusive first-person plural that Hillary Clinton deploys in a sentence like "We must stop thinking of the individual and start thinking about what is best for society." That exhortative "we" is not as strong, referentially, as the "I" you find in feminist work; I suspect that's because some of its force is dissipated by its inclusiveness. But as you see I make lots of use of it here, largely to refer to a community of academics—even if, as we all know, that "we" never includes everyone in quite the same way. As for "one," it's uncommon in American English these days, though I like it now and then for tone and mild irony, which it can produce if it replaces a highly obvious "I": "Faulkner's later work, one feels, never quite reaches the same peaks."

For me the most interesting of the pronouns these days is "you." This casual substitute for "one" or "people" has a traditionally weak rhetorical form that rarely makes an appearance in academic writing; you'll see it in phrases like Forrest Gump's "You never know what you're going to get." But a more strongly deictic "you" can startle and engage the reader by dragging him or her bodily into the text. Consider the following sentences, all from Bill Brown's *A Sense of Things*, which I have arranged in order from most rhetorical to most deictic:

You might say that all the objects on the library mantel, like the general clutter of the so-called Victorian era in America, were amassed in a hopeless effort to give substance to the abstract subject. . . . (48)

Should you begin to think about things in late nineteenth-century America, it won't be long before you stumble over Mark Twain's House in Hartford, Connecticut. (21)

Moreover, whether or not you agree with Fernand Léger's belief that fragmenting an object frees it of atmosphere even as enlarging the fragments gives them a life of their own, you can hardly deny that the objects in Strand's photograph, which seem suspended in a fragile balance, have curiously become organic or animate, have at least emerged out of their ontological status of being mere inanimate objects. (9)

Today, why do you find yourself talking to things—your car, your computer, you refrigerator? Do you grant agency to inanimate objects because you want to unburden yourself of responsibility? Or is it simply because you're lonely? Because, unlike a child, you don't have a toy to talk with? (12)

Its fingers straddling the reader's throat, this later "you" displays the engaged pronoun's immense power, its potential for sheer aggression and intimacy. Brown's is a book that touches you back and provokes, in doing so, a persistent and nagging intuition of the second person's electrifyingly cozy relation to things.

Brown thus models—for me, anyway—a committed exploration of the *here there be dragons* regions on the maps of academic prose. (You can find Mark McGurl trying something similar to activate the plural pronoun when he writes: "To bring the wellsprings of the posthuman comedy into better view we'll want to stick with these othernesses a little longer, keeping them at the center of our concern, and we can do that by first returning to Bergson" [549].) The lesson is: If you want to be bold, go where no one's going. Out on the edges of the known world you will find room to surprise, with pronouns or anything else, in ways that will make you a better writer when you stick, as mostly you must, to the well-marked and many-footed paths of our familiar interiors.

One final recommendation: you will find that as you write you use a variety of first-person markers, especially in the singular, as an emotional crutch or coping device. Having to say "I think" or "It seems to me" when drafting is a perfectly normal thing to do—it reflects your genuine uncertainty about what you think or know at that point in the writing process. As a general rule, you will want to go back and edit most of those out, since they largely diminish rhetorical authority and offer no real gains in return. What goes for obviously weak phrases like "it seems" or "I think" goes, however, just as well for "I contend," "I suggest," "I argue," or "I show," all of which *feel* stronger at first glance. What all such phrases do is to move the locus of the ideas from the historical or critical situation to the writer; they thus weaken the causal and polemical links *inside* your "diegetic" or representational space—the world, that is, of your primary and secondary texts—by referring them to an outside that, in the end, usually has little (diegetically, again) to do with them. Compare these sentences:

These changes rewrote the imaginary physical framework of human existence.

I show how these changes rewrote the imaginary physical framework of human existence.

These changes, I contend, rewrote the imaginary physical framework of human existence.

The loss in rhetorical force from the first to the third is a direct function of the intervention into the diegesis (the world, that is, in which the "changes" in the "imaginary physical framework" take place) of a first person who *doesn't need to be there for the claims to be true.*

Twenty-seven
Repetition

A simple rule: repeat all your major ideas several times.

Why? Most people read faster than they think. As you begin to lay out an idea, you will need to give the reader time to get used to it. Don't repeat everything exactly, but rework and rewrite, using subordinate clauses to reassert big ideas and independent clauses to add new material. Let the idea sink in, manage its contours, and build toward a final expression that the reader will chunk and walk away with.

This is also part of what the examples are for. They're evidence, yes, but they're also there to slow the reader down. Look at how long Susan Stewart takes to convince the reader of the single idea, expressed in the first sentence of this paragraph, that microcosmic philosophies are aesthetic and not historical (I have underlined the clearest repetitions):

> Like other forms of thought associated with the <u>miniature, microcosmic philosophies are contemplative and aesthetic rather than scientific and historical</u>. [thesis / promise] Although in Comte we find references to analogies between society and an organism, and although the theory of recapitulation is occasionally used with reference to the state, <u>microcosmic thought usually centers on the notion of the individual "specimen," whether abstract or physical</u>. [restates thesis in slightly different terms; first part of sentence manages possible counterevidence] When such theories do approach the social, they often result <u>in an aestheticization and diminution</u> of the cultural other. [here again we are manag-

ing counterevidence: when theories of the microcosm do "approach the social," this means they seem like they might be "scientific and historical"] For example, Napier's *Book of Nature* explains that "the people of the West Indies have a hot temper because their climate is hot." The alleged hot temper of the Irish gives his theory some difficulty until he realizes that "the warmth and excitability of the Irish are probably occasioned by the righteous 'stirring up' they have received, which, amongst men as amongst liquids, increases heat. As in chemistry the mixture of two or more substances occasions heat during the process, so amongst human races the greatest amount of excitement follows the union of tribes, whose infusion acts like the addition of fermenting agents. The Irish, if descending from Milesius, would be of Oriental origin, and Asia Minor, from which they are believed to have come, has a particularly fiery climate in the summer." The connection between the processes of stereotyping and caricature is obvious here: both involve the selection and exaggeration of an element of "quality," the distribution of it over quantity, and the invention of a causality to substantiate the original element chosen. [the argument is won, here, by the assertion that what looks like an explanation of a *quantity* (the Irish as a people), which would be scientific/historical, is in fact simply the extension of a *quality* (and hence is aesthetic after all)] Here we can also begin to place the <u>aestheticization of the primitive and the peasant</u> which underlies much of anthropology, particularly ethnography's impulse toward seeing the "primitive," or "peasant," community as a microcosm of larger social principles—the idea that the village is the world. [we now begin to see that a whole regime of apparently scientific microcosmic thought is in fact aesthetic in nature.] A major historian and modern proponent of microcosmic philosophies, George Conger, has suggested: "Of the persistent motivations which may be expected to keep the microcosmic theories reappearing, there need be no question that *the aesthetic motivation has possibilities* which are at once the most abundant and the least explored." [this quote just reproduces Stewart's original argument] These forms of projection of the body—the grotesque, the miniature, and the microcosm—reveal the paradoxical status of the body as both mode and object of knowing, and of <u>the self constituted outside its physical being by its image</u>. (130–31)

If that last sentence, with its sudden mention of the grotesque and the miniature alongside the microcosm, doesn't seem to fit the paragraph, that's because this closes a larger section in which those other two are addressed (the sudden leap from the 5 of the paragraph to the 5 of the section as a whole, bypassing the step-by-step structure I have shown you previously, is typical of Stewart's style in *On Longing*). But even there you can see the main line repeating in the phrase "self constituted outside its physical being by its image," which repeats the idea of the *aesthetic* construction of the self as a microcosm (the image) with which the paragraph began. Along the way we have managed possible counterevidence, helped by a reading of a long citation from Napier, and we have extended the general principle of microcosmic aestheticization both to the general field of anthropology and to the earlier concepts of the grotesque and the miniature. At no point does the reader find the paragraph repetitive. And yet, the paragraph works *because* it keeps its main line, its most basic concept, consistently in front of the reader, turning it this way and that, stretching and compressing it, and in general exposing its every facet to a public eye that is only just getting to know it.

Twenty-eight

Rhetorical Questions and Clauses

The two most common places you'll find them are: at the beginning of paragraphs, often singly, where they set up the work of that unit; and in significant introductory paragraphs, where they telegraph the outline and goals of an entire essay, and tend to appear in series.

To open paragraphs:

How, then, does Chinese art become the epitome of high craft in both Vaudoyer's review and a scene depicting a French novelist gazing at a Dutch masterpiece? (Froula 234)

So what does it mean for Hawthorne to write a romance just then of how a Congressman, with no apparent blood ties, defeated by party politics, goes to England to reconcile two branches of a family and reclaim a "consanguinity" that has been lost? (Tamarkin 81)

Why, at the moment he believes he is about to die, should the hero of Stephen Crane's 1898 story "The Five White Mice" be reminded by the insulted Mexican "of a man who had shaved him three times" years before? Is the connection between the two men as simple as the fact that one carries a knife and the other wields a razor or that both men have stared intently into the New York Kid's face? (Burrows 2)

What is money? (Giddens 23)

In series:

What, then, are some of the competing universals that underwrite Western and Chinese conceptions of the human? Given the central role of the state in so many aspects of modern social life, is it possible to conceptualize the human outside nation-states' modes of political control, economic management, and cultural production? Indeed, does the concept of the human exist only in a dialectical relationship to the state? If not, what new forms of human being—and being human—might emerge beyond such dialectic encounters on translocal, transregional, and transnational scales? (Eng, Ruskola, and Shen 6)

Larbaud's vision of her reading his own influential article in translation raises several intriguing questions: how did Spanish critics initially receive *Ulysses* and interpret Molly's character and avant-garde monologue, in contexts that dramatically contrasted those of their Anglophone and Continental counterparts? What political critiques did they see entwined in Molly's Hispanicity and in the Spanish and Irish affinities staged throughout the novel? As writers and intellectuals in Spain searched for new, foreign literary forms that would regenerate the culture of their marginalized "land of María Santísimia," what kind of map did they see in Joyce's postcolonial Ireland integrated with an imagined *post-imperial* Europe? That is to say, when Stephen Dedalus overhears the Irish man of letters Dr. George Sigerson's claim that Ireland has no "Don Quixote and Sancho Panza" and that its "national epic has yet to be written," Joyce points unawares to a challenge that many Silver Age (1898–1939) Spaniards saw for a country whose national epic from its Golden Age had become outdated, if not altogether irrelevant. How does all of this bear on present readings of Joyce, his complex cosmopolitanism, and the politics of *Ulysses*, tied as they were to a country where civil war broke out in 1922? (Rogers 256)

Rhetorical questions in series almost always have to end the paragraph they're in. (They can begin it too, as happens in the first example above, but even then they will often also end it.) They tend to appear either at the beginning of a section (see our first example again), where they perform for the section the role the single or double rhetorical question does for a single paragraph, or at the end of an introductory section (like our second example), where they both sum up and set up the rest of the piece.

In general you will want to ask only three or four rhetorical questions in a row. Any more will exhaust the reader. You'll notice that Gayle Rogers, who has four long questions, splits the third and fourth with a declarative sentence to relieve some of the pressure (though even that sentence looks like it might be a question, because of the "when"; I would have rewritten it to avoid confusion).

You should arrange your rhetorical questions in hierarchical series, going conceptually from narrower to broader, and also in terms of sentence length, usually shorter to longer. Compare these two examples, imagining that they appear at the end of an introductory section:

Why does so much of Franklin's later work strike us this way? Is it an effect of the way he writes? Does it have to do with his politics?

Why does so much of Franklin's later work strike us this way? Does what happens at the level of the sentence alter our sense of his goals and his methods as an author? How might we begin to understand the question of his entire relation to the concept of the urban with which he is so much associated as partly a function, not of his politics, but of the stylistic extravagances of his ruined prose?

For me the first instance is too choppy, too short, and not in any kind of order. The second is smoother and more engaging. Why? You'll notice there that the rhythm of the first two questions sets up a third, longer question that aims not really to ask another question but to frame (via "how might we begin to understand," which turns the whole thrust toward criticism) the coming argument. As a result the final question becomes the most rhetorical of all—it feels almost like a declarative sentence. If you go back to the earlier examples I showed you, you'll notice that they do the same thing: a strong series of rhetorical questions will rely on some kind of developmental logic to manage the reader.

You'll see one other major kind of rhetorical structure in academic writing. This one involves a use of "if" that I almost never see anywhere else.

> If the camera proves to Janie that she is black, the community attempts to prove to her that she is white. (Burrows 191)

> If the power here sits out with the people, it is also true that the semicircular plane forces the viewer to reach that site of power across a negative space. (Tamarkin 49)

> If the students of the eighteenth century were subject to the severe discipline of a clerical faculty, and the rigorous schedule of study and declamations it enforced by college law, in the nineteenth century they had considerable autonomy. (Tamarkin 259)

Honestly I'm not sure how to describe what's going on in this structure. "If" is functioning as a subordinating conjunction (its usual job, no surprises there), but it's doing so in a manner that violates the implicit causal structure of its normal use in an if/then pattern, which it resembles. Neither author means that *if* the first clause, *consequently* the second one. In all cases the part of the sentence that occupies the "conditional" space is in fact not under question—the camera *does* prove to Janie that she is black, the power here *does* sit out with the people, the students of the eighteenth century *were* subject to the severe discipline. You can tell something strange is happening because normally we'd use the subjunctive for the conditional in the *if* clause, which Tamarkin does do in her second example; but neither Burrows nor Tamarkin do so in the other ones (where it would sound very strange to write "If the camera prove to Janie that she is black," though that would be the correct form of the present subjunctive; you can check by changing the *if* to a *should*, at which point "prove" sounds quite normal, though it has the odd effect of shifting the conditional into a very strong present tense; you could fix this by abandoning the aesthetic present and putting things back in the past, finally producing "If the camera had proved . . . ").

If we abandon for a moment the attempt to describe this pattern in normative terms and instead opt for description, what I would say is that this pattern, which is as far as I know only used in academic writing, works as follows:

> If [something I have just shown is true, but whose truth-force I wish to mitigate slightly in order to adduce to it the material that appears in the next clause], [something else which is related to that initial material, and whose truth-value is increased by its being placed in opposition and subsequently to it].

This is not exactly a conditional, then, but rather something that uses the conditional structure in order to put together two elements felt to be related through mild but productive opposition (thus an x/y transition). Because it falsely suggests that a certain truth-procedure has been attempted and completed, I don't like it much. The "if" can almost always be replaced by "while" or "even as," which do the same job.

Twenty-nine
Sentence Rhythm

If you do not understand how sentences work, and especially how long sentences work, you will struggle as an academic writer.

Here I am tempted to outsource the entire discussion, however, to Joseph M. Williams's amazing *Style: Ten Lessons in Clarity and Grace*, the one book about nonfictional prose everyone who writes (and wants to write well) should own. Seriously, you should go read it and then come back here and continue.

I know you didn't really read it. But let's pretend. Among the lessons you've learned is to manage information *inside* the sentence by changing its location: to the right, as Williams suggests, to increase its importance, and to the left (toward the beginning of the sentence) to decrease it. This helps you understand why the x/y transition works the way it does—the subordinated, earlier clause, because it refracts earlier material, comes first, and the second, independent clause leads the reader into the new paragraph. It also helps clarify why I said earlier that there's a great deal of pressure in introductions on the end of the first sentence and on the end of the first paragraph: material at the *end* of any unit of prose (clause, sentence, paragraph, essay, chapter, book) will have more structural weight than the material before it (remember the "mousetrap" sentence). That means that you want to end sentences and paragraphs with their most important words and use that space, as Williams advises, "to introduce long, complex, or otherwise difficult-to-process material" (104). If you want to write that something "spectacularly unfolds into the Heideggerian, dialectical apparatus of its own clumsy becoming" and you've given up on having it tattooed on your face, then put it at the end of a sentence.

For the same reason you can use a lengthy setup, even spanning two sentences, to prepare the reader for a concise but dense conclusion. Here are a couple sentences of Mark Sussman's as an example:

> Like the fully orchestrated discursive world Bakhtin describes as the novel's essential domain, *The Damnation of Theron Ware* reproduces the affective clashes and cognitive failures of the "intellectual world" its flawed hero strives to join. The novel's representation of sociological thought and cultural criticism, its persistent disinvestment in taking a position within those domains, combine to create the novel's most spectacular and meaningful juxtaposition: the modernity of its form lies in its refusal to adopt the form of modern thought.

Knowing that he wants to get to the chiasmus of modernity / form, form / modern in the final clause, Sussman walks the reader through two versions of the final claim before summing up and announcing that chiasmus, just before the colon. You can see something similar happening across multiple sentences of Rebecca Walkowitz's, as she chunks an opposition between panoramic and microscopic perspectives in the work of W. G. Sebald:

> Sebald wants his stories to seem unfinished, so that reader will have to attempt their own order, or reckon with disorder. He proposes that a materialist history of European culture, a history attentive to the economic conditions and political contestation of values and norms, requires not only the first-person stories of natives and visitors but also the **panoramic** stories of economic relations and the researched or imagined stories of **microscopic** details. Adding **panoramic** and **microscopic** accounts (what he calls "**synoptic** and **artificial**" views ["AW" 25–26]) to

eyewitness testimony, he argues, creates more authenticity because less coherence. Sebald thus combines the **immigrant archives** and **aerial vision** of the late twentieth century—*what we know now that we could not know before*—with the critical protocols and speculative postures of early-twentieth-century modernism.

Sebald's combination of **panoramic** and **microscopic** views produces a relentless vertigo: whereas the **panoramic** view gathers context and locates agency, the **microscopic** view introduces details that resist any one context and often seem to point to a context that eludes specification. (155)

At the sentence level, I want to point you to the phrase "what we know now that we could not know before," which rewrites in a casual register the epistemological context Walkowitz refers to just before the long dash. I also want to highlight the way the initial appearance of the words "panoramic" and "microscopic," separated by eleven words, is suddenly marked and highlighted by their immediate reappearance as a pair in the following sentence. You can then watch the paragraphs walk readers through two synonyms for the panorama / microscope pair (one coming, in parentheses, from Sebald himself) before returning to them at the start of the new paragraph. That paragraph then uses the opposition between those terms to establish a new term, "vertigo," which is also in the title of the chapter: "Sebald's Vertigo." And now you see how we get there.

But now, seriously, please go read Williams. And then come back, because I still have a few short lessons on rhythm left.

1. *Hide uninteresting factual information in dependent clauses.* Things that the reader needs to hear, but can kind of ignore, should appear in dependent clauses or parenthetical structures, not as sentences on their own. When you have to get facts into the work, do so subtly. Compare these two paragraphs:

Jenson was born in 1930 in Leipzig. His novel *The White Dog's Bark* appeared in 1950. Its representation of rural Sweden, and its odd mixture of first- and second-person narration, made it a major event in Scandinavian modernism.

Jenson's *The White Dog's Bark,* which appeared twenty years after its author's 1930 birth in Leipzig, unsettled the quiet landscape of Scandinavian modernism by overlaying its representation of rural Sweden with an odd mixture of first- and second-person narration.

In a perfect world, I would take the Leipzig information out of the sentence unless I absolutely needed it there. Presumably it could go into another dependent clause elsewhere. The change would shorten the slightly uncomfortable distance between the second sentence's subject and its verb.

2. *Vary sentence style and length.* Most writers will naturally produce some variation in sentence length, though beginning writers will tend to get stuck in a groove that reflects their confidence as writers and their capacity to manage complex grammar. Even perfectly competent academic writers must be careful to avoid having all their sentences run from about eighteen to twenty-five words long—what I think of as the normative band for academic writing. If you want to become a more interesting stylist, if you want to open up space inside your prose, and if you want to create dynamic or rhythmic effects with grammar, you should practice writing sentences outside that band, either short or long.

Pairing long and short sentences can create very nice effects, as in this from Susan Stewart, where the middle sentence really makes these lines sing:

> Unlike the single miniature object, the miniature universe of the dollhouse cannot be known sensually; it is inaccessible to the languages of the body and thus is the most abstract of all miniature forms. Yet cognitively the dollhouse is gigantic. As Jonson moves from the remote to the domestic, his images become increasingly imbued with refinement. (63)

Or this from Virginia Woolf, which uses a string of semicolons to set up two shorter sentences, the second of which is the real punchline (and illustrates the rhetorical device of anadiplosis, the repetition of words at the end of one clause and the beginning of the next):

> It may be, to speak bluntly, that the daughters are in themselves deficient; that they have proved themselves untrustworthy; unsatisfactory; so lacking in the necessary ability that it is to the public interest to keep

them to the lower grades where, if they are paid less, they have less chance of impeding the transaction of public business. This solution would be easy but, unfortunately, it is denied to us. It is denied to us by the Prime Minister himself. (48)

The short clause or sentence in particular can lend itself to a nice aphoristic feel, especially when it's grammatically simple. Susan Stewart puts this to great use throughout *On Longing*, with unusually strong uses of "is" adding to the effect:

In allegory the vision of the reader is larger than the vision of the text; (3)

The movement from realism to modernism and postmodernism is a movement from the sign as material to the signifying process itself. (5)

The printed text is cinematic before the invention of cinema. (9)

The closure of the book is an illusion largely crated by its materiality, its cover. (38)

In its tableaulike form, the miniature is a world of arrested time; its stillness emphasizes the activity that is outside its borders. (67)

We want the antique miniature and the gigantic new. (86)

Aesthetic size cannot be divorced from social function and social values. (95)

The grotesque body, as a form of the gigantic, is a body of parts. (105)

Temporally, the souvenir moves history into private time. (138)

You get the idea.

At the far end of the sentence, where stunned experiment dresses the mantelpiece of beauty, you will find things like this description of the sound of a house in the night from James Agee's *Let Us Now Praise Famous Men:*

> In their prodigious realm, their field, bashfully at first, less timorous, later, rashly, all calmly boldly now, like the tingling and standing up of plants, leaves, planted crops out of the earth into the yearly approach of the sun, the noises and natures of the dark had with the ceremonial gestures of music and of erosion lifted forth the thousand several forms of their entrancement, and had so resonantly taken over the world that this domestic, this human silence obtained, prevailed, only locally, shallowly, and with the childlike and frugal dignity of a coal-oil lamp stood out on a wide night meadow and of a star sustained, unraveling in one rivery sigh its irremediable vitality, on the alien size of space. (18)

Now, that's not an academic sentence, but still. The world would be a better place if we all tried, sometimes, for this kind of effect.

3. *Use speed for effect.* Enda Duffy, whose *The Speed Handbook* co-won the 2010 Modernist Studies Association Book Prize, told me after the awards ceremony that he had rewritten his book late in the game, when he realized that it didn't *feel* fast. You can get some sense of what Duffy's revisions do from this paragraph:

> Speed politics, in the first instance, was a politics of access: this newly intense experience was offered to citizens on the basis of their ability to pay, on their gender, proximity to centers of production, consumption, and power. Next, it was a matter of national control. Everywhere speed came to be monitored by governments as traffic police. New national regulatory systems, with driver's licenses, speed limits, traffic signs, and checkpoints, were rapidly set in place. Fundamentally, however, the narratives of access to speed and its control need to be thought of in terms of how the access to all resources and pleasures has been organized in modernity. Since the mid-nineteenth century the story has been told as the matter of consumption, the desire for and the need to possess commodities. The story of national control has been one of the state's control of its land space, its territory, and the flow of traffic—in goods,

people, workers—thereupon. In both these realms, the rush to speed was profoundly disruptive. (7)

Duffy manages sentence and word length (both shorter, on average, than the academic norm) to reproduce in writing an important feature of the cultural landscape he portrays. Though not every book can, or should, express stylistically what it describes, I admire and like his book because it does, and because it thereby broadens the range of acceptable ambition in academic writing.

Duffy wanted to speed people up. You may want to slow them down. This means learning to write in ways that allow you to master phatic language—language that, like the "how ya doing?" you mumble as you pass someone on the office stairs, has primarily a social function. Phatic language in the academic sentence usually works to delay the arrival of an important idea, either to increase drama (as in the "mousetrap" sentence) or to give the reader time to adjust to a new and complex—wait for it!—weasel. No, not really: a new and complex thought. If you find yourself thinking that a paragraph needs two more sentences, just to give the reader some time to breathe, you will be writing those sentences for the animal that is your reader, for what you know of her habits and tendencies, his capacities for distraction and attention, and for what you guess of what s/he knows and needs, and needs to know, in your work. That's phatic language.

Thirty
Ventilation

I used to call this something else but Paul Saint-Amour taught me to call it "ventilation." It's how your writing breathes.

Ventilation is partly a function representational space: no matter how it's written, a book with chapters on Adorno, Lucille Ball, and the epistolary fiction of Meiji-era Japan will feel different from a book on the Meiji epistolary tradition exclusively. But even in the latter book you can imagine treatments and examples that would restrict the social amplitude of the analysis, or open it up, by for instance including comparisons to contemporary material.

But ventilation is also about sentence-level style. It results from a myriad of choices, comprising the use of pronouns, the general field and range of critical diction (from the casual to scholarly), variations in sentence length and style (more variation $\doteq$ more ventilation), shifts in tone (from the humorous to the serious), decisions about figural language (yes or no, but also what kinds of figuration), questions of voice (personal vs. impersonal), styles of reading (deconstructive vs. thematic vs. historical, for example), and the management of structural rhythm at the paragraph or chapter level. Though in some cases it may seem that ventilation will be on one or the other side of the binaries I've listed here—that, for example, writing that includes the occasional joke will be more open and airier than writing that doesn't—in each case ventilation is much more a matter of the range, or amplitudinal space, created between the extremes any work chooses within that binary. A book of jokes is no more well-ventilated than a book that has none at all. By contrast a shocking shift in matters of diction, rhythm, or style can break the reader's defenses and reveal new realms of compassion, engagement, and understanding: "Even Adorno, the great belittler of popular pleasures, can be aghast at the ease with which intellectuals shit on people who hold to a dream" (Berlant 123).

What counts as the right level of ventilation, I don't know. My own scholarship is airier than average, an effect I achieve by laddering up and down the hierarchies of style and reference, varying sentence length and style, referring to a wide array of cultural artifacts, injecting lighter units into denser ones, and shifting emotional registers with jokes and figurative language. Others do other things. Jameson, for instance, feels difficult to most readers partly because his style is relentlessly self-similar, featuring almost no significant breaks in either voice, sentence structure, or diction. He also tends to operate, especially in his later work, in a fairly narrow band of the Uneven U—or rather, the quality of his style, which does not shift depending on where in the U he is, tends to produce the feeling of a constant string of 4s and 5s. In other words, Jameson's books barely subordinate their secondary claims to their primary ones; the resulting argumentative density frustrates many attempts to build an overall understanding of the work. Together these features make his writing feel especially dense and chewy. As I've said before, I like Jameson's style, and imitate it on occasion; at the same time my own academic style is more dappled, looser, and—I hope—engaging in a different way. Your mileage may vary.

In the absence of clear moral guidance, the best advice is to at least understand what one is doing, and to develop a set of practices and preferences that help one do it. With that in mind let's compare a couple paragraphs, the first from Elisa Tamarkin's *Anglophilia,* the second from Brian Lennon's *In Babel's Shadow*:

So, to repeat, there was a style at Harvard in the mid-nineteenth century that performed in the social realm an affective doxa for the practice of intellectualism in the academy. Or, said differently, there was a way of being at college that was manifest in an attentiveness to the character one assumed there and that character expressed, in turn, a faith in the pedagogical beliefs of the college. The college believed in aimlessness:

this suggests that the emerging shape of what we now know as Arnoldian humanism and its defense of the liberal arts but also the more fugitive ends of lounging, lazing, smoking, conversing, and doing as one pleased that gave the acquisition of knowledge the college its particular manner. To the degree that these expressed the investment of higher learning in nonutilitarian values, we are reminded of any number of arguments about the anxious place of the college in an increasingly professionalized world. Asked in the 1850s what a university is, Lowell answered, "a place where nothing useful is taught." "I hope the day will come," he continued, "when a competent professor may lecture here for three years on the first three vowels of the Romance alphabet and find a fit audience, though few." Still, neither the specific character nor the full extent of academic style can be explained by accounts of the opposition between aspirations of the college and the rise of the modern research university nor between the aesthetic disposition of liberal arts and the practical ends that made literary study for Lowell by the end of the century "too much of a study and too little a pleasure." To treat the emergence of an academic style in America as a reaction formation within a familiar analysis of higher learning is not only to neglect the fascination of style itself as a means of historical response but also to assume that the distinctive character of college was ultimately determined by what it wanted to stave off. If we grant, however, that "style is properly speaking a germinative phenomenon," as Barthes writes, and so read closely for signs of how it develops and, more important, what it produces, then the ritualized and symbolic devotion to college life that we find in antebellum America beings to look rather different; we see an encompassing attention to the details of collegiate practice that celebrates even the small manners of lifestyle for how they reveal both the provenance and ambitions of the academic type. That type was recognizable to collegians then—as it is to us now—for its pretensions to Englishness. (Tamarkin 252–53)

The cross-section of the contemporary moment within which I offer my analysis exposes several layers of sedimented postwar United States cultural history. I take it for granted here that the period after 1945—a common delimiter for scholars of United States and hemispheric Euro-Atlantic literature and culture—marks the convergence of a number of developmental factors: advanced or postindustrial "postmodern" finance capitalism; the vastly expanded scale of U.S. imperial military, economic and cultural projects (and their ranks of influence); the dwindling of the British empire and the full course of the cold war, from the atomic age to what we call "globalization"; and the advent of computerization and computer science, in information theory and cold war-driven research in machine translation (the computerized transposition of human-authored documents from one rival hegemonic national language into another). I also take it for granted that in the same period, driven by new imperial technocratic imperatives, the culture of knowledge in the United States university changed significantly, largely to the benefit of applied science and to the detriment of the inapplicable humanities. The question of whether these structural changes are merely *reflected* in the cultural production of literature and the arts, or also partly produced by it is, along with the entire question of political and aesthetic vanguardism as reflective or productive of social change, an important one, to which anyone can only ever give a tentative answer. But in our culture of computerization, it seems to me that when we in literary studies make poetry—our commonsense exemplar of literary language—a figure for the untranslatable, we mean not only that poetry is the most sophisticated use of a *particular* human language, as our abiding historical Romanticism understands it (largely in national terms), but that it is the most human use of *any* language, in a world teeming with machine—that is, nondivine, yet non-human—languages. The untranslatable, as a figure for the Heideggerian "shadow" of Babel on our linguistic labor, is the *uncomputable*, that which cannot be binarized, that which best reminds us, so to speak, of human language's difference from code. (Lennon 62–63)

We're dealing here with two paragraphs whose stylistic differences also express a set of professional and intellectual affiliations and decisions. I hope it's clear to you that Lennon's paragraph is the denser of the two. How does he achieve that density, and how does Tamarkin produce her comparably ventilated prose? Largely by diction and syntax: Lennon's sentences are longer, have more "big" words, and are more frequently interrupted with parenthetical gestures (just look at his penultimate sentence, which features two interruptions between long dashes). Tamarkin's breaks and pauses, relatively lighter, tend to happen at the beginning of sentences, where they perform mainly metadiscursive tasks, some of which have a slightly chatty tone ("So, to repeat," "Or, said differently," "Still"). As for diction, compare the big words: Tamarkin has "affective doxa," "pedagogical," "humanism," "nonutilitarian," "professionalized," "germinative," and "aesthetic"; Lennon uses "postindustrial," "capitalism," "globalization," "computerization," "hegemonic," "technocratic," "vanguardism," and "untranslatable." It's not simply that Lennon is "theoretical" and Tamarkin isn't (she quotes Barthes and refers to a "reaction formation") but rather that their prose wears its relation to theory differently. You also see how Tamarkin's use of quotes lightens and opens up the paragraph, increasing amplitude by giving us variation in diction and style (the Lowell sentences in particular belong to a different world, and drop us down a level in what is otherwise a level-4 paragraph). Lennon's paragraph is tighter, with less variation in levels, holding to a single, taut structural line.

Could you rewrite Lennon's work in Tamarkin's style, or vice versa? Could you produce a denser version of Tamarkin's paragraph, or a lighter and more ventilated version of Lennon's? Surely so. But if you imagine that in that act of translation something fundamental in the work would change, that some untranslatable remainder would be left behind and gained, in both directions, then you are on your way to understanding how style knits the bones of every act of academic writing, and so, why it matters so much.

Thirty-one

Weight

Weight in writing is both external and internal. It is external when it comes from pressure induced by broad cultural norms of the type that cause readers to expect last sentences to be more significant than middle ones, last words more than first ones, and so on. It is internal when it originates from the writing's own organizational activity, where it allows you to manage emphasis at micro and macro levels to create structural and sentence rhythm. Internal weight lets you differentiate among levels of diegetic significance, allowing the close to a section to exert more gravitational pull than the close to a single paragraph, or the appearance of a major figure to feel, from the very first moments, more important than the mention of a minor one. The general variability and distribution of weight in your work will partly determine your average levels of ventilation and density.

Weight is a function of style and time. You can increase weight by adding sentences or words around a topic, allowing it to occupy a greater percentage of the work. Putting a source's name up top (instead of in a note) or using a person's first name and book title adds weight; so does putting someone's name at the beginning of a sentence or a paragraph ("Jane Smith argues that . . . " vs. " . . . , Jane Smith argues"). You increase weight when you quote someone instead of paraphrasing them, and do so even more when you re-quote something you've already cited once. Structurally, you can weight more important conclusions more heavily than lighter ones—making them "pop" out of the prose more—by making them longer (one sentence vs. two sentences vs. a paragraph) or elevating diction or sentence complexity to mark significance. You can reduce weight by folding something into a paragraph instead of giving it a paragraph of its own; you can also minimize the weight of paragraph-level transitions with weaker, extending transitions (also, similarly), or maximize them with stronger, concluding or summative ones (as a result, finally, then).

In general, you will want to match internal and external weights, making sure that your sentences and structures feel appropriately heavy or light in relation to their placement in the larger whole. But you can also usefully break that pattern, underweighting a conclusion or overweighting a piece of close reading, for dramatic effect.

Part IV

Becoming

Thirty-two

Work as Process

One of the implications of the ways of writing and of thinking about writing in this book is that the article or dissertation or book you write is never the only one you could have (or would have) written on that same topic. If I started this book over tomorrow, it would turn out differently, and the same goes for any of my other work. Probably each book has nine or ten things it could have become, the ghosts or lost children of the thing it turned out to be.

The work *becomes* itself. Writing takes a set of ideas, intuitions, acts of research, and intellectual backgrounds, and passes those through a number of refractive surfaces—your personal style and history as a writer; your disciplinary training and your job; your colleagues, friends, students, and other interlocutors; whatever's going on in your life otherwise; and, finally, the process of writing proper, the long hours of reading and thought, silent manipulation, joy, and struggle through which something final appears on the page. What is left at the end is not the only thing you could have written on the topic; but it is what you have written, what you will send out into the world to be published—and what will, prior to publication, change once again in revisions directed by some combination of external reviewers, copyeditors, editorial requirements, and, of course, your own internal process of revision, which the prospect of actual publication will kick into a higher gear. The thing that has your name and your title on it will feel, at that point, like it might never have been otherwise—like the only possible statement on the topic articulated in its explanatory subtitle. But it isn't. It never could have been.

What is it then? It is what you wrote *this time*. It owes its being, its solidity as a concept and as an object, to the process it came through. We do not like to think this way, since the emphasis on contingency and becoming undermines the basic truth-claim of the work (how could it be the truth, when you could have easily written a different truth?). But none of this means that the work is not true. Only that its truth, like all truths, is contingent upon the history of its making.

This does not liberate us to write whatever we want. Rather, it focuses our attention back on the process of making, the procedure and proceeding forward of thought, that goes into the writing of an article, a dissertation, or a book. What we trust in the final work is not the appearance of the last word in it—it is the appearance of *these* last words, final only for this project, this labor, this author, and this time. We trust the author's best and sincerest effort to make good work through a long and fraught process, and to deliver to our shores a work whose resonance beyond the world of its making ratifies, paradoxically, the world in which it was made.

The work still has to be good. But you don't have to know exactly how— you can't, and shouldn't—until it's done.

Thirty-three

Becoming a Writer

What does it take to be a writer? Or rather—since what's at stake for me is not so much what one-word description you give of your professional status, but the ideologies and rhetorics that surround writing as a social field—what would it mean to make writing a major feature of your self-image and self-production as a person?

Among other things, such a decision would, I think, entail making writing something you practice and practice often, something you conceive as an aspect of your lifelong process of self-making. We do this all the time with other things—reading cookbooks or music reviews, playing an instrument, or discussing parenting strategies with friends—in ways that reflect our understanding of ourselves as growing beings, as incomplete or unfinished versions of our best selves. How often do we do this with writing? After graduate school, almost not at all. And yet of course writing is central to the academic profession, both as a feature of our teaching and as the foundation of our scholarship.

Becoming a writer may simply entail thinking and reading actively about writing, which amounts to, at the far end, genuinely *practicing* at it. We do the latter whenever we consciously write, of course; but we can extend that practice into a more general field as we actively teach writing to our students, commit to regularly reading and discussing work with our colleagues, or take writing seriously when we describe our work, or the work of others, in professional reader's reports or book reviews.

Becoming a writer also means becoming a different kind of reader. It requires reading—at least sometimes—just for the writing, and doing so for both academic and nonacademic work, in order to broaden your perception of style or to collect, along the way, interesting syntax or new words. It means poking around the primers or blogs on style, or reading commentary on good writing in genres other than scholarly nonfiction (I recently browsed Pixar's "22 Rules for Good Storytelling"), listening to podcasts, or trying out a new piece of outlining or brainstorming software. It means keeping your ears open.

But it also—and here I think you will find this advice hardest to swallow—means becoming a different kind of writer, one who does not write as though sentences and words were mere conduits for meaning. At the level of your practice, this entails actively trying out new kinds of sentences or new structures in your own work, ones you've imagined or ones you've found elsewhere. I recommend, minimally, imitation: learning how to summarize like Moretti, to personalize like Brown, or to aphorize like Stewart, and then building a new, personal Voltron from the cobbled parts you've gleaned from others. But you can also set self-oriented constraints on your practice, deciding to make this piece lighter or heavier than the last one, trying more or fewer footnotes, or committing to a particular structure or a pattern of figuration ahead of the actual act of writing. Some of this is learning through play. At the lower frequencies, however, it involves thinking, as you work through an article or a book, about the ways your stylistic choices interact with the content of your argument, and collocating them (or dislocating them) to create the tenor of your piece.

You might also try writing outside the preferred scholarly genres. From the exotic realms—blogging! fiction!—I have heard, travelers return with new styli, new tongues. Take historian Carla Nappi, who wrote a Twitter essay titled "The Historian and the Etymologist" in a series of tweets that aimed to be readable both forwards (from the bottom of the screen up) and backwards (top–down). Whether the essay's any good makes no difference (and it's pretty good, though as Nappi herself acknowledges, it's better forwards than backwards). What matters is the active engagement with the many problems and opportunities of writing and communication (not the same thing!), all of which may one day return to affect scholarly writing. Practice gets you ready, like all practice, for the game.

In all this becoming you must avoid too much of the feeling of accomplishment which, at some point, the profession will return to you. Once you've been writing for long enough there's a floor beneath which you can't really fall: you've published, so you have every reason to believe you will continue to be able to write publishable things. Frankly, it's a wonderful moment, one in which you can abandon much of the professional anxiety and fear that has thus far governed your career. It is tempting at that moment to decide that you've really become a writer, and that the rest is just the search for new things to write about. Fair enough. But it's a terrible example for everyone else, including your students, to make a certain *efficiency* the model of adequate practice, while treating reflection, struggle, and change as the accoutrements of weakness or youth ("I have learned to do this. Now I can stop learning."). Staying committed to them as necessary appurtenances of the writer's being, incorporating as necessary a certain unhappy dissatisfaction and striving, honors not only those who are still fighting to be recognized, but also your former, struggling self.

Thirty-four

From the Workshop to the World
(as Workshop [as World])

To be a writer is to be among writers, among readers. No one writes into a void; we owe every act of narration and description to the panoply of norms into which, like newborns into language, we all emerge. What we are as writers, what we can imagine being or doing with prose, we owe to the others who have made the world in which we become.

This is true even if you work alone. There is still, against your solitude, out there a reader who waits for you, whose presence makes your work viable, possible, even desirable. The workshop of writing is wide, including all in the realm of the living and the not-yet-born (if not, or at least not literally, the dead).

This praise for the basic sociality of writing is meant to remind you—and, at this late hour, me—of the importance of the group of people who make all writing meaningful and worth doing. In the throes of (self-)contempt or despair, you have the people you admire to write for. You too are a social writer.

So build your society! Work with others, teach as you can teach, learn as you can learn. Talk with us, with them, with whoever you can talk to, about the importance of this practice to your work, your professional life, your sense of self. Cut from the existing cloth the social fabric of your practice, and use it to sustain and encourage you. I would never have started this book had it not been for Andrea Bachner, who told me, as we discussed her book manuscript in the spring of 2011, that she would read a book on writing if I wrote one, and has read every word as promised. Along the way my friends Paul

Saint-Amour, Mara de Gennaro, Victoria Rosner, Steve Yao, and Sean Goudie read huge chunks of what you see here, helping shape its tone and pushing here and there on the balance between the personally interesting and the publically useful. A number of other friends responded to queries about their favorite academic writers, personally encouraged the project, or engaged in long conversations about institutional structure and prosaic style; here I must especially thank current and former Angelenos Christopher Bush, Mark McGurl, Wendy Belcher, Haun Saussy, Sianne Ngai, Shu-mei Shih, Elizabeth Deloughrey, and Tara Fickle. And I should also thank Rachel Adams, who at the last minute saved me from a deeply thoughtless omission.

The society of this book also includes a wide variety of other friends, colleagues, and audiences who participated in the making of it. If I refer to them here, above the waterline—outside, that is, the structure of exclusion and inclusion that is the formal "acknowledgments" section, which follows—it is in order to violate the boundary that separates the decorously academic acknowledgment of engagement or influence that is codified in the citations and footnotes of scholarly work and the more relaxed and personal recognition of influence normally relegated to the "acknowledgments." The boundary between them, which estranges what one might think of as a kind of metaintellectual support (some of which can be institutional or personal, as when people thank their families) from the work of actual thought, is—like all boundaries—a scar, a certainty. Like all certainties it denies—as it must, to organize—the resemblances and similarities that might violate it, and reduces complex relations to their simpler, opposed parts: these over here, these over there. But the similarities are always there, in two dimensions: first in the fact that one's formal citations represent—in addition to their intellectual work, of course—patterns of friendship, enmity, generation, or affiliation (just note, for instance, how often students of the same advisor will cite one another's work); second in the fact that the folks in the acknowledgments have—in addition to their friendship and emotional support, of course—often shaped or even written specific sentences, paragraphs, entire ideas or sections, given the writer the title of the book, and so on. "All errors are, of course, my own": this cliché of responsibility is a lie. Some of the errors (if errors there be) are probably someone else's fault. We cannot acknowledge this truth, for it would disrupt the entire process whereby the work is assigned, finally, to a single signature—and that signature, in turn, to a career, a reputation, a tenure decision, and so on. But it is a truth nonetheless.

The point is not to say that all books should be assigned to multiple authors (as in the sciences), but to note once again that the very institutional structure within which we work predisposes us to think about writing practices a certain way. My argument throughout this book has been that we can gain—in ambition, in confidence, in calm, in craft, and in, finally, respect for our work as writers and scholars—if we think of writing otherwise, that small shifts in the ways we conceive of writing as a feature of the profession can change the ways we (each individually and all together) practice writing in our (personal and professional) lives. Recognizing the social world of your work; understanding the difference between how you work and how you must, given professional norms, present that process to the world; acknowledging and taking advantage of the forms of engaged communal practice in which you already take part—these are steps in the re-theorization of writing practice and writing community that never just begins, or ends, with each of us alone in front of a legal pad or a computer. The work begins in the workshop; it moves into the world; back to the workshop; then into the world, and back again.

This is how it is, and how it should be: the work in round, spiraling, as you spiral with it.

Thirty-five
Acknowledgments

I include, in addition to the folks I've already mentioned, the audiences and panelists at three Modernist Studies Association sessions devoted to writing in the social life of the making of this book. I am especially grateful to Helen Sword, who organized two of the sessions and has done so much to make visible writing's importance to academic life, and to Erin Carlston and Nico Israel, whose honesty and thoughtfulness model a public relation to writing. My society also involved UCLA's Mellon postdoctoral fellows and the faculty and graduate students in English and comparative literature at Yale (especially John Williams and Jordan Brower, who also read over parts of the manuscript), with whom I did seminars on scholarly writing; the audiences for "Academic Writing, I Love You. Really, I Do," a talk I gave at the University of Chicago (thanks to Lauren Berlant) and the University of Pennsylvania (thanks to Jim English and Kevin Platt) in spring 2013; and the participants in the summer school of the Asia/Europe Center at the University of Heidelberg (organized by Joachim Kurtz, Martin Hoffman, and Pablo Blitstein).

After I'd drafted the outline (which turned out, inevitably, not to be the final outline), I sent it around to a group of current and former students, through and with whom I learned many of the lessons here. They were Anne Brooksher-Yen, Mark Sussman, Sarah Osment, Megan Massino, Helena Ribeiro, Matt Cook, Neetu Khanna, Michelle Decker, Grace Wu, Matt Price, and Darwin Tsen. I also talked through the book with students in a graduate seminar on academic style and, late in the game, worked through some of the appendix exercises with Lea Pao. Their fingerprints appear variously here. Sarah in particular spent a day improving the first section with me. These few names stand in, somewhat inadequately, for the hundreds of students I've taught since my first class on composition in 1995, with whom I learned how to teach writing at the most basic levels. And they figure, as well, my long history of learning writing, which began as it does for all of us in grade school and continued through college (Henry Schwarz, John Glavin, Bruce Smith), my brief period of intense interest in creative writing (and the classes I took around that), my tiny career in journalism (and the editors and teachers that helped me), and into graduate school, where Herbert Blau, Gregory Jay, and Christopher Lane left their marks on my habits and my prose.

At Columbia University Press, Philip Leventhal, the book's editor, helped see this book through to completion, helped pick the title, reframed some its ideas, and helped me resist a few suggestions from friends and colleagues for specific changes. I'm also grateful to the press's two anonymous reviewers, one of whom I am sad to disappoint by having retained the word "amaroidal," but with whom I share nonetheless, I suspect, a predilection for the dark reaches of the dictionary. Kathryn Jorge's copyediting has improved the prose and saved me from a number of sad mistakes; she and Irene Pavitt advised me on structure and kept the entire publication process moving along smoothly.

I would never have been interested in academic writing had I not grown up in a profession with so many fantastic and admirable writers. Many of these belong to the generation of scholars and critics I read in graduate school, including Roland Barthes (in French, but also in the lovely English translations by Richard Howard, Richard Miller, and Annette Lavers), Jameson, the two Millers (D. A. and Nancy K.), Eve Sedgwick, Leo Bersani, Rey Chow, Jonathan Culler, Stephen Greenblatt, and many others. I tried in this book to cite some other folks, especially ones nearer to my generation, to register academic writing's eternally surprising, vernal beauty. Quoting my favorites was usually just a question of wandering over to the office bookshelf, but I also found great writing by people I'd never heard of by poking through recent journal issues.

The less direct conditions of this book's possibility are both institutional and personal, and include my department at Penn State and my

223

friends and colleagues here. This is true especially of Shuang Shen, Chris Castiglia, and Chris Reed, with whom I often share writing, but also of the amazingly long list of people from whom I receive personal and professional support: Carey Eckhardt, Tom Beebee, Jon Abel, Charlotte Eubanks, Sophia McClennen, Jon Eburne, Christopher Moore, Lisa Sternlieb, Derek Fox, Jonathan Marks, Erica Brindley, Hester Blum, Ben Schreier, Michael Elavsky, Lee Ahern, Denise Solomon, Janet Lyon, Robert Caserio, Debbie Hawhee, Tina Chen, Gabeba Baderoon, Dan Purdy, Kate Baldanza, On-cho Ng, and Jessamyn Abel.

Having Jane Gallop as a teacher changed my life—my whole life. The lessons she taught me are half of what I still teach my students and half, dear reader, of what you have gotten here. Jane, my *advisadora*, this book is for you.

Appendix

A Writer's Workbook

One of the things you might reasonably want to do, having read this book, is to practice a few of the things you've just learned. In fact we probably should agree that, following the general rule that ideas only matter when in material forms, unless you put these lessons into practice, you can't really learn them.

In this appendix, I offer a series of exercises which are keyed to individual chapters. I've used some of these with individual students, or with groups of them. In other cases I'm guessing at what might work for you, or drawing from my personal experience.

Before we get started, though, one thing: I think this will all go *much* more smoothly if you find another person to do these exercises with. Hard things get easier when you're not alone, and it's easier to maintain a habit when you've included someone else in it. Plus, teaching something to someone else—or explaining to someone else what you've learned—is often the best way to actually learn it yourself.

Chapter 3: Habit Formation

When can you work? Construct a chart of your typical schedule to find out. Before deciding when and where to write, spend a typical week tracking your time expenditures, fifteen-minute chunk by fifteen-minute chunk. Be sure to include all your breaks, downtime, sleeping, and so on. If you can track your time over two typical weeks, that's even better. Your goal is to produce a chart that will show you exactly how much free time you usually have during a given week. To make it easier to figure this out, try coloring various pieces of it in red (for actions or tasks that can't be moved, such as sleeping and eating), yellow (for time that is to some extent under your control, like office hours), and green (for time that belongs entirely to you, which you use for studying, reading, course preparation, leisure, etc.). You may even want to use a different color (say, blue) for what I think of as "mandatory" leisure: the three times a week you work out, the regular meeting of your knitting club, and so on.

You want to find at least thirty minutes per day that you can block off for writing (and more, if you're making a schedule for times when you're not teaching). Ideally this block of time will occur at the same time daily, preferably in the morning. If you can, include time for a five- to ten-minute warm-up period, during which you'll sit down, open the file, maybe stare at things a bit, and freewrite for two or three minutes, writing a few sentences about where you stopped yesterday and where you think you're going next.

At the end of this process you should be able to produce a weekly calendar that includes your writing periods, labeled in whatever color will make them seem most unmovable.

Look forward in the long-term with a calendar of meet-able goals. This comes in two flavors: the multi-year calendar and the semester- or year-long calendar. The multi-year calendar is best discussed with your advisor, your department head, or a trusted colleague, and is especially useful for pre-tenure scholars. Simply put, it's a list of what you think you will do when: how you will spend your summers, any available leave, and the like. Charting this long-term calendar will help you keep yourself organized and undistracted as you move through the process of evaluation. Divide your year into three periods: Fall, Spring, and Summer. For each period write down the major project or projects you'll be working on. For semester- or year-long calendars, organize time week-by-week. Hang it on the wall above your desk so that you see it daily and refer to it often.

Remember in both cases to include "empty" weeks (or months) that you can use either as breaks or to meet unexpected challenges or events. You never want to schedule yourself so tightly that you cannot deal with surprises or overruns. A calendar you can't stick to does you no good.

You can refer to the examples below as a guide to get you started.

MULTI-YEAR CALENDAR

Academic Year	Fall	Spring	Summer
Year 1 (2014–15)	Mann article	Mann article ACLA conference	Send Mann article out Research Proust chapter
Year 2 (2015–16)	Research Proust Second-year review	Start Proust	Finish Proust Plan book revisions
Year 3 (2016–17)	Start revising book	Revise book	Finalize revisions
Year 4 (2017–18)	Write book proposal Research new article	Contact presses Conference talk	Start new article

SEMESTER-LONG CALENDAR

Week (Weekdays Only)	Travel/Other	Work
Oct. 14–18		Teaching starts/Auerbach
Oct. 21–25	Bremen (23rd–24th)	Korea talk
Oct. 28–Nov. 1	Kids no school (1st)	Korea talk
Nov. 4–8	Seoul (5th–10th)	Korea talk/Scale article
Nov. 11–15		Scale
Nov. 18–22		Scale
Nov. 25–29		Read job applications
Dec. 2–6		Scale
Dec. 9–13		Scale/Prep for Mainz talk
Dec. 16–20	Mainz (17th)	Work on MLA talk
Dec. 23–27	School vacation	Vacation
Dec. 30–Jan. 3	School vacation	Try to find some time for MLA talk

Chapters 8–10: Structure and the Uneven U

Chart the Uneven U in action. Pick an academic article in your field. Chart three individual paragraphs according to the five levels of the Uneven U. Pay attention to how individual sentences manage the reader, passing him or her along as they move up, forward, or down. Make a visual map of each paragraph to get a better idea of this movement as you read through the prose.

Then chart the entire article at the paragraph level. Your goal is to see the larger structures that compose the article's sections, and to observe the way these sections interact. Next, make a map of the essay as a whole. Discuss with your partner.

Map out the structural rhythm of a section. Let's focus on sections rather than entire articles or books. Chart out the pattern of section structures in three articles in your field. What's the function of each section in relation to the others? How long are they? How are they subordinated? Map this out, if you can. Then discuss with your partner which section pattern/structure works best and why.

Perform the same exercise, this time for books. Pick two academic books that you like and read only the chapter titles and the first and last paragraphs of each chapter. How has the book organized the chapters? Do they constitute a coherent line? A developmental (rising) arc? A series of concentric circles? Make a map of their relations, noting along the way relative length and subordination.

Like surgery, this kind of thing is best first practiced on others. Now that you have done so, try these exercises out on your own work.

Reconstruct the Uneven U. Ask a friend (preferably one not part of your writing group) to take apart five paragraphs from a recent piece of scholarly writing in your field. Ask him or her to return those paragraphs to you with the paragraphs out of order, and the sentences out of order within each paragraph as well. Work with your partner to reconstruct the paragraphs. Do not worry about getting things exactly right; the point here is to think and talk about why things might go one way or another, to externalize your sense of structure.

Write the Uneven U. Have someone give you a piece of level-1 evidence (for example, a description of a film scene, or a quotation, or an image). Next, write the paragraph that surrounds it in an imaginary paper. Start high in the U, move down and in, and then build your way back out.

Another way to practice using the Uneven U in your writing is to give your partner the structuring framework of a series of sentences in a paragraph, like this:

> But [. . .]. That's because [. . .]. The entire relationship, in fact, [. . .]. We see as much later in the novel, when [. . .]. [Requote from the quotation in previous sentence]: with these words [...]. And though it is perhaps too late for [. . .] to say so, what appears here shows that [. . .]. This amounts to a radical shift in direction, since [. . .]. In fact the novel can be understood in no other way.

This template could become a thousand paragraphs. The goal, however, is to understand that by writing three or four genuinely different versions. Finish up this exercise by each of you writing a *new* framework paragraph for the other person to practice with.

For a shorter version of this exercise, practice writing sentences in a particular spot within a paragraph. Take any paragraph from any piece of work and recopy its first sentence. Then write three second sentences that *could* follow it. Try the same thing for the third, fourth, and fifth sentences, observing each time how the constraints of what came before shape the possibilities of what's next.

This last exercise works well also for your own work as a freewriting drill. If you are stuck somewhere, open a new document or grab a blank piece of paper. Start with one to three sentences that immediately precede the place where you're currently stuck. For ten minutes, come up with at least three alternative sentences (or more if you can). You'll often find that you'll hit upon the right one—you'll just *feel* it when you do—and then it will become impossible to continue the freewriting because you'll be excited about going on. In a worst-case scenario, you can get yourself started by arbitrarily forcing yourself to begin with the building blocks of a legitimate sentence: "This allows us to see that. . . . " Come up with four sentences that could end that beginning and you could be on your way to finishing the U.

Chapters 11, 14, and 17: Introductions, Transitions, and Conclusions

Explore the range of styles for introductions and conclusions. Go through two different articles from your field, reading only the first two introductory sentences for each section. Try, if you can, to reverse engineer and typologize them—figure out not only *what* they're doing but *how* they're doing it. Be on the look-out for patterns, similarities, and differences. When you're finished, compare the general patterns of introduction between the two articles. It's best to do the reading alone, but the comparative and typological work with a partner.

Repeat the exercise, this time with two books. Read only the introductory paragraphs for each chapter.

Repeat this exercise with all sentence-level transitions in an article, or all the major transitional paragraphs in a book. In this case, you should mainly look at the first paragraphs of chapters, but you might also focus on the first paragraphs of major sections.

Now try out this exercise again, this time with conclusions. Look at the conclusions of all of the articles in a single issue of a journal, and then all of the chapter conclusions in a book. Each time try to find patterns of similarity and difference, but also patterns or techniques you admire. Think about how you could copy them in a future work. "Which one of these do I like best?" is always a great way to begin, since your gut feelings will eventually carry you to critical judgment.

Practice identifying and using transitions. Go through something you've written and pick out places where you have used transitions. Make every transition into an x/y transition. Try to change at least two transitions into two-sentence x/y structures.

Then work on your transitions so that at least two of them are short, punchy sentences (ten words at most, no commas) that follow the longer, more elaborate final sentences of previous paragraphs.

As a final exercise, make at least three transitions lexical, with at least one of these a pure sonic match.

Chapter 15: Showing Your Iceberg

Make a list like the one on pages 116–18 for your next project, describing what you need to know for your specific task and genre. Organize this knowledge under these headings: Archival, Critical, Theoretical, Biographical, Historical, Aesthetic, Documentary, and Linguistic. Doing this helps you get a more specific idea what you need to know and do.

If you're working on a dissertation or book, make similar charts for each chapter. For each chapter, you should also start building a bibliography that will help you learn and look for what you need.

Repeat this exercise for an article in your field. Note all the places where the author shows (whether directly or indirectly) the background necessary to justify the arguments he or she makes. Pay special attention to how the author handles theoretical material.

Chapter 16: Metalanguage

Work through someone else's article (whether your partner's or something already published) and underline all instances of explicit, signposting metalanguage. Make sure you mark textual instances ("In what follows") and paratextual or unvoiced ones (chapter numbers, headings, etc.). Describe each piece of metalanguage by its major function.

Take a second pass through the same text to find instances of implicit metalanguage, especially instances that use rhythm or sentence length to communicate opening or concluding movement.

Finally, to develop a sense of how things work in other academic fields and spaces, redo this exercise once for something from history or philosophy, once for an article from psychology, and once for an article in your home field but originally written in a language other than English. Talk with your partner about differences among fields. Your goal is to develop a clearer understanding of the norms in your own disciplinary space.

Chapter 19: Citational Practice

Take a piece of writing you've done recently. Go through it and practice turning one type of quotation you've used into another. Try transforming a block quote into a partial quote, a partial quote into a full quote, and so on. Do this for five quotations, being sure to move both big to small (block to full) and small to big (partial to full).

Now take two quotations. Rewrite their citational paratext in three different ways, so that the paratext prepares the reader for a fuller treatment of the quote, a middle treatment, and a lighter one.

Chapter 22: Figurative Language

Experiment with similes to liven up your arguments. Commit yourself to putting at least three similes into your next essay. When you come to a place where you think you could possibly use a simile, make it up *then* rather than later. Allow that simile to change what happens next, letting the specificity of the concretion you've invented shape your idea.

Also try shifting your simile around in the sentence (beginning, middle, end). Note how in each position the image clarifies things differently. (You can see in the list of Jameson's similes examples of each type.)

Use an extended metaphor to link ideas and terms together in your piece. In your next essay, try your hand at an extended metaphor. Look back at the examples from Porter, McGurl, and Saint-Amour. Their metaphors usually last no more than two sentences. See how two of the three (Porter on alchemy, Saint-Amour on honey) depend on a slightly esoteric knowledge of the vocabulary associated with the primary image, which both writers deploy (Porter: elements, explosive, spark, illuminates; Saint-Amour: hive, cells) to good effect. Like a Slinky making its happy way down a staircase, these new words extend the energy of the first image, releasing it in progressively smaller kinetic bursts.

Chapter 23: Footnotes and Endnotes

Typologize notes in your field. Go through two articles and characterize the notes by their function. Compare the balance between articles. (As a variation of this exercise, do the same between two *journals* in your field.)

Also compare the function and number of notes in a book with footnotes against a book with endnotes. Pick out (and then discuss with your partner) your favorite or least favorite notes, trying to describe why exactly they appeal (or don't) to you as notes. Focus on their form rather than on their content—look at how they reflect or shape the line of the upstairs argument, and think about how they organize the argumentative force of the book as a whole.

Practice making notes. In your next seminar paper, make an effort to use notes the ways published articles do. One of the most important functions of footnotes and endnotes is to allow you to clean up the main line of your argument while gesturing toward other ideas. As you revise, see if you can find places to move material down into the footnotes to streamline your piece.

Now reread your work, this time with an eye to the things that are interesting but don't really belong in the top line. Keep a running tally of interesting connections, thoughts, and digressions. Turn at least two of these connections into notes that either elaborate the main argument or send the reader beyond the text.

Chapter 24: Jargon

Expand your diction. Ask around among your friends and colleagues for a couple names of people they consider good writers. Search these people out and read two articles or chapters of their work, keeping an eye out for interesting or interestingly used words. Make a list of the ten best ones you find. Talk with your partner about why certain words are especially cool or striking. Use them in new work.

Do the same exercise to identify interesting usages of syntax, marking out two or three favorite sentences at minimum. For each sentence, break it down into its pieces. Next, think about ways to change the nouns and verbs to make it your own. This way, you can begin to identify sentence structures you like, which you can then reconfigure and use in your own work.

As always, it helps to keep a paper journal or digital file in which you simply note down as you read things that you like.

Chapters 25 and 28: Parentheticals and Rhetorical Questions

Chart the use of parenthetical structures and rhetorical questions. Work your way through a piece of writing, highlighting all parenthetical structures. Many of these will be marked with punctuation, but be sure to pay attention to phrasal parentheticals such as "by the way." Describe them by function or type. Do the same for rhetorical questions and if-clauses.

Put your new knowledge of parentheticals and rhetorical questions into practice. In your next piece of writing, use at least two parentheticals or rhetorical structures of each type. Don't be afraid to experiment. Play with punctuation and clause/sentence length, noting the differences in rhythm and tone in each case.

As a warm-up, try rewriting the Barthes paragraph that closes chapter 25. Follow its structure exactly, but build it into a piece you're already writing. Do the same thing to practice using rhetorical structures, this time rewriting the Eng, Ruskola, and Shen paragraph in chapter 28.

Chapter 29: Sentence Rhythm

Chart and change sentence length in your writing. Go through something you're working on and count the number of words per sentence. Compute the average. Then compare your average to my rough guide for academic prose in literature and cultural studies: 0–10 words = very short; 10–15 words = short; 16–25 words = average; 25–32 words = long, 33 or more words = very long. (You may have to adjust this to fit the conventions of your field.)

Note any places in the piece where you have three or more sentences in a row that belong to the same length group. Mark or highlight places where two or more successive sentences jump two or more length levels (average to very short, or short to long, e.g.). Circle all very short and very long sentences.

Now, double your number of very short and very long sentences. Revise so that you do not have more than three sentences in a row of the same type.

Learn by imitation. Pick a writer you like. (This person may not necessarily write in your academic field, or write academic prose at all.) Read a piece of his or her work for a while, and then, with that work open next to you, sit down and try write two pages in imitation of that style. Practice forming exact copies of sentence and paragraph structure (including changing the words).

Simply inhale and exhale the style as closely as you can. To do this, you may just want to read a few pages to fill your mind with the patterns, and then quickly turn to your notebook or screen and start writing. Take another hit after every few sentences you write. (Some writers seem to *provoke* this kind of response automatically. Derrida and Heidegger, for instance, are hard to write about without stylistic osmosis.)

Part of the reason this exercise works (and not just for students) is that imitation first begins with an understanding and capturing of style. That understanding will include a sense of diction, sentence structure, structural rhythm, citational practice, the use of jargon or figurative language, and so on. This exercise thus brings together all the major lessons of this book.

Chapters 30 and 31: Ventilation and Weight

Identify ventilation and weight in writing. Read through an issue of a recently published journal and pick out the two pieces that seem to you most different in style. Compare one typical paragraph from each essay. You can begin by deciding which piece is airier, explaining (to your partner) *why* it is so. Track patterns of diction and rhythm, noticing the way that ventilation can change via content (what the author writes about) and form (how the author writes about it). Refer to the comparison between Lennon and Tamarkin in chapter 30 as a starting point on how to approach this exercise.

Within those same paragraphs, also note moments of particular weight (where the author is increasing attention to a subject) and moments of comparative lightness (where something is brought up, used quickly, and dropped).

Weight can also be seen at the level of a whole article. Find a piece from your academic field and look at ways in which stylistic intensity (jokes, figurative language, rhetorical flourishes) increase weight, or the ways the author uses repetition and time to make something heavier. Mark three instances of each pattern.

Use ventilation and weight. Compare a piece of your own writing to the paragraphs in this book and the ones you used for the exercise above. Is it denser or airier? Why?

Rewrite a couple paragraphs of your partner's work to make them denser. Next, take those same paragraphs and rewrite for airiness. Weight can come from a variety of techniques and usage, including diction, sentence structure, citational range and practice, and tone. Try to use most or all those tools to alter the prose. Then sit down, exchange paragraphs with your partner, and talk about the results.

Chapter 33: Becoming a Writer

Read more widely. Read other writing just for the writing. That means reading with an attention to style, and a keen eye for tricks, moves, patterns, and choices that you can borrow in your own prose. Do this both inside and outside your field; I especially recommend nonfiction essays (like the ones in *Best American Essays*) and prose fiction, in addition to scholarly work.

Write more widely. Find a way to write outside of your scholarship. Take *Printculture*, which I created with a few friends almost a decade ago.

It has proven to be an incredibly flexible and open outlet for other kinds of thoughts and work, from the memoir-like and personal to the quasi-academic. For me the site functions as an open, free space for experimentation, expression, and play. If you can find something like that for yourself, public or private, you'll be a happier and better writer.

Share more widely. Don't be afraid to share your work and your writing practice with others. Talk on a regular basis with someone about writing, whether with a friend, colleague, or an advisor. Co-write a paper for a class, or an article for a journal. Participate in your university's dissertation boot camp (search online for "dissertation boot camp" for examples). Create a small writing group, or a group that reads scholarly writing and discusses how it's made. Organize a writing camp or writing weekend with a friend. Read and work through this book with someone. Teach and institutionalize writing well. And so on . . .

Works Cited

Agee, James. *Let Us Now Praise Famous Men, A Death in the Family, and Shorter Fiction*. New York: Library of America, 2008.

Appiah, Kwame Anthony. "*Geist* Stories." *Comparative Literature in the Age of Multiculturalism*. Ed. Charles Bernheimer. Baltimore: Johns Hopkins University Press, 1994.

Auerbach, Erich. *Mimesis: The Representation of Reality in Western Literature*. Trans. Willard R. Trask. Princeton: Princeton University Press, 2003.

Bachner, Andrea. *Ethics of Inscription: Poststructuralist Prehistories*. 2013. MS in progress.

Banta, Martha. *Taylored Lives: Narrative Productions in the Age of Taylor, Veblen, and Ford*. Chicago: University of Chicago Press, 1995.

Barthes, Roland. *A Lover's Discourse: Fragments*. Trans. Richard Howard. New York: Hill and Wang, 2010.

——. *S/Z: An Essay*. Trans. Richard Miller. New York: Hill and Wang, 1974.

Bell, Dorian. "Hannah Arendt, the Jews, and the Labor of Superfluity." *PMLA* 127.4 (2012): 800–808.

Berlant, Lauren. *Cruel Optimism*. Durham, N.C.: Duke University Press, 2011.

Bersani, Leo. "Is the Rectum a Grave?" *AIDS: Cultural Analysis / Cultural Activism* 43 (1987): 197–222.

Brown, Bill. *A Sense of Things: The Object Matter of American Literature*. Chicago: University of Chicago Press, 2004.

Burrows, Stuart. *A Familiar Strangeness: American Fiction and the Language of Photography, 1839–1945*. Athens: University of Georgia Press, 2010.

Bush, Christopher. "The Ethnicity of Things in America's Lacquered Age." *Representations* 99 (Summer 2007): 74–98.

Butler, Judith. *Frames of War: When is Life Grievable?* New York: Verso, 2010.

Cadava, Eduardo. *Words of Light: Theses on the Photography of History.* Princeton: Princeton University Press, 1997.

Cleary, Joe. "Realism After Modernism and the Literary World-System" *Modern Language Quarterly* 73.3 (2012): 255–68.

Coats, Emma, and Dino Ignacio. "Pixar's 22 Rules of Storytelling." http://imgur.com/a/MRfTb. Accessed October 17, 2013.

Cohen, Jeffrey Jerome. *Animal, Vegetable, Mineral: Ethics and Objects.* Washington, D.C.: Punctum Books, 2012.

Cohn, Norman. *Europe's Inner Demons: The Demonization of Christians in Medieval Christendom.* Chicago: University of Chicago Press, 2001.

——. *The Pursuit of the Millennium: Revolutionary Millenarians and Mystical Anarchists of the Middle Ages.* Rev. and expanded ed. London: Oxford University Press, 1970.

Cole, Sarah. *At the Violet Hour: Modernism and Violence in England and Ireland.* New York: Oxford University Press, 2012.

Derrida, Jacques. *Archive Fever: A Freudian Impression.* Trans. Eric Prenowitz. Chicago: University of Chicago Press, 1998.

——. *Of Grammatology.* Trans. Gayatri Chakravorty Spivak. Baltimore: Johns Hopkins University Press, 1998.

——. *Limited Inc.* Ed. Gerald Graff. Trans. Samuel Weber. Evanston: Northwestern University Press, 1988.

——. *The Monolingualism of the Other: or, The Prosthesis of Origin.* Trans. Patrick Mensah. Stanford, Calif.: Stanford University Press, 1998.

Ding, Ling. *Miss Sophie's Diary and Other Stories.* Trans. W. J. F. Jenner. Beijing: Panda, 1985.

Duarte, Eduardo de Assis, and Dawn Taylor. "Jorge Amado: Exile and Literature." *Comparative Literature Studies* 49.3 (2012): 382–94.

Duffy, Enda. *The Speed Handbook: Velocity, Pleasure, Modernism.* Durham, N.C. Duke University Press, 2009.

Edelman, Lee. *Homographesis: Essays in Gay Literary and Cultural Theory.* New York: Routledge, 1994.

Eng, David L., Teemu Ruskola, and Shuang Shen. "Introduction: China and the Human." *Social Text* 29.4 (2012): 1–26.

Ertürk, Nergis. *Grammatology and Literary Modernity in Turkey.* New York: Oxford University Press, 2011.

Feuerbach, Ludwig. *Das Wesen des Christentums.* Leipzig: Alfred Kroner Verlag, 1909.

Foucault, Michel. *Discipline and Punish: The Birth of the Prison.* Trans. Alan Sheridan. New York: Vintage, 1995.

Frank, Joseph. *The Idea of Spatial Form: Essays on Twentieth-Century Culture*. New Brunswick, N.J.: Rutgers University Press, 1991.

Froula, Christine. "Proust's China." *Modernism/Modernity* 19.2 (2012): 227–54.

Frye, Northrop. *Anatomy of Criticism: Four Essays*. Princeton: Princeton University Press, 2000.

Gallop, Jane. *Reading Lacan*. Ithaca, N.Y.: Cornell University Press, 1987.

Gasché, Rodolphe. The *Stelliferous Fold: Toward a Virtual Law of Literature's Self-Formation*. New York: Fordham University Press, 2011.

Giddens, Anthony. *The Consequences of Modernity*. Stanford, Calif.: Stanford University Press, 1991.

Goble, Mark. *Beautiful Circuits: Modernism and the Mediated Life*. New York: Columbia University Press, 2010.

Goldman, Jonathan. *Modernism Is the Literature of Celebrity*. Austin: University of Texas Press, 2012.

Hayles, N. Katherine. *How We Became Posthuman: Virtual Bodies in Cybernetics, Literature, and Informatics*. Chicago: University of Chicago Press, 1999.

Hayot, Eric. *Chinese Dreams: Pound, Brecht, Tel Quel*. Ann Arbor: University of Michigan Press, 2011.

——. *The Hypothetical Mandarin: Sympathy, Modernity, and Chinese Pain*. New York: Oxford University Press, 2009.

——. *On Literary Worlds*. New York: Oxford University Press, 2012.

Heller-Roazen, Daniel. *Echolalias: On the Forgetting of Language*. New York: Zone Books, 2005.

Jameson, Fredric. *Postmodernism: or, the Cultural Logic of Late Capitalism*. Durham, N.C.: Duke University Press, 1990.

——. *The Political Unconscious: Narrative as a Socially Symbolic Act*. Ithaca: Cornell University Press, 1982.

Jin, Wen. *Pluralist Universalism: An Asian Americanist Critique of U.S. and Chinese Multiculturalisms*. Columbus: Ohio State University Press, 2012.

Johnson, B. S. *The Unfortunates*. New York: New Directions, 2009.

Johnson, Eleanor. "The Poetics of Waste: Medieval English Ecocriticism." *PMLA* 127.3 (2012): 460–76.

Kaiser, Birgit Mara. *Figures of Simplicity: Sensation and Thinking in Kleist and Melville*. Albany: State University of New York Press, 2011.

Kaplan, Alice. *French Lessons: A Memoir*. Chicago: University of Chicago Press, 1994.

Kincaid, James R. "Resist Me, You Sweet Resistible You." *PMLA* 118.5 (2003): 1325–33.

Lally, Phillippa, et al. "How Are Habits Formed: Modelling Habit Formation in the Real World." *European Journal of Social Psychology* 40.6 (2010): 998–1009.

Lennon, Brian. *In Babel's Shadow: Multilingual Literatures, Monolingual States.* Minneapolis: University of Minnesota Press, 2010.

Loh, Jules. "A Better Mousetrap and More." *Finger Lake Times*, February 15, 1979, 1.

Machor, James. *Reading Fiction in Antebellum America: Informed Response and Reception Histories, 1820–1865.* Baltimore: Johns Hopkins University Press, 2011.

Marks, Laura U. *Touch: Sensuous Theory and Multisensory Media.* Minneapolis: University of Minnesota Press, 2002.

McCrea, Barry. *In the Company of Strangers: Family and Narrative in Dickens, Conan Doyle, Joyce, and Proust.* New York: Columbia University Press, 2011.

Mcgonigal, Kelly. *The Willpower Instinct: How Self-Control Works, Why It Matters, and What You Can Do to Get More of It.* New York: Avery, 2011.

McGurl, Mark. "The Posthuman Comedy." *Critical Inquiry* 38.3 (2012): 533–53.

Michaels, Walter Benn. *The Gold Standard and the Logic of Naturalism: American Literature at the Turn of the Century.* Berkeley: University of California Press, 1988.

Moretti, Franco. *Graphs, Maps, Trees: Abstract Models for Literary History.* New York: Verso, 2007.

Nappi, Carla. "The Historian and the Etymologist: An Experimental Twitter Essay." November 28, 2012. http://carlanappi.com/2012/11/28/the-historian-and-the-etymologist-an-experimental-twitter-essay/. Accessed October 17, 2013.

Ngai, Sianne. *Our Aesthetic Categories: Zany, Cute, Interesting.* Cambridge, Mass.: Harvard University Press, 2012.

——. *Ugly Feelings.* Cambridge, Mass.: Harvard University Press, 2007.

Pascal, Blaise. "Letter 16." *The Provincial Letters.* Trans. Rev. Thomas McCrie. New York: Derby & Jackson, 1859. 392–418.

Perera, Sonali. "Working-Class Writing and the Use Value of the Literary." *PMLA* 127.4 (2012): 932–38.

Phillips, Siobhan. "Elizabeth Bishop and the Ethics of Correspondence." *Modernism/ modernity* 19.2 (2012): 343–63.

Pick, Anat. *Creaturely Poetics: Animality and Vulnerability in Literature and Film.* New York: Columbia University Press, 2011.

Poovey, Mary. *Genres of the Credit Economy: Mediating Value in Eighteenth- and Nineteenth-Century Britain.* Chicago: University of Chicago Press, 2008.

Porter, David L. "The Comparative Return." Paper presented at the Modern Language Association conference, Boston, Mass., January 5, 2013.

Rogers, Gayle. "Joyce and the Spanish *Ulysses.*" *Modernism/modernity* 19.2 (2012): 255–75.

Rollo, David. *Kiss My Relics: Hermaphroditic Fictions of the Middle Ages.* Chicago: University of Chicago Press, 2011.

Rosenthal, Laura J. "Obscenity and Work in Early-Eighteenth-Century British Fictions." *PMLA* 127.4 (2012): 947–53.

Saint-Amour, Paul K. "Modernism and the Lives of Copyright." *Modernism and Copyright*, edited by Paul K. Saint-Amour. New York: Oxford University Press, 2010. 1–38.

——. *Tense Future: Modernism, Total War, Encyclopedic Form.* New York. Oxford University Press, forthcoming.

Sanchez, Melissa E. "'Use Me But as Your Spaniel': Feminism, Queer Theory, and Early Modern Sexualities." *PMLA* 127.3 (2012): 493–511.

Santos, Irene Ramalho. *Atlantic Poets: Fernando Pessoa's Turn in Anglo-American Modernism.* Hanover, N.H.: Dartmouth College, 2003.

Saussy, Haun. *Great Walls of Discourse and Other Adventures in Cultural China.* Cambridge, Mass.: Harvard University Asia Center, 2002.

Seigneurie, Ken. *Standing by the Ruins: Elegiac Humanism in Wartime and Postwar Lebanon.* New York: Fordham University Press, 2011.

Siraganian, Lisa. *Modernism's Other Work: The Art Object's Political Life.* New York: Oxford University Press, 2012.

Spivak, Gayatri Chakravorty. "Three Women's Texts and a Critique of Imperialism." *Critical Inquiry* 12.1 (1985): 243–61.

Spurr, David. *Architecture and Modern Literature.* Ann Arbor: University of Michigan Press, 2012.

Steedman, Carolyn. "On a Horse." *PMLA* 127.4 (2012): 809–819.

Stewart, Susan. *On Longing: Narratives of the Miniature, the Gigantic, the Souvenir, the Collection.* Durham, N.C.: Duke University Press, 1993.

Sussman, Mark. "Cynicism and *The Damnation of Theron Ware." Novel*. Forthcoming.

Tamarkin, Elisa. *Anglophilia: Deference, Devotion, and Antebellum America.* Chicago: University of Chicago Press, 2008.

Tiffany, Daniel. *Toy Medium: Materialism and Modern Lyric.* Berkeley: University of California Press, 2000.

Tsu, Jing. *Failure, Nationalism, and Literature: The Making of Modern Chinese Identity, 1895–1937.* Stanford, Calif.: Stanford University Press, 2005.

Walkowitz, Rebecca. *Cosmopolitan Style: Modernism Beyond the Nation.* New York: Columbia University Press, 2007.

Wallace, Mark, and Steven Marks, eds. *Telling It Slant: Avant Garde Poetics of the 1990s.* Tuscaloosa: University of Alabama Press, 2001.

Watt, Ian. *The Rise of the Novel: Studies in Defoe, Richardson, and Fielding.* Berkeley: University of California Press, 1960.

Woolf, Virginia. *Three Guineas.* 1938. New York: Mariner Books, 2006.

Bibliography

Barzun, Jacques. *Simple and Direct: A Rhetoric for Writers*. 1975. New York: Harper & Row, 1985.

Belcher, Wendy Laura. *Writing Your Journal Article in Twelve Weeks: A Guide to Academic Publishing Success*. Thousand Oaks, Calif.: Sage, 2009.

Billig, Michael. *Learn to Write Badly: How to Succeed in the Social Sciences*. New York: Cambridge University Press, 2013.

Boice, Robert. *Professors as Writers: A Self-Help Guide to Productive Writing*. Stillwater, Okla.: New Forums Press, 1990.

Bolker, Joan. *Writing Your Dissertation in Fifteen Minutes a Day: A Guide to Starting, Revising, and Finishing Your Doctoral Thesis*. New York: Owl Books, 1998.

Carlston, Erin. "How We Write and How We Feel About It." Roundtable discussion at the Modernist Studies Association Annual Conference, Las Vegas, October 19, 2012.

Cirillo, Francesco. *The Pomodoro Technique*. San Francisco: Creative Commons, 2007.

Clark, Roy Peter. *Writing Tools: 50 Essential Strategies for Every Writer*. New York: Little, Brown, 2006.

Crewe, Jennifer. "Caught in the Middle: The Humanities." *Revising Your Dissertation: Advice from Leading Editors*. Ed. Beth Luey. Berkeley: University of California Press, 2007. 131–47.

Elbow, Peter. *Writing Without Teachers*. New York: Oxford University Press, 1998.

Germano, William. *From Dissertation to Book*. Chicago: University of Chicago Press, 2005.

——. *Getting It Published: A Guide for Scholars and Anyone Else Serious About Serious Books*. Chicago: University of Chicago Press, 2008.

Goldberg, Natalie. *Writing Down the Bones: Freeing the Writer Within.* Boston: Shambhala, 2005.

Graff, Gerald, and Cathy Birkenstein. *They Say, I Say: The Moves That Matter in Academic Writing.* 2nd ed. New York: Norton, 2009.

Harman, Eleanor, et al. *The Thesis and the Book: A Guide for First-Time Academic Authors.* 2nd ed. Toronto: University of Toronto Press, 2003.

Luey, Beth, ed. *Revising Your Dissertation: Advice from Leading Editors.* Berkeley: University of California Press, 2007.

Plotnik, Arthur. *Spunk & Bite: A Writer's Guide to Punchier, More Engaging Language and Style.* New York: Random House, 2005.

Silvia, Paul. *How to Write a Lot: A Practical Guide to Productive Academic Writing.* Washington, D.C.: American Psychological Association, 2007.

Strunk, William, and E. B. White. *The Elements of Style.* 4th ed. Boston: Allyn and Bacon, 1999.

Sword, Helen. *Stylish Academic Writing.* Cambridge, Mass.: Harvard University Press, 2012.

Williams, Joseph. *Style: Toward Clarity and Grace.* Chicago: University of Chicago Press, 1990.

Zinsser, William. *On Writing Well: The Classic Guide to Writing Nonfiction.* 1973. New York: HarperCollins, 2001.